ISBN 0-8373-2428-9

C-2428 CAREER EXAMINATION SERIES

This is your PASSBOOK® for...

Environmental Conservation Officer

Test Preparation Study Guide

Questions & Answers

NATIONAL LEARNING CORPORATION

National Learning Corporation

212 Michael Drive, Syosset, New York 11791

(516) 921-8888
(800) 645-6337
FAX: (516) 921-8743
www.passbooks.com
sales @ passbooks.com
info @ passbooks.com

PRINTED IN THE UNITED STATES OF AMERICA

PASSBOOK®

NOTICE

This book is *SOLELY* intended for, is sold *ONLY* to, and its use is *RESTRICTED* to *individual,* bona fide applicants or candidates who qualify by virtue of having seriously filed applications for appropriate license, certificate, professional and/or promotional advancement, higher school matriculation, scholarship, or other legitimate requirements of educational and/or governmental authorities.

This book is *NOT* intended for use, class instruction, tutoring, training, duplication, copying, reprinting, excerption, or adaptation, etc., by:

(1) Other Publishers
(2) Proprietors and/or Instructors of "Coaching" and/or Preparatory Courses
(3) Personnel and/or Training Divisions of commercial, industrial, and governmental organizations
(4) Schools, colleges, or universities and/or their departments and staffs, including teachers and other personnel
(5) Testing Agencies or Bureaus
(6) Study groups which seek by the purchase of a single volume to copy and/or duplicate and/or adapt this material for use by the group as a whole without having purchased individual volumes for each of the members of the group
(7) Et al.

Such persons would be in violation of appropriate Federal and State statutes.

PROVISION OF LICENSING AGREEMENTS. — Recognized educational commercial, industrial, and governmental institutions and organizations, and others legitimately engaged in educational pursuits, including training, testing, and measurement activities, may address a request for a licensing agreement to the copyright owners, who will determine whether, and under what conditions, including fees and charges, the materials in this book may be used by them. In other words, a licensing facility *exists* for the legitimate use of the material in this book on other than an individual basis. However, it is asseverated and affirmed here that the materials in this book *CANNOT* be used without the receipt of the express permission of such a licensing agreement from the Publishers.

NATIONAL LEARNING CORPORATION
212 Michael Drive
Syosset, New York 11791

Inquiries re licensing agreements should be addressed to:
The President
National Learning Corporation
212 Michael Drive
Syosset, New York 11791

PASSBOOK SERIES®

THE *PASSBOOK SERIES®* has been created to prepare applicants and candidates for the ultimate academic battlefield – the examination room.

At some time in our lives, each and every one of us may be required to take an examination – for validation, matriculation, admission, qualification, registration, certification, or licensure.

Based on the assumption that every applicant or candidate has met the basic formal educational standards, has taken the required number of courses, and read the necessary texts, the *PASSBOOK SERIES®* furnishes the one special preparation which may assure passing with confidence, instead of failing with insecurity. Examination questions – together with answers – are furnished as the basic vehicle for study so that the mysteries of the examination and its compounding difficulties may be eliminated or diminished by a sure method.

This book is meant to help you pass your examination provided that you qualify and are serious in your objective.

The entire field is reviewed through the huge store of content information which is succinctly presented through a provocative and challenging approach – the question-and-answer method.

A climate of success is established by furnishing the correct answers at the end of each test.

You soon learn to recognize types of questions, forms of questions, and patterns of questioning. You may even begin to anticipate expected outcomes.

You perceive that many questions are repeated or adapted so that you can gain acute insights, which may enable you to score many sure points.

You learn how to confront new questions, or types of questions, and to attack them confidently and work out the correct answers.

You note objectives and emphases, and recognize pitfalls and dangers, so that you may make positive educational adjustments.

Moreover, you are kept fully informed in relation to new concepts, methods, practices, and directions in the field.

You discover that you are actually taking the examination all the time: you are preparing for the examination by "taking" an examination, not by reading extraneous and/or supererogatory textbooks.

In short, this PASSBOOK®, used directedly, should be an important factor in helping you to pass your test.

ENVIRONMENTAL CONSERVATION OFFICER

DUTIES

As an Environmental Conservation Officer, you would be a sworn police officer and be involved in the enforcement of environmental conservation law in order to protect the State's natural resources and environment. You would investigate complaints from concerned individuals in order to detect and document environmental conservation law felonies, misdemeanors and violations. You would meet with school groups, service groups, and hunter's and angler's clubs to promote compliance with environmental conservation law, which includes fish and wildlife law. At times, you would be expected to work long and irregular hours on outdoor patrols. You would be required to carry a firearm in the performance of your duties.

SCOPE OF THE EXAMINATION

The written test will be designed to test for abilities in such areas as:

1. Memory for facts and information;
2. Preparing written material;
3. Reading, understanding and interpreting written information; and
4. Applying written information (rules, regulations, policies, procedures, directives, etc.).

HOW TO TAKE A TEST

I. YOU MUST PASS AN EXAMINATION

A. WHAT EVERY CANDIDATE SHOULD KNOW

Examination applicants often ask us for help in preparing for the written test. What can I study in advance? What kinds of questions will be asked? How will the test be given? How will the papers be graded?

As an applicant for a civil service examination, you may be wondering about some of these things. Our purpose here is to suggest effective methods of advance study and to describe civil service examinations.

Your chances for success on this examination can be increased if you know how to prepare. Those "pre-examination jitters" can be reduced if you know what to expect. You can even experience an adventure in good citizenship if you know why civil service exams are given.

B. WHY ARE CIVIL SERVICE EXAMINATIONS GIVEN?

Civil service examinations are important to you in two ways. As a citizen, you want public jobs filled by employees who know how to do their work. As a job seeker, you want a fair chance to compete for that job on an equal footing with other candidates. The best-known means of accomplishing this two-fold goal is the competitive examination.

Exams are widely publicized throughout the nation. They may be administered for jobs in federal, state, city, municipal, town or village governments or agencies.

Any citizen may apply, with some limitations, such as the age or residence of applicants. Your experience and education may be reviewed to see whether you meet the requirements for the particular examination. When these requirements exist, they are reasonable and applied consistently to all applicants. Thus, a competitive examination may cause you some uneasiness now, but it is your privilege and safeguard.

C. HOW ARE CIVIL SERVICE EXAMS DEVELOPED?

Examinations are carefully written by trained technicians who are specialists in the field known as "psychological measurement," in consultation with recognized authorities in the field of work that the test will cover. These experts recommend the subject matter areas or skills to be tested; only those knowledges or skills important to your success on the job are included. The most reliable books and source materials available are used as references. Together, the experts and technicians judge the difficulty level of the questions.

Test technicians know how to phrase questions so that the problem is clearly stated. Their ethics do not permit "trick" or "catch" questions. Questions may have been tried out on sample groups, or subjected to statistical analysis, to determine their usefulness.

Written tests are often used in combination with performance tests, ratings of training and experience, and oral interviews. All of these measures combine to form the best-known means of finding the right person for the right job.

II. HOW TO PASS THE WRITTEN TEST

A. NATURE OF THE EXAMINATION

To prepare intelligently for civil service examinations, you should know how they differ from school examinations you have taken. In school you were assigned certain definite pages to read or subjects to cover. The examination questions were quite detailed and usually emphasized memory. Civil service exams, on the other hand, try to discover your present ability to perform the duties of a position, plus your potentiality to learn these duties. In other words, a civil service exam attempts to predict how successful you will be. Questions cover such a broad area that they cannot be as minute and detailed as school exam questions.

In the public service similar kinds of work, or positions, are grouped together in one "class." This process is known as *position-classification.* All the positions in a class are paid according to the salary range for that class. One class title covers all of these positions, and they are all tested by the same examination.

B. FOUR BASIC STEPS

1) Study the announcement

How, then, can you know what subjects to study? Our best answer is: "Learn as much as possible about the class of positions for which you've applied." The exam will test the knowledge, skills and abilities needed to do the work.

Your most valuable source of information about the position you want is the official exam announcement. This announcement lists the training and experience qualifications. Check these standards and apply only if you come reasonably close to meeting them.

The brief description of the position in the examination announcement offers some clues to the subjects which will be tested. Think about the job itself. Review the duties in your mind. Can you perform them, or are there some in which you are rusty? Fill in the blank spots in your preparation.

Many jurisdictions preview the written test in the exam announcement by including a section called "Knowledge and Abilities Required," "Scope of the Examination," or some similar heading. Here you will find out specifically what fields will be tested.

2) Review your own background

Once you learn in general what the position is all about, and what you need to know to do the work, ask yourself which subjects you already know fairly well and which need improvement. You may wonder whether to concentrate on improving your strong areas or on building some background in your fields of weakness. When the announcement has specified "some knowledge" or "considerable knowledge," or has used adjectives like "beginning principles of..." or "advanced ... methods," you can get a clue as to the number and difficulty of questions to be asked in any given field. More questions, and hence broader coverage, would be included for those subjects which are more important in the work. Now weigh your strengths and weaknesses against the job requirements and prepare accordingly.

3) Determine the level of the position

Another way to tell how intensively you should prepare is to understand the level of the job for which you are applying. Is it the entering level? In other words, is this the position in which beginners in a field of work are hired? Or is it an intermediate or advanced level? Sometimes this is indicated by such words as "Junior" or "Senior" in the class title. Other jurisdictions use Roman numerals to designate the level – Clerk I, Clerk II, for example. The word "Supervisor" sometimes appears in the title. If the level is not indicated by the title, check the description of duties. Will you be working under very close supervision, or will you have responsibility for independent decisions in this work?

4) Choose appropriate study materials

Now that you know the subjects to be examined and the relative amount of each subject to be covered, you can choose suitable study materials. For beginning level jobs, or even advanced ones, if you have a pronounced weakness in some aspect of your training, read a modern, standard textbook in that field. Be sure it is up to date and has general coverage. Such books are normally available at your library, and the librarian will be glad to help you locate one. For entry-level positions, questions of appropriate difficulty are chosen – neither highly advanced questions, nor those too simple. Such questions require careful thought but not advanced training.

If the position for which you are applying is technical or advanced, you will read more advanced, specialized material. If you are already familiar with the basic principles of your field, elementary textbooks would waste your time. Concentrate on advanced textbooks and technical periodicals. Think through the concepts and review difficult problems in your field.

These are all general sources. You can get more ideas on your own initiative, following these leads. For example, training manuals and publications of the government agency which employs workers in your field can be useful, particularly for technical and professional positions. A letter or visit to the government department involved may result in more specific study suggestions, and certainly will provide you with a more definite idea of the exact nature of the position you are seeking.

III. KINDS OF TESTS

Tests are used for purposes other than measuring knowledge and ability to perform specified duties. For some positions, it is equally important to test ability to make adjustments to new situations or to profit from training. In others, basic mental abilities not dependent on information are essential. Questions which test these things may not appear as pertinent to the duties of the position as those which test for knowledge and information. Yet they are often highly important parts of a fair examination. For very general questions, it is almost impossible to help you direct your study efforts. What we can do is to point out some of the more common of these general abilities needed in public service positions and describe some typical questions.

1) General information

Broad, general information has been found useful for predicting job success in some kinds of work. This is tested in a variety of ways, from vocabulary lists to questions about current events. Basic background in some field of work, such as sociology or economics, may be sampled in a group of questions. Often these are principles which have become familiar to most persons through exposure rather than through formal training. It is difficult to advise you how to study for these questions; being alert to the world around you is our best suggestion.

2) Verbal ability

An example of an ability needed in many positions is verbal or language ability. Verbal ability is, in brief, the ability to use and understand words. Vocabulary and grammar tests are typical measures of this ability. Reading comprehension or paragraph interpretation questions are common in many kinds of civil service tests. You are given a paragraph of written material and asked to find its central meaning.

3) Numerical ability

Number skills can be tested by the familiar arithmetic problem, by checking paired lists of numbers to see which are alike and which are different, or by interpreting charts and graphs. In the latter test, a graph may be printed in the test booklet which you are asked to use as the basis for answering questions.

4) Observation

A popular test for law-enforcement positions is the observation test. A picture is shown to you for several minutes, then taken away. Questions about the picture test your ability to observe both details and larger elements.

5) Following directions

In many positions in the public service, the employee must be able to carry out written instructions dependably and accurately. You may be given a chart with several columns, each column listing a variety of information. The questions require you to carry out directions involving the information given in the chart.

6) Skills and aptitudes

Performance tests effectively measure some manual skills and aptitudes. When the skill is one in which you are trained, such as typing or shorthand, you can practice. These tests are often very much like those given in business school or high school courses. For many of the other skills and aptitudes, however, no short-time preparation can be made. Skills and abilities natural to you or that you have developed throughout your lifetime are being tested.

Many of the general questions just described provide all the data needed to answer the questions and ask you to use your reasoning ability to find the answers. Your best preparation for these tests, as well as for tests of facts and ideas, is to be at your physical and mental best. You, no doubt, have your own methods of getting into an exam-taking mood and keeping "in shape." The next section lists some ideas on this subject.

IV. KINDS OF QUESTIONS

Only rarely is the "essay" question, which you answer in narrative form, used in civil service tests. Civil service tests are usually of the short-answer type. Full instructions for answering these questions will be given to you at the examination. But in case this is your first experience with short-answer questions and separate answer sheets, here is what you need to know:

1) Multiple-choice Questions

Most popular of the short-answer questions is the "multiple choice" or "best answer" question. It can be used, for example, to test for factual knowledge, ability to solve problems or judgment in meeting situations found at work.

A multiple-choice question is normally one of three types—

- It can begin with an incomplete statement followed by several possible endings. You are to find the one ending which *best* completes the statement, although some of the others may not be entirely wrong.
- It can also be a complete statement in the form of a question which is answered by choosing one of the statements listed.
- It can be in the form of a problem – again you select the best answer.

Here is an example of a multiple-choice question with a discussion which should give you some clues as to the method for choosing the right answer:

When an employee has a complaint about his assignment, the action which will *best* help him overcome his difficulty is to

A. discuss his difficulty with his coworkers
B. take the problem to the head of the organization
C. take the problem to the person who gave him the assignment
D. say nothing to anyone about his complaint

In answering this question, you should study each of the choices to find which is best. Consider choice "A" – Certainly an employee may discuss his complaint with fellow employees, but no change or improvement can result, and the complaint remains unresolved. Choice "B" is a poor choice since the head of the organization probably does not know what assignment you have been given, and taking your problem to him is known as "going over the head" of the supervisor. The supervisor, or person who made the assignment, is the person who can clarify it or correct any injustice. Choice "C" is, therefore, correct. To say nothing, as in choice "D," is unwise. Supervisors have and interest in knowing the problems employees are facing, and the employee is seeking a solution to his problem.

2) True/False Questions

The "true/false" or "right/wrong" form of question is sometimes used. Here a complete statement is given. Your job is to decide whether the statement is right or wrong.

SAMPLE: A person-to-person long-distance telephone call costs less than a station-to-station call to the same city.

This statement is wrong, or false, since person-to-person calls are more expensive.

This is not a complete list of all possible question forms, although most of the others are variations of these common types. You will always get complete directions for answering questions. Be sure you understand *how* to mark your answers – ask questions until you do.

V. RECORDING YOUR ANSWERS

For an examination with very few applicants, you may be told to record your answers in the test booklet itself. Separate answer sheets are much more common. If this separate answer sheet is to be scored by machine – and this is often the case – it is highly important that you mark your answers correctly in order to get credit.

An electric scoring machine is often used in civil service offices because of the speed with which papers can be scored. Machine-scored answer sheets must be marked with a pencil, which will be given to you. This pencil has a high graphite content which responds to the electric scoring machine. As a matter of fact, stray dots may register as answers, so do not let your pencil rest on the answer sheet while you are pondering the correct answer. Also, if your pencil lead breaks or is otherwise defective, ask for another.

Since the answer sheet will be dropped in a slot in the scoring machine, be careful not to bend the corners or get the paper crumpled.

The answer sheet normally has five vertical columns of numbers, with 30 numbers to a column. These numbers correspond to the question numbers in your test booklet. After each number, going across the page are four or five pairs of dotted lines. These short dotted lines have small letters or numbers above them. The first two pairs may also have a "T" or "F" above the letters. This indicates that the first two pairs only are to be used if the questions are of the true-false type. If the questions are multiple choice, disregard the "T" and "F" and pay attention only to the small letters or numbers.

Answer your questions in the manner of the sample that follows:

32. The largest city in the United States is
    A. Washington, D.C.
    B. New York City
    C. Chicago
    D. Detroit
    E. San Francisco

1) Choose the answer you think is best. (New York City is the largest, so "B" is correct.)
2) Find the row of dotted lines numbered the same as the question you are answering. (Find row number 32)
3) Find the pair of dotted lines corresponding to the answer. (Find the pair of lines under the mark "B.")
4) Make a solid black mark between the dotted lines.

VI. BEFORE THE TEST

Common sense will help you find procedures to follow to get ready for an examination. Too many of us, however, overlook these sensible measures. Indeed, nervousness and fatigue have been found to be the most serious reasons why applicants fail to do their best on civil service tests. Here is a list of reminders:

- Begin your preparation early – Don't wait until the last minute to go scurrying around for books and materials or to find out what the position is all about.
- Prepare continuously – An hour a night for a week is better than an all-night cram session. This has been definitely established. What is more, a night a

week for a month will return better dividends than crowding your study into a shorter period of time.

- Locate the place of the exam – You have been sent a notice telling you when and where to report for the examination. If the location is in a different town or otherwise unfamiliar to you, it would be well to inquire the best route and learn something about the building.
- Relax the night before the test – Allow your mind to rest. Do not study at all that night. Plan some mild recreation or diversion; then go to bed early and get a good night's sleep.
- Get up early enough to make a leisurely trip to the place for the test – This way unforeseen events, traffic snarls, unfamiliar buildings, etc. will not upset you.
- Dress comfortably – A written test is not a fashion show. You will be known by number and not by name, so wear something comfortable.
- Leave excess paraphernalia at home – Shopping bags and odd bundles will get in your way. You need bring only the items mentioned in the official notice you received; usually everything you need is provided. Do not bring reference books to the exam. They will only confuse those last minutes and be taken away from you when in the test room.
- Arrive somewhat ahead of time – If because of transportation schedules you must get there very early, bring a newspaper or magazine to take your mind off yourself while waiting.
- Locate the examination room – When you have found the proper room, you will be directed to the seat or part of the room where you will sit. Sometimes you are given a sheet of instructions to read while you are waiting. Do not fill out any forms until you are told to do so; just read them and be prepared.
- Relax and prepare to listen to the instructions
- If you have any physical problem that may keep you from doing your best, be sure to tell the test administrator. If you are sick or in poor health, you really cannot do your best on the exam. You can come back and take the test some other time.

VII. AT THE TEST

The day of the test is here and you have the test booklet in your hand. The temptation to get going is very strong. Caution! There is more to success than knowing the right answers. You must know how to identify your papers and understand variations in the type of short-answer question used in this particular examination. Follow these suggestions for maximum results from your efforts:

1) Cooperate with the monitor

The test administrator has a duty to create a situation in which you can be as much at ease as possible. He will give instructions, tell you when to begin, check to see that you are marking your answer sheet correctly, and so on. He is not there to guard you, although he will see that your competitors do not take unfair advantage. He wants to help you do your best.

2) Listen to all instructions

Don't jump the gun! Wait until you understand all directions. In most civil service tests you get more time than you need to answer the questions. So don't be in a hurry.

Read each word of instructions until you clearly understand the meaning. Study the examples, listen to all announcements and follow directions. Ask questions if you do not understand what to do.

3) Identify your papers

Civil service exams are usually identified by number only. You will be assigned a number; you must not put your name on your test papers. Be sure to copy your number correctly. Since more than one exam may be given, copy your exact examination title.

4) Plan your time

Unless you are told that a test is a "speed" or "rate of work" test, speed itself is usually not important. Time enough to answer all the questions will be provided, but this does not mean that you have all day. An overall time limit has been set. Divide the total time (in minutes) by the number of questions to determine the approximate time you have for each question.

5) Do not linger over difficult questions

If you come across a difficult question, mark it with a paper clip (useful to have along) and come back to it when you have been through the booklet. One caution if you do this – be sure to skip a number on your answer sheet as well. Check often to be sure that you have not lost your place and that you are marking in the row numbered the same as the question you are answering.

6) Read the questions

Be sure you know what the question asks! Many capable people are unsuccessful because they failed to *read* the questions correctly.

7) Answer all questions

Unless you have been instructed that a penalty will be deducted for incorrect answers, it is better to guess than to omit a question.

8) Speed tests

It is often better NOT to guess on speed tests. It has been found that on timed tests people are tempted to spend the last few seconds before time is called in marking answers at random – without even reading them – in the hope of picking up a few extra points. To discourage this practice, the instructions may warn you that your score will be "corrected" for guessing. That is, a penalty will be applied. The incorrect answers will be deducted from the correct ones, or some other penalty formula will be used.

9) Review your answers

If you finish before time is called, go back to the questions you guessed or omitted to give them further thought. Review other answers if you have time.

10) Return your test materials

If you are ready to leave before others have finished or time is called, take ALL your materials to the monitor and leave quietly. Never take any test material with you. The monitor can discover whose papers are not complete, and taking a test booklet may be grounds for disqualification.

VIII. EXAMINATION TECHNIQUES

1) Read the general instructions carefully. These are usually printed on the first page of the exam booklet. As a rule, these instructions refer to the timing of the examination; the fact that you should not start work until the signal and must stop work at a signal, etc. If there are any *special* instructions, such as a choice of questions to be answered, make sure that you note this instruction carefully.

2) When you are ready to start work on the examination, that is as soon as the signal has been given, read the instructions to each question booklet, underline any key words or phrases, such as *least, best, outline, describe* and the like. In this way you will tend to answer as requested rather than discover on reviewing your paper that you *listed without describing*, that you selected the *worst* choice rather than the *best* choice, etc.

3) If the examination is of the objective or multiple-choice type – that is, each question will also give a series of possible answers: A, B, C or D, and you are called upon to select the best answer and write the letter next to that answer on your answer paper – it is advisable to start answering each question in turn. There may be anywhere from 50 to 100 such questions in the three or four hours allotted and you can see how much time would be taken if you read through all the questions before beginning to answer any. Furthermore, if you come across a question or group of questions which you know would be difficult to answer, it would undoubtedly affect your handling of all the other questions.

4) If the examination is of the essay type and contains but a few questions, it is a moot point as to whether you should read all the questions before starting to answer any one. Of course, if you are given a choice – say five out of seven and the like – then it is essential to read all the questions so you can eliminate the two that are most difficult. If, however, you are asked to answer all the questions, there may be danger in trying to answer the easiest one first because you may find that you will spend too much time on it. The best technique is to answer the first question, then proceed to the second, etc.

5) Time your answers. Before the exam begins, write down the time it started, then add the time allowed for the examination and write down the time it must be completed, then divide the time available somewhat as follows:
   - If 3-1/2 hours are allowed, that would be 210 minutes. If you have 80 objective-type questions, that would be an average of 2-1/2 minutes per question. Allow yourself no more than 2 minutes per question, or a total of 160 minutes, which will permit about 50 minutes to review.
   - If for the time allotment of 210 minutes there are 7 essay questions to answer, that would average about 30 minutes a question. Give yourself only 25 minutes per question so that you have about 35 minutes to review.

6) The most important instruction is to *read each question* and make sure you know what is wanted. The second most important instruction is to *time yourself properly* so that you answer every question. The third most

important instruction is to *answer every question.* Guess if you have to but include something for each question. Remember that you will receive no credit for a blank and will probably receive some credit if you write something in answer to an essay question. If you guess a letter – say "B" for a multiple-choice question – you may have guessed right. If you leave a blank as an answer to a multiple-choice question, the examiners may respect your feelings but it will not add a point to your score. Some exams may penalize you for wrong answers, so in such cases *only*, you may not want to guess unless you have some basis for your answer.

7) Suggestions

   a. Objective-type questions

      1. Examine the question booklet for proper sequence of pages and questions
      2. Read all instructions carefully
      3. Skip any question which seems too difficult; return to it after all other questions have been answered
      4. Apportion your time properly; do not spend too much time on any single question or group of questions
      5. Note and underline key words – *all, most, fewest, least, best, worst, same, opposite,* etc.
      6. Pay particular attention to negatives
      7. Note unusual option, e.g., unduly long, short, complex, different or similar in content to the body of the question
      8. Observe the use of "hedging" words – *probably, may, most likely,* etc.
      9. Make sure that your answer is put next to the same number as the question
      10. Do not second-guess unless you have good reason to believe the second answer is definitely more correct
      11. Cross out original answer if you decide another answer is more accurate; do not erase until you are ready to hand your paper in
      12. Answer all questions; guess unless instructed otherwise
      13. Leave time for review

   b. Essay questions

      1. Read each question carefully
      2. Determine exactly what is wanted. Underline key words or phrases.
      3. Decide on outline or paragraph answer
      4. Include many different points and elements unless asked to develop any one or two points or elements
      5. Show impartiality by giving pros and cons unless directed to select one side only
      6. Make and write down any assumptions you find necessary to answer the questions
      7. Watch your English, grammar, punctuation and choice of words
      8. Time your answers; don't crowd material

8) Answering the essay question

Most essay questions can be answered by framing the specific response around several key words or ideas. Here are a few such key words or ideas:

M's: manpower, materials, methods, money, management
P's: purpose, program, policy, plan, procedure, practice, problems, pitfalls, personnel, public relations

a. Six basic steps in handling problems:
   1. Preliminary plan and background development
   2. Collect information, data and facts
   3. Analyze and interpret information, data and facts
   4. Analyze and develop solutions as well as make recommendations
   5. Prepare report and sell recommendations
   6. Install recommendations and follow up effectiveness

b. Pitfalls to avoid
   1. *Taking things for granted* – A statement of the situation does not necessarily imply that each of the elements is necessarily true; for example, a complaint may be invalid and biased so that all that can be taken for granted is that a complaint has been registered
   2. *Considering only one side of a situation* – Wherever possible, indicate several alternatives and then point out the reasons you selected the best one
   3. *Failing to indicate follow up* – Whenever your answer indicates action on your part, make certain that you will take proper follow-up action to see how successful your recommendations, procedures or actions turn out to be
   4. *Taking too long in answering any single question* – Remember to time your answers properly

IX. AFTER THE TEST

Scoring procedures differ in detail among civil service jurisdictions although the general principles are the same. Whether the papers are hand-scored or graded by machine we have described, they are nearly always graded by number. That is, the person who marks the paper knows only the number – never the name – of the applicant. Not until all the papers have been graded will they be matched with names. If other tests, such as training and experience or oral interview ratings have been given, scores will be combined. Different parts of the examination usually have different weights. For example, the written test might count 60 percent of the final grade, and a rating of training and experience 40 percent. In many jurisdictions, veterans will have a certain number of points added to their grades.

After the final grade has been determined, the names are placed in grade order and an eligible list is established. There are various methods for resolving ties between those who get the same final grade – probably the most common is to place first the name of the person whose application was received first. Job offers are made from the eligible list in the order the names appear on it. You will be notified of your grade and your rank as soon as all these computations have been made. This will be done as rapidly as possible.

People who are found to meet the requirements in the announcement are called "eligibles." Their names are put on a list of eligible candidates. An eligible's chances of getting a job depend on how high he stands on this list and how fast agencies are filling jobs from the list.

When a job is to be filled from a list of eligibles, the agency asks for the names of people on the list of eligibles for that job. When the civil service commission receives this request, it sends to the agency the names of the three people highest on this list. Or, if the job to be filled has specialized requirements, the office sends the agency the names of the top three persons who meet these requirements from the general list.

The appointing officer makes a choice from among the three people whose names were sent to him. If the selected person accepts the appointment, the names of the others are put back on the list to be considered for future openings.

That is the rule in hiring from all kinds of eligible lists, whether they are for typist, carpenter, chemist, or something else. For every vacancy, the appointing officer has his choice of any one of the top three eligibles on the list. This explains why the person whose name is on top of the list sometimes does not get an appointment when some of the persons lower on the list do. If the appointing officer chooses the second or third eligible, the No. 1 eligible does not get a job at once, but stays on the list until he is appointed or the list is terminated.

X. HOW TO PASS THE INTERVIEW TEST

The examination for which you applied requires an oral interview test. You have already taken the written test and you are now being called for the interview test – the final part of the formal examination.

You may think that it is not possible to prepare for an interview test and that there are no procedures to follow during an interview. Our purpose is to point out some things you can do in advance that will help you and some good rules to follow and pitfalls to avoid while you are being interviewed.

What is an interview supposed to test?

The written examination is designed to test the technical knowledge and competence of the candidate; the oral is designed to evaluate intangible qualities, not readily measured otherwise, and to establish a list showing the relative fitness of each candidate – as measured against his competitors – for the position sought. Scoring is not on the basis of "right" and "wrong," but on a sliding scale of values ranging from "not passable" to "outstanding." As a matter of fact, it is possible to achieve a relatively low score without a single "incorrect" answer because of evident weakness in the qualities being measured.

Occasionally, an examination may consist entirely of an oral test – either an individual or a group oral. In such cases, information is sought concerning the technical knowledges and abilities of the candidate, since there has been no written examination for this purpose. More commonly, however, an oral test is used to supplement a written examination.

Who conducts interviews?

The composition of oral boards varies among different jurisdictions. In nearly all, a representative of the personnel department serves as chairman. One of the members of the board may be a representative of the department in which the candidate would work. In some cases, "outside experts" are used, and, frequently, a businessman or some other representative of the general public is asked to serve. Labor and management or other special groups may be represented. The aim is to secure the services of experts in the appropriate field.

However the board is composed, it is a good idea (and not at all improper or unethical) to ascertain in advance of the interview who the members are and what groups they represent. When you are introduced to them, you will have some idea of their backgrounds and interests, and at least you will not stutter and stammer over their names.

What should be done before the interview?

While knowledge about the board members is useful and takes some of the surprise element out of the interview, there is other preparation which is more substantive. It *is* possible to prepare for an oral interview – in several ways:

1) Keep a copy of your application and review it carefully before the interview

This may be the only document before the oral board, and the starting point of the interview. Know what education and experience you have listed there, and the sequence and dates of all of it. Sometimes the board will ask you to review the highlights of your experience for them; you should not have to hem and haw doing it.

2) Study the class specification and the examination announcement

Usually, the oral board has one or both of these to guide them. The qualities, characteristics or knowledges required by the position sought are stated in these documents. They offer valuable clues as to the nature of the oral interview. For example, if the job involves supervisory responsibilities, the announcement will usually indicate that knowledge of modern supervisory methods and the qualifications of the candidate as a supervisor will be tested. If so, you can expect such questions, frequently in the form of a hypothetical situation which you are expected to solve. NEVER go into an oral without knowledge of the duties and responsibilities of the job you seek.

3) Think through each qualification required

Try to visualize the kind of questions you would ask if you were a board member. How well could you answer them? Try especially to appraise your own knowledge and background in each area, *measured against the job sought*, and identify any areas in which you are weak. Be critical and realistic – do not flatter yourself.

4) Do some general reading in areas in which you feel you may be weak

For example, if the job involves supervision and your past experience has NOT, some general reading in supervisory methods and practices, particularly in the field of human relations, might be useful. Do NOT study agency procedures or detailed manuals. The oral board will be testing your understanding and capacity, not your memory.

5) Get a good night's sleep and watch your general health and mental attitude

You will want a clear head at the interview. Take care of a cold or any other minor ailment, and of course, no hangovers.

What should be done on the day of the interview?

Now comes the day of the interview itself. Give yourself plenty of time to get there. Plan to arrive somewhat ahead of the scheduled time, particularly if your appointment is in the fore part of the day. If a previous candidate fails to appear, the board might be ready for you a bit early. By early afternoon an oral board is almost invariably behind schedule if there are many candidates, and you may have to wait.

Take along a book or magazine to read, or your application to review, but leave any extraneous material in the waiting room when you go in for your interview. In any event, relax and compose yourself.

The matter of dress is important. The board is forming impressions about you – from your experience, your manners, your attitude, and your appearance. Give your personal appearance careful attention. Dress your best, but not your flashiest. Choose conservative, appropriate clothing, and be sure it is immaculate. This is a business interview, and your appearance should indicate that you regard it as such. Besides, being well groomed and properly dressed will help boost your confidence.

Sooner or later, someone will call your name and escort you into the interview room. *This is it.* From here on you are on your own. It is too late for any more preparation. But remember, you asked for this opportunity to prove your fitness, and you are here because your request was granted.

What happens when you go in?

The usual sequence of events will be as follows: The clerk (who is often the board stenographer) will introduce you to the chairman of the oral board, who will introduce you to the other members of the board. Acknowledge the introductions before you sit down. Do not be surprised if you find a microphone facing you or a stenotypist sitting by. Oral interviews are usually recorded in the event of an appeal or other review.

Usually the chairman of the board will open the interview by reviewing the highlights of your education and work experience from your application – primarily for the benefit of the other members of the board, as well as to get the material into the record. Do not interrupt or comment unless there is an error or significant misinterpretation; if that is the case, do not hesitate. But do not quibble about insignificant matters. Also, he will usually ask you some question about your education, experience or your present job – partly to get you to start talking and to establish the interviewing "rapport." He may start the actual questioning, or turn it over to one of the other members. Frequently, each member undertakes the questioning on a particular area, one in which he is perhaps most competent, so you can expect each member to participate in the examination. Because time is limited, you may also expect some rather abrupt switches in the direction the questioning takes, so do not be upset by it. Normally, a board member will not pursue a single line of questioning unless he discovers a particular strength or weakness.

After each member has participated, the chairman will usually ask whether any member has any further questions, then will ask you if you have anything you wish to add. Unless you are expecting this question, it may floor you. Worse, it may start you off on an extended, extemporaneous speech. The board is not usually seeking more information. The question is principally to offer you a last opportunity to present further qualifications or to indicate that you have nothing to add. So, if you feel that a significant qualification or characteristic has been overlooked, it is proper to point it out in a sentence or so. Do not compliment the board on the thoroughness of their examination – they have been sketchy, and you know it. If you wish, merely say, "No thank you, I have nothing further to add." This is a point where you can "talk yourself out" of a good impression or fail to present an important bit of information. Remember, *you close the interview yourself.*

The chairman will then say, "That is all, Mr. ______, thank you." Do not be startled; the interview is over, and quicker than you think. Thank him, gather your belongings and take your leave. Save your sigh of relief for the other side of the door.

How to put your best foot forward

Throughout this entire process, you may feel that the board individually and collectively is trying to pierce your defenses, seek out your hidden weaknesses and embarrass and confuse you. Actually, this is not true. They are obliged to make an appraisal of your qualifications for the job you are seeking, and they want to see you in your best light. Remember, they must interview all candidates and a non-cooperative candidate may become a failure in spite of their best efforts to bring out his qualifications. Here are 15 suggestions that will help you:

1) Be natural – Keep your attitude confident, not cocky

If you are not confident that you can do the job, do not expect the board to be. Do not apologize for your weaknesses, try to bring out your strong points. The board is interested in a positive, not negative, presentation. Cockiness will antagonize any board member and make him wonder if you are covering up a weakness by a false show of strength.

2) Get comfortable, but don't lounge or sprawl

Sit erectly but not stiffly. A careless posture may lead the board to conclude that you are careless in other things, or at least that you are not impressed by the importance of the occasion. Either conclusion is natural, even if incorrect. Do not fuss with your clothing, a pencil or an ashtray. Your hands may occasionally be useful to emphasize a point; do not let them become a point of distraction.

3) Do not wisecrack or make small talk

This is a serious situation, and your attitude should show that you consider it as such. Further, the time of the board is limited – they do not want to waste it, and neither should you.

4) Do not exaggerate your experience or abilities

In the first place, from information in the application or other interviews and sources, the board may know more about you than you think. Secondly, you probably will not get away with it. An experienced board is rather adept at spotting such a situation, so do not take the chance.

5) If you know a board member, do not make a point of it, yet do not hide it

Certainly you are not fooling him, and probably not the other members of the board. Do not try to take advantage of your acquaintanceship – it will probably do you little good.

6) Do not dominate the interview

Let the board do that. They will give you the clues – do not assume that you have to do all the talking. Realize that the board has a number of questions to ask you, and do not try to take up all the interview time by showing off your extensive knowledge of the answer to the first one.

7) Be attentive

You only have 20 minutes or so, and you should keep your attention at its sharpest throughout. When a member is addressing a problem or question to you, give him your undivided attention. Address your reply principally to him, but do not exclude the other board members.

8) Do not interrupt

A board member may be stating a problem for you to analyze. He will ask you a question when the time comes. Let him state the problem, and wait for the question.

9) Make sure you understand the question

Do not try to answer until you are sure what the question is. If it is not clear, restate it in your own words or ask the board member to clarify it for you. However, do not haggle about minor elements.

10) Reply promptly but not hastily

A common entry on oral board rating sheets is "candidate responded readily," or "candidate hesitated in replies." Respond as promptly and quickly as you can, but do not jump to a hasty, ill-considered answer.

11) Do not be peremptory in your answers

A brief answer is proper – but do not fire your answer back. That is a losing game from your point of view. The board member can probably ask questions much faster than you can answer them.

12) Do not try to create the answer you think the board member wants

He is interested in what kind of mind you have and how it works – not in playing games. Furthermore, he can usually spot this practice and will actually grade you down on it.

13) Do not switch sides in your reply merely to agree with a board member

Frequently, a member will take a contrary position merely to draw you out and to see if you are willing and able to defend your point of view. Do not start a debate, yet do not surrender a good position. If a position is worth taking, it is worth defending.

14) Do not be afraid to admit an error in judgment if you are shown to be wrong

The board knows that you are forced to reply without any opportunity for careful consideration. Your answer may be demonstrably wrong. If so, admit it and get on with the interview.

15) Do not dwell at length on your present job

The opening question may relate to your present assignment. Answer the question but do not go into an extended discussion. You are being examined for a *new* job, not your present one. As a matter of fact, try to phrase ALL your answers in terms of the job for which you are being examined.

Basis of Rating

Probably you will forget most of these "do's" and "don'ts" when you walk into the oral interview room. Even remembering them all will not ensure you a passing grade. Perhaps you did not have the qualifications in the first place. But remembering them will help you to put your best foot forward, without treading on the toes of the board members.

Rumor and popular opinion to the contrary notwithstanding, an oral board wants you to make the best appearance possible. They know you are under pressure – but they also want to see how you respond to it as a guide to what your reaction would be under the pressures of the job you seek. They will be influenced by the degree of poise you display, the personal traits you show and the manner in which you respond.

EXAMINATION SECTION

EXAMINATION SECTION

TEST 1

DIRECTIONS: Each question or incomplete statement is followed by several suggested answers or completions. Select the one that BEST answers the question or completes the statement. *PRINT THE LETTER OF THE CORRECT ANSWER IN THE SPACE AT THE RIGHT.*

1. Generally, when energy passes from one trophic level to another in the food chain or food web, about _____% of the usable energy is transferred. 1.___
   A. 10 B. 20 C. 33 D. 50

2. Of the following organic elements, which is the most unreactive? 2.___
   A. Oxygen B. Carbon C. Nitrogen D. Hydrogen

3. The *first law of human ecology* states that 3.___
   A. uncontrolled population growth is the greatest threat to the planet's ecological integrity
   B. one cannot get more energy out of something than is put into it
   C. nature exists for all the earth's species
   D. any intrusion into nature has numerous effects

4. Which of the following federal laws established the requirement that all major federal projects that might affect the quality of the human environment be preceded by an evaluation of the project and its potential impact on the environment? 4.___
   A. Multiple Use Sustained Yield Act of 1968
   B. National Environmental Policy Act (NEPA) of 1969
   C. Resource Conservation and Recovery Act of 1976
   D. Comprehensive Environmental Response, Compensation, and Liability Act (CERCLA) of 1986

5. What is the term for a land area that delivers water, sediment, and dissolved substances to a major stream or river via small streams? 5.___
   A. Riparian zone B. Divide
   C. Buffer zone D. Watershed

6. Of the 7 billion tons of carbon that were released into the atmosphere throughout the 1980s, only about 3.2 billion tons remained in the atmosphere. The current hypothesis among scientists is that the bulk of this *missing carbon* is 6.___
   A. dissolved in freshwater resources
   B. stored in forests of the northern hemisphere
   C. locked into agricultural runoff
   D. dissolved in the oceans

7. What is the term for noxious, mineralized liquids that are capable of transmitting bacterial pollutants? 7.____
   A. Effluent B. Leachate C. Tailings D. Dioxin

8. Which of the following statements about pesticides is generally FALSE? 8.____
   A. The health risks of pesticides are negligible compared with their health benefits.
   B. They remain fairly immobile once applied.
   C. They work faster and better than alternatives.
   D. They lower food costs.

9. A lake with a low supply of plant nutrients is described as 9.____
   A. atrophic B. mesotrophic
   C. oligotrophic D. eutrophic

10. Which of the following compounds is associated with the earliest stage in the carbon-silicate cycle? 10.____
   A. Carbonic acid B. Hydrocarbon
   C. Calcium carbonate D. Bicarbonate ion

11. Probably the most important step toward slowing the global warming phenomenon would be to 11.____
   A. more carefully use nitrogen-containing fertilizers
   B. increase the overall efficiency of energy utilization
   C. completely ban the use of all CFCs
   D. plant multitudes of trees to help remove CO_2 from the atmosphere

12. Which of the following is NOT a product of aerobic respiration? 12.____
   A. Carbon dioxide B. Energy
   C. Water D. Glucose

13. Biological diversity is universally thought to consist of each of the following concepts EXCEPT _____ diversity. 13.____
   A. climatic B. genetic C. habitat D. species

14. When a material is removed from the earth's surface or subsurface by mining, dredging, quarrying, and excavation, the unwanted rock and other waste materials produced are referred to as 14.____
   A. gangue B. tailings C. spoils D. substrata

15. Each of the following elements is found in every living thing on the planet and is recycled when an organism dies EXCEPT 15.____
   A. calcium B. phosphorus
   C. nitrogen D. hydrogen

16. The concept that the growth or survival of a population is directly related to the life requirement that is in least supply, and not to a combination of factors, is known as the 16.____

A. law of succession
B. competitive exclusion principle
C. law of tolerance
D. law of the minimum

17. Which of the following is an example of a cosmopolitan species? 17.___
A. Monterey cypress
B. Moose
C. Polar bear
D. Humans

18. The term *overburden* refers to 18.___
A. an excess of the threshold of stress -- from chemical fertilizers and natural depletion -- that an agricultural soil can tolerate
B. the layer of soil and rock overlying a mineral deposit
C. the point at which water can no longer flow from one underground pore space to another
D. the point at which an ecosystem's resources can no longer sustain the current population of a species

19. Nearly all the carbon stored in the earth's lithosphere exists as 19.___
A. methane
B. igneous rocks
C. metamorphic rocks
D. sedimentary rocks

20. What is the term for any close, long-lasting physical relationship between two different species of organisms? 20.___
A. Affinity
B. Commensalism
C. Synergy
D. Symbiosis

21. The primary component of industrial smog is 21.___
A. ozone
B. sulfur dioxide
C. chlorofluorocarbons (CFCs)
D. carbon monoxide

22. In flowing streams, which of the following factors contribute to the fact that downstream ecosystems generally contain less dissolved oxygen than those further upstream? 22.___
I. Slower flow
II. Thinner tree canopy
III. Lower altitude
IV. Agricultural runoff

The CORRECT answer is:
A. I, II
B. III, IV
C. I, II, IV
D. II, III, IV

23. Which of the following factors would tend to increase species diversity in an ecosystem? 23.___
A. Frequent and extreme disturbance
B. The introduction of exotic species
C. The middle stages of ecological succession
D. Geographic isolation

24. Of the following methods for removing particulates from the exhaust gases of electric power and industrial plants, a(n) _____ is also useful for reducing sulfur dioxide emissions. 24.___
    A. wet scrubber
    B. baghouse filter
    C. cyclone separator
    D. electrostatic precipitator

25. What is the term for the process of separating an ore mineral from waste mineral material? 25.___
    A. Beneficiation
    B. Gangue
    C. Eutrophication
    D. Tailing

KEY (CORRECT ANSWERS)

1. A
2. C
3. D
4. B
5. D

6. D
7. B
8. B
9. C
10. A

11. B
12. D
13. A
14. C
15. A

16. D
17. D
18. B
19. D
20. D

21. B
22. C
23. C
24. A
25. A

TEST 2

DIRECTIONS: Each question or incomplete statement is followed by several suggested answers or completions. Select the one that BEST answers the question or completes the statement. *PRINT THE LETTER OF THE CORRECT ANSWER IN THE SPACE AT THE RIGHT.*

1. Which of the following is a term for a stage in ecological succession? 1.___
   A. Trophic level B. Sere
   C. Echelon D. Steppe

2. In general, as the amount of organic waste in a body of water increases, the 2.___
   A. biological oxygen demand (BOD) increases
   B. greater the risk of oligotrophy
   C. biological oxygen demand (BOD) decreases
   D. risk of die-off increases

3. According to the National Academy of Sciences and most other members of the scientific community, the most important priority in adopting a low-waste approach should be to 3.___
   A. recycle and compost as much waste as possible
   B. reduce the production of waste and pollution
   C. treat or incinerate waste that can't otherwise be prevented or transformed
   D. reuse as many things as possible

4. Which of the following is not a product of the nitrogen fixation process? 4.___
   A. Molecular nitrogen B. Ammonia
   C. Nitrate ion D. Amino acids

5. Of the following, the most important group of rock-forming minerals are the 5.___
   A. pyroxines B. carbonates
   C. phosphates D. silicates

6. The active decomposition zone of a stream is associated with 6.___
   A. waterborne pathogens
   B. a minimum dissolved oxygen content
   C. eutrophication
   D. reduced biological oxygen demand (BOD)

7. The third layer of the atmosphere, found above the stratosphere, is the 7.___
   A. thermosphere B. mesosphere
   C. troposphere D. ionosphere

8. Which of the following types of pesticides tend to be most persistent in the environment? 8.___
   A. Soil sterilants B. Botanicals
   C. Chlorinated hydrocarbons D. Carbamates

9. Which of the following pollutants is most likely to effect changes in the distribution of wildlife population? 9.___
   A. Asbestos B. Arsenic
   C. Nitrogen oxides D. Fluoride

10. The primary stage in oil field production typically recovers about _____% of the oil contained within the reservoir. 10.___
   A. 10 B. 25 C. 50 D. 75

11. A system's ability to maintain favorable internal conditions, despite changes in external conditions, is specifically known as 11.___
   A. homogeneity B. constancy
   C. homeostasis D. inertia

12. Which of the following international environmental summits resulted in agreements to reduce the air pollutants that destroy stratospheric ozone? 12.___
   A. Antarctic Treaty of 1961
   B. 1979 Conference on Long-Range Transboundary Air Pollution
   C. Montreal Protocol of 1987
   D. U.N. Earth Summit of 1992

13. Which of the following is a general term for all the organisms of all species living in an area or region? 13.___
   A. Biota B. Fauna C. Biome D. Biomass

14. Which of the following is NOT a step described in the traditional demographic transition model of human populations? 14.___
   A. Initially, countries have an unstable population with a low birth rate and a low death rate.
   B. Improved economic and social conditions bring about a period of rapid growth.
   C. As countries become industrialized, birth rates drop as people make use of contraceptives.
   D. Eventually, birth rates and deaths become balanced.

15. As a pollutant, which site on the human body will cadmium affect to the greatest degree? 15.___
   A. Bones B. Heart C. Liver D. Skin

16. Of the topsoil that erodes away each day in the United States, what percentage comes from land that is used to graze cattle or to raise crops to feed cattle? 16.___
   A. 20 B. 45 C. 60 D. 85

17. Which of the following is the clearest example of a primary consumer? 17.___
    A. Pine tree B. Wolf C. Deer D. Trout

18. In the control of industrial pollution, the scrubbing process is used primarily to remove _____ from gases emitted from power plants burning coal. 18.___
    A. calcium B. carbon C. load D. sulfur

19. Of the following, the greatest drawback to conservation-tillage farming is 19.___
    A. the potential for increased pesticide requirements with certain crops
    B. greater overall expense
    C. lower overall yield
    D. the potential for compaction of soil

20. Which of the following is NOT a commonly applied definition of biomass? 20.___
    A. Dry weight of all organic matter in plants and animals in an ecosystem
    B. Plant materials and animal wastes used as fuel
    C. Zone of the earth where life is found
    D. Organic matter produced by plants and other photosynthetic producers

21. The kind of ecological succession that occurs after the destruction or disturbance of an existing ecosystem is known as _____ succession. 21.___
    A. primary B. secondary
    C. pioneer D. seral

22. Species that are introduced into a new area by human action are described as 22.___
    A. hostile B. endemic C. alien D. exotic

23. Which of the following pollutants is caused by the incomplete burning of fossil fuels? 23.___
    A. Particulates B. Hydrocarbons
    C. Sulfur dioxide D. Nitrogen compounds

24. An interaction of two or more factors or processes, in which the combined effect is greater than the sum of their separate effects, is described as 24.___
    A. synergistic B. entropic
    C. alchemistic D. post-threshold

25. In the carbon cycle, carbon frequently enters the atmosphere through each of the following processes or events EXCEPT 25.___
    A. the respiration of living things
    B. fires that burn organic compounds
    C. winds that lift small sediments
    D. diffusion from the ocean

KEY (CORRECT ANSWERS)

1. B
2. A
3. B
4. A
5. D

6. B
7. B
8. C
9. D
10. B

11. C
12. C
13. A
14. A
15. B

16. D
17. C
18. D
19. A
20. C

21. B
22. D
23. B
24. A
25. C

EXAMINATION SECTION

TEST 1

DIRECTIONS: Each question or incomplete statement is followed by several suggested answers or completions. Select the one that BEST answers the question or completes the statement. *PRINT THE LETTER OF THE CORRECT ANSWER IN THE SPACE AT THE RIGHT.*

1. Which of the following natural resources is classified as inexhaustible/immutable, or incapable of much change or alteration through human activity? 1.___
   A. Agricultural products
   B. Atomic energy
   C. Waterpower of flowing streams
   D. Mineral resources

2. Each of the following practices is a current method for maintaining the utility of cattle grazing rangeland EXCEPT 2.___
   A. manipulating stock herds
   B. reseeding
   C. firing
   D. maintaining constant grazing pressure

3. The one of the following considered to be an ADVANTAGE of monocultural forest harvesting is 3.___
   A. superior wood quality
   B. makes use of built-in ecological balancing mechanisms
   C. allows nurturing of shade-intolerant species
   D. decreased susceptibility to fires

4. The type of soil that is BEST able to hold water is 4.___
   A. silt B. sandy clay
   C. silty clay D. loam

5. The practice of *chipping*, or breaking the forest harvest down into smaller particles that can be compressed into useful products, can INCREASE the forest yield by ______%. 5.___
   A. 25 B. 50 C. 100 D. 200

6. The ______ industry generates the MOST revenue in the United States. 6.___
   A. steel B. cattle
   C. textiles D. automobile

7. Which of the following is NOT considered to be a guiding principle in the current model for conserving natural resources? 7.___
   A. Balancing individual privilege with individual responsibility
   B. Ultimate government control of conservation efforts
   C. Concentrated, singular use of particular resources
   D. Frequent inventory and projection of resource use

8. One of soil's macronutrients is 8.____
   A. cobalt B. calcium C. zinc D. copper

9. Food production in the United States is currently hindered by all of the following factors EXCEPT the 9.____
   A. loss of farmland to land development
   B. gradually increasing average temperatures
   C. huge fossil fuel input requirement for production
   D. transfer of water to urban populations

10. The bark of trees, long discarded as useless by loggers, has proven to be a useful resource for all of the following purposes EXCEPT 10.____
   A. medical uses
   B. construction of building frames
   C. production of chemicals for tanning leather
   D. oil-well drilling compounds

11. Of the following, the one that is NOT generally considered to be an advantage associated with the use of organic fertilizers is 11.____
   A. increased rate of water release
   B. prevention of leaching
   C. improved soil structure
   D. maximum aeration of root zone

12. APPROXIMATELY _____ percent of the earth's freshwater supply is underground. 12.____
   A. 30 B. 50 C. 75 D. 95

13. Which of the following is NOT generally considered to be part of the ocean's contribution as a natural resource? A 13.____
   A. highway for international transport
   B. replenisher of oxygen supply through algeal photosynthesis
   C. major source of important vitamins in the human diet
   D. major source of important proteins in the human diet

14. The natural resource GENERALLY considered to be inexhaustible, but whose quality can be impaired by misuse, is 14.____
   A. rangeland B. marine fish and mammals
   C. static mineral resources D. solar energy

15. The one of the following resources that can be converted into methane gas by high-pressure steam heating is 15.____
   A. high-sulfur coal
   B. solid animal wastes
   C. petroleum
   D. human garbage and solid wastes

16. Given the current methods of using fossil fuels, the LEAST defensible (most wasteful), according to scientists, is 16.___
    A. synthetic or bacterial food production
    B. heating
    C. petrochemicals
    D. synthetic polymers

17. The BEST way to restore soil fertility is by 17.___
    A. organic fertilizers
    B. inorganic fertilizers
    C. crop rotation
    D. strip cropping

18. The MINIMUM amount of time that toxic material will remain in a given groundwater supply is generally considered to be _____ years. 18.___
    A. 10
    B. 30
    C. 200
    D. 1,000

19. What is considered to be the MOST influential factor governing the occurrence and behavior of aquatic life? 19.___
    A. Availability of food
    B. Availability of sunlight
    C. Availability of oxygen
    D. Temperature

20. Which of the following has NOT proven to be a consequence involved in the use of solar energy? 20.___
    A. Toxicity of working fluids
    B. Decrease in photosynthetic rates of surrounding flora
    C. Climatic change
    D. Marine pollution

21. More than 50% of the coal that has ever been mined from the earth has been extracted in the last _____ years. 21.___
    A. 100
    B. 50
    C. 25
    D. 10

22. The natural resource classified as exhaustible but renewable, meaning that its permanence is dependent on how it is used by humans, is 22.___
    A. fossil fuels
    B. wildlife species
    C. solar energy
    D. soil

23. The one of the following that is NOT a limiting power held by the International Whaling Commission over commercial whalers is 23.___
    A. protecting certain species
    B. deciding minimum length for permissible kill
    C. protecting breeding grounds
    D. protecting calves and nursing cows

24. Which of the following is generally accepted as the MOST promising solution to the increasing worldwide food shortage? 24.___
    A. Development of more effective fertilizers
    B. Vigorous human population control
    C. More efficient pest control
    D. Decreased reliance on meat as a food source

25. The contaminants PRIMARILY responsible for the depletion of the earth's atmospheric ozone are 25.___
   A. carbon monoxide
   B. chlorinated fluorocarbons
   C. dioxins
   D. steam

KEY (CORRECT ANSWERS)

1. B
2. D
3. C
4. B
5. D

6. B
7. C
8. B
9. B
10. B

11. A
12. D
13. C
14. D
15. A

16. B
17. A
18. C
19. D
20. B

21. C
22. D
23. C
24. B
25. B

TEST 2

DIRECTIONS: Each question or incomplete statement is followed by several suggested answers or completions. Select the one that BEST answers the question or completes the statement. *PRINT THE LETTER OF THE CORRECT ANSWER IN THE SPACE AT THE RIGHT.*

1. Which of the following is currently the MOST promising method for the management of the earth's wildlife resources? 1.___
   A. Introduction of exotics B. Habitat development
   C. Predator control D. Game laws

2. The element of American society that is MOST responsible for consuming the largest share of energy resources is 2.___
   A. industry B. home construction
   C. transportation D. recreation

3. Of all the water drawn and transported for irrigation purposes in the United States, APPROXIMATELY _____ percent is eventually absorbed by the root systems of crops. 3.___
   A. 10 B. 25 C. 50 D. 75

4. The APPROXIMATE rate at which the Mississippi River currently carries topsoil into the Gulf of Mexico is _____ tons per _____. 4.___
   A. thirty; minute B. one hundred; minute
   C. fifteen; second D. fifty; hour

5. According to current projections, it will be approximately _____ years before the world's fossil fuel resources are completely exhausted, given current methods of use. 5.___
   A. thirty-five B. fifty
   C. seventy-five D. one hundred

6. Each of the following is considered to be a disadvantage to monocultural systems for forest harvesting EXCEPT 6.___
   A. long harvesting rotations
   B. inefficiency in growing and harvesting large crops
   C. runoff from intensive chemical use
   D. creation of oversimplified ecosystems

7. _____ is considered to be among soil's micronutrients. 7.___
   A. Manganese B. Nitrate
   C. Potassium D. Calcium

8. In relation to the population growth of the United States, what is the increase in per capita rate energy consumption? It is increasing at about _____ rate of population growth. 8.___
   A. half the B. the same
   C. twice the D. five times the

9. Which of the following is NOT considered to be a disadvantage associated with the damming of flowing streams and rivers? 9.___
   A. Decreased energy potential
   B. Increased flooding
   C. Sedimentation of reservoirs
   D. Complications with the irrigating process

10. Given the topography of most United States farmland, the one of the following which has NOT proven an efficient method for the control of soil erosion by water is 10.___
   A. contour farming B. gully reclamation
   C. terracing D. planting shelterbelts

11. Of the following natural resources, the one classified as a consumptively used resource, or one whose eventual exhaustion is CERTAIN given current use patterns, is 11.___
   A. gem minerals B. freshwater fish
   C. stationary water sources D. natural gas

12. In forestry, a sustained-yield harvest program, one that produces a moderate crop that can be harvested year after year, is called 12.___
   A. silvicultural B. clear-cutting
   C. agricultural D. monocultural

13. Approximately _____ tons of soil are washed away ANNUALLY from the United States. 13.___
   A. fourteen million B. fifty-five million
   C. one billion D. three billion

14. Each of the following is considered to be a disadvantage associated with *channelization*, or the artificial widening of rivers and streams, EXCEPT 14.___
   A. loss of hardwood timber
   B. loss of wildlife habitat
   C. lowering of water table
   D. increased flood risk

15. The MOST defensible (least wasteful) use of aquifer water, according to most current scientists, is to 15.___
   A. irrigate monocultural crop systems
   B. relieve drought
   C. provide for industrial cleaning processes
   D. fill existing reservoirs

16. Given the current methods of using fossil fuels, the MOST defensible (least wasteful) one, according to scientists, is 16.___
   A. essential liquid fuels B. heating
   C. industrial purposes D. electricity

17. The annual allotment of _____ acres of rangeland per head is considered to be universally standard for a single cattle animal's grazing. 17.___
   A. two B. four C. eight D. twelve

18. APPROXIMATELY _____ percent of the extracted forest product in the United States is used for lumber. 18.___
   A. 30 B. 50 C. 70 D. 95

19. _____ is NOT considered to be an influential factor in the depletion of American soil nutrients. 19.___
   A. Cropping B. Erosion
   C. Pesticide use D. Fertilization

20. Which of the following is NOT considered to be a factor contributing to the decline of our freshwater fish resources? 20.___
   A. Decreasing habitat temperatures
   B. Toxic industrial waste
   C. Oxygen depletion
   D. Siltation

21. Of the following uses of a metallic natural resource, the one which is NOT generally considered to be consumptive or exhausting is 21.___
   A. zinc in galvanized iron
   B. tin in toothpaste tubes
   C. aluminum in cans and containers
   D. lead in gasoline

22. Each of the following is an effect of oil pollution on marine ecosystems EXCEPT 22.___
   A. introduction of carcinogens into food chain
   B. acceleration of photosynthetic rates
   C. concentration of chlorinated hydrocarbons
   D. immediate mortality of marine animals

23. The forestry practice of *clear-cutting* is defensively used in the 23.___
   A. old-growth firs of the Pacific Northwest
   B. oak groves throughout the Midwest
   C. sequoia groves of Northern California
   D. pine barrens of New Jersey

24. Each of the following is a factor that affects the erosion of soil by water EXCEPT 24.___
   A. volume of precipitation
   B. wind patterns
   C. topography of land
   D. type of vegetational cover

25. Which of the following is classified as an inorganic soil fertilizer? 25.___
   A. Legumes B. Manure C. Sewage D. Nitrates

KEY (CORRECT ANSWERS)

1. B
2. A
3. B
4. C
5. A

6. B
7. A
8. D
9. C
10. C

11. D
12. A
13. C
14. D
15. B

16. A
17. C
18. A
19. D
20. A

21. C
22. B
23. A
24. B
25. D

EXAMINATION SECTION

DIRECTIONS: Each question or incomplete statement is followed by several suggested answers or completions. Select the one that BEST answers the question or completes the statement. *PRINT THE LETTER OF THE CORRECT ANSWER IN THE SPACE AT THE RIGHT.*

1. *Which* of the following statements are TRUE of stream improvement? 1. ___
   I. The term denotes procedures for correcting an environmental deficiency or man-made problem
   II. Its prime purpose is increased fishfood production.
   III. It includes any treatment of the watershed that results in a favorable influence upon fish habitat.
   IV. It corrects conditions that continue to be aggravated by damaging floods.
   V. It may, under favorable conditions, improve shelter and spawning conditions.

   The CORRECT answer is:
   A. I,II,III B. I,III C. I,III,IV D. I,II,III,V
   E. All of the above

2. *Why* are deflectors preferable to dams? They 2. ___
   I. are less subject to destruction
   II. are less disturbing to the stream bottom
   III. allow vegetation to be established on deposits formed to one side of the stream
   IV. help to protect eroding banks
   V. cut off side channels or direct the flow to a more suitable channel

   The CORRECT answer is:
   A. II,IV,V B. III,IV,V C. I,II D. II,IV
   E. All of the above

3. Fishways may *not* be justified *where:* 3. ___
   I. There is not enough satisfactory upstream area to justify the cost
   II. Streams are populated with anadromous species
   III. There are insurmountable problems in getting a satisfactory return of downstream migrants to the ocean
   IV. The flow fluctuates considerably
   V. It is more economical to provide hatching channels below a dam

   The CORRECT answer is:
   A. I,II,IV B. II,III,V C. III,IV D. I,III,V E. II,IV

4. The *most* expensive structure used to prevent bank erosion next to roads is: 4. ___
A. Parking nodes B. Log revetments
C. Gabion revetments D. Gabion matting E. Riprap

5. All of the following are harmful effects of turbidity EXCEPT: 5. ___
A. Sight-feeders are disadvantaged
B. There is a decrease in dissolved nitrogen levels
C. There is a reduction in bottom organisms
D. There is destruction of sedimentation in spawning areas
E. Removal of algae and plants occurs

6. When erosion products reach streams, they 6. ___
I. fill ponds
II. cause the removal of algae, plants, and bottom food organisms
III. block fish passage
IV. destroy cover
V. increase turbidity

The CORRECT answer is:
A. I,V B. II,III,V C. III,V D. I,IV,V E. II,IV,V

7. *Which* of the following prescriptions should guide random boulder placement? 7. ___
I. Boulder placement is most effective in narrow, shallow, and moderate-to-low velocity stream channels
II. Boulder placement should be avoided in narrow channels with unstable banks
III. Boulders should be two-thirds of a cubic yard or larger
IV. All boulders should be placed so that they may be operational in high water periods
V. The number of boulders placed should be at least one per 300 square feet of channel

The CORRECT answer is:
A. I,II,IV B. II,III C. II,III,IV,V D. III,V
E. I,II,III,V

8. A type of fish ladder that consists of a series of ascending boxes set in a chute is: 8. ___
A. Pool and weir ladders B. Pool and orifice ladders
C. Denils D. Alaskan steeppasses
E. Fish locks and elevators

9. *What* is the MAIN reason for providing fish cover in lakes? It 9. ___
A. helps lower water temperatures
B. offers protection from bird and mammal predators
C. attracts fish
D. produces greater natural reproduction
E. decreases evaporation

10. Turbidity control for stream improvement is usually accomplished by 10. ___
A. increasing water flow B. removal of shade
C. use of instream devices D. chemical treatment
E. improvement of riparian vegetation

11. Direct channel improvement projects have been unsuccessful for all of the following reasons EXCEPT: 11. ___
A. Methods well-adapted to a one region gave poor results elsewhere
B. Limitations imposed by steep gradients and extreme fluctuations in flow were ignored
C. Abused watersheds were treated before or during the stream project work
D. Improper devices were selected
E. Devices were improperly installed

12. *One* of the MOST expensive deflectors is a ________ deflector. 12. ___
A. sheet piling B. rock C. trash piling
D. cabled tree E. gambion

13. *What* type of fish ladder is used *mainly* for passing small runs of fish over high barriers? 13. ___
A. Denils B. Alaskan steeppasses
C. Pool and weir ladders D. Pool and orifice ladders
E. Fish locks and elevators

14. *How* may the buildup of undesirable fish population be determined? By: 14. ___
I. Installing natural or artificial barriers
II. Creel censuses
III. Netting surveys
IV. Draining small lakes and ponds
V. Trapping surveys

The CORRECT answer is:
A. I,IV B. I,III,IV C. I,III D. II,III,V E. III,V

15. All of the following may deplete oxygen supplies EXCEPT: 15. ___
A. Decrease in temperature
B. Respiration of plants and animals
C. Reactions with other gases and chemicals
D. Decomposition of organic matter
E. Presence of iron

16. *Which* of the following guidelines should be considered in planning a direct channel improvement project? 16. ___
I. The need for improvement should be obvious
II. Bank deflectors are more susceptible to flood damage than dams
III. Log and sheet piling installations are better suited to streams with steeper gradients and larger flows than gambion structures
IV. Improvements should not be concentrated in one area but should be placed where they are most needed
V. When possible, structures should be located where solid bedrock occurs a few inches below the rubble

The CORRECT answers is:
A. I,IV B. I,III,V C. III,V D. II,III,V
E. None of the above

17. Cabled tree deflectors: 17. ___

I. Use only long trees
II. Use only trees with a large trunk circumference
III. Cable the trees parallel to the bank
IV. Must have the butt of the tree pointing downstream
V. Increase deflection by using trees with a maximum number of limbs

The CORRECT answer is:
A. I,II,III B. III,IV C. III,V D. I,II,III,IV
E. All of the above

18. *What* is the PRINCIPAL disadvantage of pool and orifice ladders? 18. ___

A. They are unable to function where the flow fluctuates considerably.
B. Too much flashboard adjustment is required.
C. They have a tendency to plug with debris at high flows and are difficult to clean.
D. Mechanical problems and heavy maintenance often cause high operating costs.
E. They are too expensive.

19. Stratified dispersal of toxicants are required in 19. ___

A. heterothermous lakes
B. lakes that cannot be completely drained
C. very deep lakes
D. lakes with both desirable and undesirable species
E. lakes with heavy cover

20. Carbon dioxide is removed from water by: 20. ___

I. Reaction with other chemicals
II. Inflow of subterranean water
III. Photosynthesis
IV. Agitation of water
V. Evaporation

The CORRECT answer is:
A. III,V B. II,III C. I,II,III D. I,II E. III,IV,V

21. *Which* of the following are the MOST practical to use in the creation or improvement of pools? 21. ___

I. Mechanical excavation II. Digging logs
III. Deflectors IV. Blasting V. Dams

The CORRECT answer is:
A. I,II B. III,IV D. III,V D. II,V E. I,IV

22. *Which* of the following statements are TRUE of improving gravel bed for trout and salmon propagation? 22. ___

I. The objective is to remove materials too small for spawning use.
II. Selected sites should not be subject to sediment from upstream sources.
III. The survival rate in cleaned riffles is 40-60% greater than before treatment.
IV. Bed stability must be controlled before cleaning procedures begin.
V. Cleaning procedures are followed by maintenance of sustained minimum flows.

The CORRECT answer is:
A. I,II,III B. I,IV,V C. I,III,V D. I,II,IV
E. All of the above

23. *Which* of the following are true of denils? They 23. ___
I. constitute an improved version of the Alaskan steeppass
II. are usually built over low barriers
III. are portable
IV. have good entrance characteristics
V. pass debris well

The CORRECT answer is:
A. I,II,III B. II,IV,V C. I,II,IV
D. All of the above E. None of the above

24. *What* are the disadvantages of aquatic plants in lakes? 24. ___
I. Certain types trap the eggs of insects and fish
II. The decomposition of dead plants consumes oxygen
III. Decomposing plants sometimes produce toxins which kill fish
IV. Less fish-food is available per unit area
V. Certain types increase turbidity

The CORRECT answer is:
A. I,III,V B. II,IV,V C. II,III D. I,III
E. II,V

25. *What* is the BEST *single* indicator of productivity? 25. ___
A. pH B. Total hardness C. Carbon dioxide
D. Oxygen E. Turbidity

26. *Most* dam failures are due to: 26. ___
I. Omitting to brace log dams behind trees or large boulders or extending them at least six feet into the bank
II. Construction of low dams that are more subject to destruction by floods than high ones
III. Building dams so high that floodwaters are forced over the bank at either end
IV. Constructing or directing the flow through wide notches, greater than one-fourth the total width of the dam
V. Restricting log-type dams to channel widths of 20 feet or less

The CORRECT answer is:
A. I,II,III B. I,III C. I,II,IV D. I,V
E. All of the above

27. Debris jams should be removed because they: 27. ___
I. Block fish passage
II. Are responsible for sedimentation of channels
III. Are unsightly
IV. Damage fish habitat
V. Prevent further sediment deposition downstream

The CORRECT answer is:
A. I,II,V B. I,II,III C. I,IV,V D. II,III
E. II,III,IV,V

28. Fish screens are particularly valuable in situations involving 28. ___
A. harmful debris
B. small streams with large volume diversions
C. artificial spawning channels
D. high water velocities
E. fishways of the denil or Alaskan steeppass type

29. What is the purpose of regulating dams? To 29. ___
A. decrease the velocity of stream channels
B. provide hiding places for fish during construction projects
C. permit scouring spring flows to remove silt and gravel
D. correct situations where normal stream flows have been pre-empted by irrigation or power diversions
E. supply satisfactory streamflows during the driest months

30. Carbon dioxide is removed from water by: 30. ___
I. Reaction with other chemicals
II. Inflow of subterranean water
III. Photosynthesis
IV. Agitation of water
V. Evaporation

The CORRECT answer is:
A. III,V B. II,III C. I,II,III D. I,III E. III,IV,V

31. What type of dam is well suited to large, fast-flowing streams? The 31. ___
A. gambion B. simple log C. board D. K
E. trash-catcher

32. Ladders may not pass fish if: 32. ___
I. The pools are too large
II. The slope is too shallow
III. Resting areas are inadequate
IV. Hydraulic conditions are unsatisfactory
V. The entrance does not attract fish

The CORRECT answer is:
A. I,III,IV B. I,II,III C. III,IV,V D. IV,V
E. All of the above

33. Riparian vegetation is important to the fish habitat in all of the following ways EXCEPT: 33. ___
A. It serves as a buffer strip to block soil movements and to trap and filter out silt
B. The root mats bind the soil in place to provide soil stability
C. When roots extend into the stream, small pools result
D. When shade is provided, it helps keep the water temperature low
E. It provides a habitat for insects

34. All of the following are *true* of streamflow maintenance dams EXCEPT: 34. ___
A. Sites must have sufficient storage capacity
B. Sites must be accessible to motor transportation
C. Sites must have an adequate amount of water that can be stored at a reasonable cost
D. The stream should have physical characteristics capable of supporting fish in reasonable quantity
E. Streams without pools do not justify development

35. *What* is the *most commonly* used method for control of undesirable fish? 35. ___
A. Chemicals B. Netting C. Trapping D. Electrical barriers
E. Physical barriers

36. All of the following emphasize low-stream gradients EXCEPT the ________ dam. 35. ___
A. K B. board C. trash-catcher
D. simple log E. gambion

37. All of the following are requirements of a good fishway EXCEPT: 36. ___
A. It must not create velocities which exceed the swimming capacity of the fish
B. It must dampen rapid changes in flow patterns
C. It should be deep enough so that fish may remain hidden from view
D. Those in which energy is dissipated by steeppass require resting areas about every two feet of vertical rise
E. It should operate at all stages of the river without need for manual controls

38. *What* is the MAIN purpose of thinning sites of dense thickets of woody riparian vegetation? 37. ___
A. It improves the stand
B. It reduces the area of shade
C. It makes the site more attractive to some animals
D. The site is more productive of insects
E. It allows new species to be introduced

39. The ability of any given body of water to produce plants and animals depends MAINLY upon: 38. ___
I. Its size II. Water movement III. Waterside
IV. Water quality V. Its shape

The CORRECT answer is:
A. I,IV.V B. I,II,III,IV C. II,III,IV D. I,V
E. I,II,IV

40. *Which* of the following statements are TRUE of planning water impoundments? 39. ___
I. The site should readily lend itself to dam and spillway construction.
II. A minimum lake depth of 30-40 feet is recommended for greater productivity.
III. Sites which involve flooding of substantial sections of good quality trout stream habitat generally have high priority.
IV. Anticipated sediment deposition in the reservoir basin should be low.

V. Sites at lower mountain elevations are preferable.

The CORRECT answer is:
A. I,IV,V B. I,II,III C. III,IV,V D. I,II,V
E. III,IV

41. *Which* of the following dams are considered to be relatively inexpensive? 41. ___
I. K II. Board III. Gambion IV. Trash-catch
V. I

The CORRECT answer is:
A. I,II,IV B. II,IV C. IV,V D. I,III,IV E. II,III,V

42. *What* is the MOST important factor of a fishway? 42. ___
A. The angle of the slope
B. The location of the rest areas
C. The hydraulic conditions
D. Adequate maintenance
E. The location of the entrance

43. *Which* of the following statements are TRUE of steambank plantings of willows? 43. ___
I. Successful cuttings result if made while the willows are dormant.
II. When beaver and muskrat are abundant, "hardened" cuttings should be used.
III. Best results are obtained when cuttings are planted on mud or silt bars.
IV. The lower end of the cutting should never be exposed to permanently wet soil.
V. Rooting success may be increased by dipping the cutting stub into a commercial root-growth hormone.

The CORRECT answer is:
A. I,II,III B. I,III,V C. I,II,IV D. II,III,IV,V
E. All of the above

44. Warm-water fish do *best* at summer water temperatures near 44. ___
A. 60°F. B. 70°F. C. 75°F. D. 80°F. E. 90°F.

45. *Which* of the following techniques produce greater natural reproduction of lake fish? 45. ___
I. Placing shallow spawning boxes filled with sand and gravel
II. Artificially graveled lake bottoms
III. Manipulating water levels
IV. Manipulating water temperature
V. Placing artificial "holes" on the lake bottom

The CORRECT answer is:
A. I,IV B. I,II,V C. II,III D. II,V
E. None of the above

46. *Which* of the following characteristics are TRUE of gambion dams? 46. ___

I. Highly effective on streams where the flow is very small
II. Best suited to rocky streams where the banks can be excavated to strata sufficiently hard to support the weight of the dam
III. Particularly well adapted to remote stream sections
IV. Extremely effective in protecting stream banks below culverts which accommodate large and high-velocity discharges
V. Extremely effective when restricted to streams less than 10 or 15 feet wide

The CORRECT answer is:
A. I,II,V B. II,III C. I,V D. II,III,IV
E. III,IV

47. *Which* of the following factors are important in designing weir and pool fishways? 47. ___

I. Small fishways should have a water depth of 6-12 inches over the top of the weir
II. Pools that are too large increase the discharge and make the pools very turbulent
III. Fish prefer shaded and dark areas while traveling through fishways
IV. Notches in the weir crests have the effect of increasing the quantity of water required for fish passage
V. Increasing the crest differential decreases the upper limit of plunging flow

The CORRECT answer is:
A. I,II,III B. I,III,IV C. II,IV,V D. I,II,IV,V
E. All of the above

48. *Which* of the following are benefits of stream bottom fences? They 48. ___

I. collect bedload material
II. aid in the establishment of streamside vegetation
III. reduce water velocity
IV. are important to stream improvement by their protection of existing vegetation
V. serve as allotment pasture division fences and aid in the management of livestock

The CORRECT answer is:
A. I,II,III,IV B. II,IV C. I,III,IV D. II,IV,V
E. All of the above

49. *Which* of the following statements are TRUE of water temperature? 49. ___

I. Temperatures affect the water's ability to carry dissolved oxygen.
II. Increasing the temperature in several small tributaries usually does not affect the temperature of the larger receiving stream.
III. Removal of riparian vegetation has little effect on raising water temperature.
IV. Water temperature manipulation may be achieved by regulating reservoir outflows.
V. Both water temperature and streamflow may be increased by the clearcutting of timber in a major portion of a drainage.

The CORRECT answer is:
A. I,V B. II,III,IV C. I,IV,V D. II,IV
E. IV,V

50. *Which* of the following are advantages of rotenone for selective kills? It 50. ___

I. is relatively inexpensive
II. has excellent vertical dispersal through stratified density in lakes
III. is effective in both warm and cold waters
IV. has a low toxicity level to other environmental forms of life
V. is not overly dangerous to the applicator

The CORRECT answer is:
A. I,II,IV B. I,IV C. II,III,IV D. IV,V
E. III,IV,V

KEY (CORRECT ANSWERS)

1.	B	11.	C	21.	C	31.	A	41.	D
2.	E	12.	C	22.	A	32.	C	42.	E
3.	D	13.	E	23.	B	33.	C	43.	B
4.	E	14.	D	24.	C	34.	B	44.	D
5.	B	15.	A	25.	B	35.	A	45.	B
6.	D	16.	A	26.	B	36.	E	46.	E
7.	B	17.	C	27.	D	37.	D	47.	A
8.	A	18.	C	28.	B	38.	D	48.	D
9.	C	19.	A	29.	E	39.	A	49.	C
10.	E	20.	E	30.	E	40.	A	50.	D

EXAMINATION SECTION

DIRECTIONS: Each question or incomplete statement is followed by several suggested answers or completions. Select the one that BEST answers the question or completes the statement. *PRINT THE LETTER OF THE CORRECT ANSWER IN THE SPACE AT THE RIGHT.*

1. All of the following are *true* of parking nodes EXCEPT: 1. ___
   A. They should be limited to straight or long sweeping curved sections of channel
   B. They should be limited to channels whose width does not exceed fifty feet
   C. Minimum distance between nodes should not be less than 400 feet
   D. Channel flow should not be directed into the opposite bank
   E. The general shape of nodes should be streamlined

2. *Which* of the following methods is MOST successful in eliminating undesirable fish in lakes? 2. ___
   A. Netting B. Trapping C. Spearfishing
   D. Commercial fishing E. Liberalized harvest regulations

3. *What* is the MAIN disadvantage of sodium arsenite in the control of aquatic weeds? 3. ___
   A. It is only really effective under acid conditions
   B. Results are too variable
   C. It is very corrosive
   D. It is highly toxic to fish, birds, and mammals
   E. Polyneuritis results from prolonged skin contact

4. *What* is the PRINCIPAL target species of greentree reservoirs? 4. ___
   A. Turkey B. Deer C. Quail D. Raccoon E. Duck

5. *What* is the MOST practical way of reducing algae growth in guzzlers? By: 5. ___
   A. *Maintaining* adequate chemical levels in the tank
   B. *Locating* them under a cover of trees
   C. *Facing* the open end of the tank in a northerly direction
   D. *Placing* the guzzler in a gully where it will collect silt
   E. *Adding* synthetic dyes to the cistern

6. All of the following are *good* herbaceous marsh plants *EXCEPT* 6. ___
   A. cattails B. arrowheads C. bulrushes D. smartweed
   E. snowberry

7. *Which* of the following aquatic plants are classified as emersed plants? 7. ___

I. Cattails II. Pondweeds III Bulrushes
IV. Waterweed V. Sedges

The CORRECT answer is:
A. I,IV,V B. I,III,V C. I,IV D. I,II,III
E. II,III,IV,V

8. *What* are the *most common* chemicals used to control emersed plants? 8. ___

I. 2,4-D ester formulations II. Silvex III. Dalapon
IV. Copper sulfate V. Dichlone

The CORRECT answer is:
A. I,IV B. I,II,III D. I,III D. I,III,V
E. I,II,IV

9. All of the following are *true* of the selection of a site for a greentree reservoir EXCEPT: The 9. ___

A. area should be close to a low gradient stream
B. area should be flat
C. area should contain absorbent soil
D. area should have a mast-bearing oak timber that is adapted to flooding
E. water supply must be ample and dependable

10. *Where* do guzzlers have their greatest value? In 10. ___

A. areas with sufficient rainfall to supply them
B. semi-arid regions where natural water is widely spread
C. areas where the soil is heavy clay and difficult to drain
D. areas that can be managed for a variety of wildlife
E. areas that do not offer the required arrangement of nearby cover and not—too—distant foods

11. *Which* tree species is probably the *single most important* mast producer through the country? 11. ___

A. Oak B. Hickory C. Beech D. Gum E. Cherry

12. *Which* of the following are floating-leafed plants? 12. ___

I. Water buttercups II. Duck weed III. Water shield
IV. Pond weed V. Water weed

The CORRECT answer is:
A. I,III,IV B. I,IV V. C. II,III,IV
D. II,III E. II,IV,V

13. *Why* is fishing water fertilized? To 13. ___

I. produce more game fish poundage
II. control or eliminate submersed aquatic weeds
III. control or eliminate algal growths
IV. decrease turbidity
V. produce greater natural reproduction of lake fish

The CORRECT answer is:
A. I,II B. I,III C. I,IV,V D. I,V E. I,II,III,V

14. *Which* of the following species of trees are considered *good* food producers for waterfowl? 14. ___
I. Cherrybark oak II. Elm III. Hackberry
IV. Sycamore V. Willow oak

The CORRECT answer is:
A. I,V B. I,II,IV C. II,III,IV D. II,IV
E. I,III,V

15. A guzzler is *similar to* a 15. ___
A. corridor B. dugout C. spillway D. cistern
E. cesspool

16. *Where* should a wood duck nest be placed so that it is *least likely* to be usurped by starlings? 16. ___
A. On trees B. On stumps C. On posts over water
D. In open parklike woods E. In dense woods

17. *Which* of the following are *true* of phytoplankton in lakes and ponds? 17. ___
I. They are tiny one-celled plants
II. They are attached to the bottom or lie on submerged objects
III. They can cause taste or odor problems in the water
IV. When they die or are broken loose, they entrap gas bubbles and are floated upward to accumulate on the surface
V. They produce toxins capable of killing fish, birds, and mammals

The CORRECT answer is:
A. I,II,III B. I,III,IV C. I,III,V D. I,III
E. I,II,III,IV

18. *What* dangers are involved in the use of fertilizers? 18. ___
I. The resulting increase in plankton production may cause serious depletion of oxygen
II. Inorganic fertilizers may cause clay particles to settle out of muddy ponds
III. Use of commercial fertilizers in nesting areas of spiny-ray fish may cause some of the embryos to die
IV. Fertilization may upset an efficient natural food chain
V. Fertilization may result in excessive production of filamentous algae

The CORRECT answer is:
A. I,II,III B. II,III C. I,II,IV,V D. I,IV,V
E. II,III,IV,V

19. *Which* species of trees should be *avoided* for use in a green-tree reservoir? 19. ___
I. Boxelder II. Pine III. Soft maple IV. Pin oak
V. Tupelo

The CORRECT answer is:
A. II,IV B. I,II,III C. II,III,IV D. II,IV,V
E. I,II,V

20. The tanks used for guzzlers are usually made of 20. ___
I. concrete II. rubber III. asphalt IV. plastic
V. plywood

The CORRECT answer is:
A. I,III B. II,IV,V C. IV,V D. II,IV E. I,IV

21. *What* is the MAJOR drawback of beechnut mast? 21. ___
A. The nuts are bitter
B. Few species prefer them
C. The nuts do not withstand freezing
D. The nuts do not last through the critical season
E. Production is not consistent

22. *What* type of algal growth forms a floating surface mat and is referred to as "pond scum?" 22. ___
A. Phytoplankton B. Filamentous algae C. Branched algae
D. Submersed algae E. Macrophytes

23. *Which* of the following are *true* of direct lake fertilization with lime? 23. ___
I. In areas where total water hardness is low, lime should be applied prior to general fertilization projects
II. Calcium is almost immediately available when agricultural lime is used in place of hydrated lime
III. Liming is recommended for unproductive, acid, highly-colored bog lakes
IV. Lime may eliminate fish parasites
V. Best results are obtained when lime and phosphate are added at the same time

The CORRECT answer is:
A. I,IV,V B. III,IV,V C. I,II,IV D. I,III,IV,V
E. I,III,IV

24. *What* is the MOST important consideration in providing artificial nesting sites for water fowl? 24. ___
A. Placement B. Construction C. Installation
D. Design E. Maintenance

25. *What* determines the size of the water-collecting apron to fill a guzzler? 25. ___
A. Minimum annual rainfall B. Average annual rainfall
C. Maximum annual rainfall D. The water shed's target species
E. The site location

26. The procedure used to release durable browse plants from the competition of less desirable species *mainly* depends upon 26. ___
A. geological formation
B. the time and intensity of the application
C. plant ecology
D. the action of biological agents
E. climate conditions

27. *Which* of the following are submersed plants? 27. ___
I. Pond weed II. Waterweed III. Pickerel weed
IV. Cattails V. Coontails

The CORRECT answer is:
A. I,II,III B. I,II C. IV,V D. II,IV
E. I,III,V

28. All of the following are the results of dry fall of drainable basins EXCEPT: 28. ___
A. Release of phosphates and other fertilizers from insoluble bonds with iron and other minerals
B. Control of overpopulations of forage fish
C. Increase in decomposition
D. pH is increased
E. Release of various fertilizers from organic colloidal systems

29. *Which* of the following are *true* of nesting cover for waterfowl? 29. ___
I. Bare shorelines should be replaced with closely-grazed pastures
II. Openings should be created when lakes or ponds are closely surrounded with dense brush cover
III. Reservoir drawdown is an effective method of manipulating cover
IV. Aquatic vegetation can be improved with deep water along the shoreline
V. The easiest way to provide brook cover is to leave trees and shrub growth uncut when the reservoir is constructed

The CORRECT answer is:
A. I,III,V B. I,II,III C. I,IV,V D. II,III
E. All of the above

30. Reservoirs intended for use by water fowl should 30. ___
I. have gently sloping shorelines
II. have shllow areas with mud flats
III. have desirable emergent vegetation
IV. have tree cover
V. not offer a desirqble habitat for small game

The CORRECT answer is:
A. I,II,V B. I,II,III,V C. I,III,III,IV
D. I,II,IV E. All of the above

31. The field width of a chaining operation intended to release browse is determined by all of the following EXCEPT 31. ___
A. density of the vegetation
B. type of vegetation
C. weight and length of the anchor chain
D. size of the tractors used
E. topography

32. Physical control of aquatic weeds involves: 32. ___

I. Adding synthetic dyes to lakes
II. Using a hand sickle or scythe
III. Adding nutrients to the water
IV. Spreading opaque black polyethylene sheeting over the surface or bottom of the pond or lake
V. Stocking water with herbivores of aquatic vegetation

The CORRECT answer is:
A. I,II B. II,V C. II,IV D. I,II,IV E. I,III,IV

33. An ideal wetland for water fowl has ________ open water, ________ marsh. 33. ___

A. 1/2, 1/2 B. 1/4, 3/4 C. 1/3, 2/3
D. 2/3, 1/3 E. 3/4, 1/4

34. *Which* of the following are the *essential* elements of the wildlife habitat? 34. ___

I. Food II. Topography III. Water IV. Soil
V. Cover

The CORRECT answer is:
A. II,III,IV B. I,III,V C. I,II,III D. I,II
E. II,IV,V

35. *Which* of the following are *true* for selecting reservoir sites? 35. ___

I. Reservoirs for wildlife should be no longer than are needed to serve the forage area
II. The most suitable soil is straight, clay soils
III. The watershed above the dam should not be large enough for flood damage to occur
IV. The channel grade immediately above the dam should have a fairly steep slope
V. Access to the water should be limited to the target species

The CORRECT answer is:
A. I,II,III B. I,II,III,V C. I,III D. I,III,IV
E. III,IV,V

36. *What* determines the size of the chain used to thin browse? The 36. ___

A. width of the field B. topography
C. degree of kill desired D. density of the target species
E. size of the tractors used

37. *What* are the disadvantages of creating organic turbidity as a means of aquatic weed control? It 37. ___

I. results in reduced use of the lake by swimmers and fishermen
II. is not practical on waters larger than small ponds or pot holes
III. can cause winterkill of fish
IV. is only practical for control of emersed plants
V. can cause development of filamentous algae

The CORRECT answer is:
A. I,II,III B. I,II,IV C. I,V D. III,V
E. I,II,V

38. *What* are the MOST important items to consider in a pond or pothole program? 38. ___

I. Soil type II. Slope of the pond margins
III. Water quality and quantity IV. Nesting sites
V. Plant species

The CORRECT answer is:
A. I,II B. III,IV C. I,II,III D. I,II,IV
E. All of the above

39. *Which* of the following are important to the design of spring developments? 39. ___

I. At least one escape route to and from the water should be provided
II. Protective fences should be negotiable by wildlife
III. Fenceposts should be pointed to discourage perching by avian predators
IV. Natural cover should be cleared from the watering area surroundings
V. Protective fences should be negotiable by domestic livestock

The CORRECT answer is:
A. I,III,V B. I,IV C. I,II,III D. I,III,IV
E. All of the above

40. *What* is the *minimum* width of the top of all dams constructed for reservoir sites? ____________ feet. 40. ___

A. 5 B. 10 C. 20 D. 30 E. 40

41. Browse is *most effectively* thinned by chaining when 41. ___

A. moisture has thoroughly saturated the soil
B. the ground is not frozen
C. there is no danger of frost
D. the first several inches of soil are devoid of moisture
E. soil moisture is minimal

42. *Which* of the following methods are *most effective* in controlling duckweeds? Use of 42. ___

I. wild ducks II. domestic muscovy ducks
III. 2,4-D ester mormulations in an oil carrier IV. kerosene
V. minnow seine

The CORRECT answer is:
A. I,III,V B. II,III C. I,II,III D. III,IV,V
E. I,III

43. *What* are the benefits of ditching marshes? It 43. ___

I. *increases* the variety of habitat for furbearers and waterfowl
II. *helps* animals find food and cover during dry periods
III. *facilitates* access for hunters
IV. *provides* necessary openings
V. *protects* prey fish from predators

The CORRECT answer is:
A. I,III,IV B. I,III,IV,V C. III,IV,V D. I,II,III
E. All of the above

44. *What* is the purpose of installing ramps in the drinking troughs of spring developments? To 44. ___

A. make them accessible to the target species
B. control access to them by wildlife
C. allow access to the public
D. provide access for maintenance purposes
E. provide safety from wildlife drownings

45. *Which* of the following are *essential* to constructing spillways of reservoirs? 45. ___

I. The spillway should have a capacity equaling that required to handle the largest known volume of runoff
II. It should be designed to allow the water level to rise just to the top of the dam
III. It should be wide and flat-bottomed
IV. It should be protected from washing by riprapping
V. The entrance should be narrow, and the grade of the spillway channel steep so that the water will pass through rapidly

The CORRECT answer is:
A. I,II,IV B. I,IV C. I,II,V D. III,IV
E. II,III,IV

46. *Which* of the following methods can effectively be used to remove competition from rocky browse sites? 46. ___

A. A hula dozer B. Mechanical scalping
C. A wheatland plow D. Hand scalping
E. Cabling

47. *What* is the *most common* algacide? 47. ___

A. Copper sulfate B. Sodium arsenite compounds
C. Sodium and potassium salts of endothal
D. Silvex E. Diquat

48. *What* are the *advantages* of dredging as a method of ditch construction? 48. ___

I. Dredged ditches are shallower than blasted ditches
II. There are lesser quantities of muck loosened along the edge of the ditch
III. High spoil banks are not created
IV. It is more expeditious and economical than blasting
V. Ditches are less susceptible to wave and wind erosion

The CORRECT answer is:
A. I,III B. II,V C. I,II,IV,V D. I,II,III
E. None of the above

49. *Which* of the following principles should guide the installation of a guzzler? 49. ___

I. It should not be placed in a gully
II. The tank should be placed with its open end toward the prevailing wind
III. It is more effective if an escape cover of trees is immediately adjacent
IV. When possible, the open end of the tank should face away from a northerly direction
V. The size of the water-collecting apron should be proportioned so that the tank will maintain an adequate water supply

The CORRECT answer is:
A. I,V B. II,III,IV C. III,V D. II,IV
E. All of the above

50. When reservoirs are built in drainages where the chances are high that the tank will be filled with sand, 50. ___
A. the bottom should be salted to encourage "puddling" the soil by livestock trampling
B. bentonite should be spread over the bottom and sides of the pit and face of the dam
C. a pipeline should be installed through the dam during construction
D. the reservoir should be built for the greatest possible ratio of depth to area
E. utilize fencing specifications which will prevent the tank from becoming clogged.

KEY (CORRECT ANSWERS)

1.	B	11.	A	21.	E	31.	B	41.	E
2.	D	12.	D	22.	B	32.	E	42.	B
3.	D	13.	A	23.	E	33.	C	43.	D
4.	E	14.	E	24.	A	34.	B	44.	E
5.	C	15.	D	25.	A	35.	C	45.	D
6.	E	16.	E	26.	B	36.	C	46.	D
7.	B	17.	C	27.	B	37.	D	47.	A
8.	B	18.	D	28.	A	38.	E	48.	B
9.	C	19.	B	29.	D	39.	C	49.	A
10.	B	20.	E	30.	C	40.	B	50.	C

MEMORY FOR FACTS AND INFORMATION

EXAMINATION SECTION

TEST 1

DIRECTIONS: Questions 1 through 15 test your ability to remember key facts and details. You are given a rather long reading passage, which you will have approximately ten minutes to read. The reading selection should then be turned over. Then immediately answer the fifteen questions that refer to this passage. Please do NOT refer back to the reading passage at any time while you are answering the questions. Select the letter that represents the BEST of the four possible choices.

THE CASE OF THE MISSING OVERTIME WAGES

Melba Tolliber is a new Labor Standards Investigator assigned to investigate a complaint of nonpayment of some overtime wages. The complaint came in the form of a telephone call from Albert Brater, employed by the Whizzer Audio and Video Store in Dorchester. Whizzer Audio and Video, Inc. is a fast-growing and very successful chain in the Northeast. Their headquarters is in Dorchester.

Melba Tolliber drives the eight miles to Dorchester on a breezy Monday morning. She meets with Albert Brater, the employee who called. He is employed in the warehouse unit.

Hello, Mr. Brater, my name is Melba Tolliber, and I'm here to investigate whether you've been paid the proper amount of overtime wages.

Nice to meet you, Ms. Tolliber. I'm not the only one with this problem. Two salesclerks in the Dorchester store, Mary and Martin, have also gotten less for overtime than they should have.

Can I talk with them, too? Melba asks.

Well, the problem is, we're worried about getting into a lot of trouble with the company. We were hoping you could talk just to me. I'm a little worried about talking with you myself.

This is a confidential interview; don't worry. It would be very helpful, however, if I could at least get copies of their paystubs.

Albert hesitates and then says, *Gee, I hope I can find my last paystub. Anyway, we've been working forty-six hours a week the last four weeks, but only getting paid our usual rate of $5.25 an hour.*

Melba says, *But that's below the minimum wage.*

Maybe it's $5.35; I get confused; I'll have to check. I think it's $5.35. Yeah, I'm pretty sure it's $5.35. But you know what else? I was promised a raise of $.50 per hour after eight months of working here, and that's up next week. We'll see if I get it or not.

Have the other employees here gotten the raises they were promised?

Yeah, I think they have. But I know of at least one person, a truckdriver, who hasn't gotten his raise yet.

Do you know his name?

Just his first name. But the next time I see him, I'll ask him if he's gotten the raise yet. I'll let you know if he hasn't.

What day would be good for you to drop off the paystubs and have a second interview?

Well, you have to give me some time to get them from Mary and Martin, too. How about this Thursday afternoon at one?

Fine, here's my card. I'll see you this Thursday at one.

At the beginning of their next meeting, Albert gives Melba the paystubs for the last month's work for all three employees.

Let's do you first, Albert. What have your hours been each week for the last four weeks?

I've worked the same schedule for the past month, my usual forty hours - 8 to 5 with an hour for lunch, which I don't like, on Mondays, Tuesdays, and Thursdays. Wednesdays and Fridays I've worked from 8 A.M. to 9 P.M. because those are the days we do our most shipping. They give us from 5 to 6 P.M. as a dinner break on those days.

So that adds up to forty-six hours. Give me a few minutes to go over these figures with my calculator.

That's a great calculator; it's so small. Looks like a credit card.

Thanks, but I have to be careful how I hit the numbers; there's not much room.... Well, according to my calculations, you're owed $48.15 in overtime pay for the last four weeks. But there's something else wrong, too. It looks like they've been taking out a little too much money for Social Security. Let me recheck this.

1. In the passage, Melba Tolliber visited 1.____
   A. Midwood
   B. Dorchester
   C. Midale
   D. Midville

2. In the passage, Melba talked with 2.____
   A. Albert who works in the warehouse unit
   B. Albert who works in the warehouse unit and in the store
   C. Robert who works in the warehouse
   D. Robert, Martin, and Mary who work in the warehouse and the store

3. The organization whose payment of overtime wages is in question 3.____
   A. is struggling to succeed
   B. is the most successful of the new audio-visual store chains in the Northeast
   C. has its headquarters in the town that Melba travels to
   D. has successfully switched from selling just records to selling records, tapes, and video equipment

4. During their initial discussion, how sure of his rate of pay was the employee to whom Melba spoke? 4.____
   A. Not sure at all
   B. Very sure
   C. Pretty sure
   D. Totally unsure

5. What day of the week did Melba conduct the initial interview? 5.____
   A. Monday
   B. Wednesday
   C. Tuesday
   D. Thursday

6. When did Melba conduct the second interview? 6.____
   A. Monday at 1 P.M.
   B. Thursday at 1 P.M.
   C. Wednesday at 1 P.M.
   D. Friday at 1 P.M.

7. In order to calculate how much money the employee should have received, Melba used a 7.____
   A. credit card
   B. calculator
   C. credit card/calculator/watch combination
   D. desk top personal computer

8. According to the passage, what did Melba do to try to make the employee feel more at ease? 8.____
   She
   A. gave him time to collect his thoughts
   B. assured him that she believed what he said
   C. assured him that the interview was confidential
   D. asked if she could speak with the other two employees affected

9. The initial complaint from the employee 9.___
   A. resulted in his receiving back pay
   B. came in the form of a phone call
   C. was anonymous
   D. resulted in a large-scale investigation

10. The name of the establishment the employee works for is the 10.___
   A. Whizzer
   B. Genuine Article
   C. Electronic Era
   D. Gizmos etcetera

11. The other two employees who have questions about their overtime pay 11.___
   A. are truckdrivers
   B. work in the warehouse
   C. are salesclerks
   D. work in maintenance

12. The organization told the employee he would receive a 12.___
   A. $.60 per hour raise after eight months
   B. $.60 per hour raise after five months
   C. $.50 per hour raise after six months
   D. $.50 per hour raise after eight months

13. How many hours a week have the employees who are questioning their pay been working for the last month? 13.___
   A. Forty-four
   B. Forty-five
   C. Forty-six
   D. Forty-eight

14. In the last month, what hours did the employee Melba interviewed work on Wednesdays? 14.___
   A. 8 A.M. to 5 P.M.
   B. 9 A.M. to 10 P.M.
   C. 9 A.M. to 5 P.M.
   D. 8 A.M. to 9 P.M.

15. At the start of the second interview, 15.___
   A. the employee gives Melba the paystubs for the last month for all three workers involved
   B. the employee gives Melba the paystubs for the last month for all three workers involved, with the exception of his last paystub
   C. the employee gives Melba only his paystubs from the last month
   D. it cannot be determined if the employee gives Melba any paystubs

---

KEY (CORRECT ANSWERS)

1. B	6. B	11. C
2. A	7. B	12. D
3. C	8. C	13. C
4. C	9. B	14. D
5. A	10. A	15. A

TEST 2

DIRECTIONS: Questions 1 through 15 test your ability to remember key facts and details. You are given a rather long reading passage, which you will have approximately ten minutes to read. The reading selection should then be turned over. Then immediately answer the fifteen questions that refer to this passage. Please do NOT refer back to the reading passage at any time while you are answering these questions. Select the letter that represents the BEST of the four possible choices.

THE CASE OF THE DELINQUENT TAXPAYER

David Owens has been a Tax Investigator for five years. His unit has received another anonymous tip about possible sales tax abuse, and David's supervisor, William, has assigned David to conduct the investigation. The organization in question is Bob's News, a 24-hour newsstand and variety store. The store is located in Hillsdell, five miles away. The anonymous caller did not provide details, but stated that she was an employee, and that there was widespread *abuse in the collection and reporting of sales tax by the store*. The agency has had a series of crank calls regarding sales tax abuse in Hillsdell.

For this investigation, David has been instructed not to work undercover, but to go in, identify himself, and discuss the situation with the owner and some employees without divulging the reason for the visit. On Wednesday, David drives to the store in a government car, a 2004 Plymouth.

David arrives at the store and buys a magazine for which he is properly not charged sales tax. He speaks to the employee whose name tag says Susan.

Hello, Susan, my name is David Owens, and I'm from the State Tax Department. Here's my identification. We're doing a routine check-up to see if things are in order with regard to sales tax collection and reporting. Is the owner around?

No, Bob is out of town today. He'll be back tomorrow. You seem surprised that his name is Bob. Some people think he must not exist, sort of like a Betty Crocker or something. Can I help you with anything? I'm the Assistant Manager.

Well, it would be helpful if you could answer a few questions for me.

As long as it doesn't get me in trouble with my boss, I'd be glad to, Susan replied.

Don't worry, I won't ask you anything that could get you in trouble.

OK, then.

Did someone tell employees how to go about collecting sales tax on items?

Bob has a list of items we're not allowed to collect tax on. It's right next to the cash register. Would you like to see it?

If you don't mind. Thanks. It says here not to collect tax on magazines, but there's no mention of newspapers.

I guess that's because he probably assumes we know better than that. I'll ask him to add it to the list.

This is a pretty good list, but what's this written on the bottom here about toilet paper? That's a taxable item.

Oh, I know. Henry who works nights put that in as a joke because he says toilet paper is a necessity, not a luxury, and shouldn't be taxed. I agree. So does Bob. But don't worry, we collect sales tax on it. Nine percent, right?

No, the rate is eight percent.

Just kidding, David. We know that. I guess I shouldn't joke about something like that; I don't want to end up in jail. What else do you need to know?

Who keeps the records and submits the sales tax money to Metro City every quarter?

Bob does that himself, but I'd rather you come back tomorrow to talk with him about that end of it....I think that would be best. I don't know much about it, except that he yells if I don't have everything - the records and stuff - ready for him when he wants it.

What time do you think Bob will be in tomorrow?

I think the morning would be best; you'll be sure to catch him then.

OK, I'll drop by tomorrow around nine. See you then. Thanks again.

The next day, David drives back to the store to meet with Bob at the time stated earlier. When he arrives, Susan immediately introduces him to Bob.

It's nice to meet you, Bob. Nice store you have here. How long have you been in business?

We've been open for five years. Time really flies, doesn't it?

It sure does. As Susan probably mentioned, I'm here on a routine type check-up about sales tax collection.

Sure thing.

Well, I just noticed you're not displaying the Sales Tax Certificate of Authority that you need to show in order to collect sales tax.

That's strange; it was there yesterday. Here it is. It fell under the counter. We're off to a great start. Let me tape this thing back up.

How many employees work here, Bob?

We have six full-time and three part-time employees, plus myself. I understand you'd like to see our books. Come on in to my office. Stay in here as long as you need. I've got it all laid out for you.

Thanks.

Several hours later, David finishes looking through the books.

Well, Bob, things look in order. The only question I have is why your receipts for 2004 were so much lower than in other years?

A chain store moved in about eight blocks away, and we initially lost a lot of business. But eventually our customers started coming back. We do the little things - save them the Boston papers, things like that. The chain moved downtown in early 2005.

Well, listen, thanks very much for all of your time. I really appreciate it.

No problem. Anytime. Well, I wouldn't go that far, but it's been nice meeting you.

1. What was the name of the Tax Investigator in the above passage? 1.____
   A. David Allen B. Bob Williams
   C. Derwin Williams D. David Owens

2. What was the name of the city the investigator visited? 2.____
   A. Hillsville B. Hillsdale
   C. Hicksville D. Hillsdell

3. The store under investigation is a 3.____
   A. department store
   B. 24-hour massage parlor
   C. newsstand and variety store
   D. sporting goods store

4. The phone call received by the agency was 4.____
   A. placed by an anonymous employee of the store being accused of sales tax fraud
   B. received by the investigator handling the case
   C. placed by an anonymous caller
   D. received by the investigator's supervisor

5. The investigator on this case 5.____
   A. did not work undercover
   B. was instructed to work undercover, but refused because of the nature of the case
   C. worked undercover
   D. pretended to his supervisor that he worked undercover

6. According to the above passage, it is 6.____
   A. not correct to charge sales tax for a magazine
   B. correct to charge sales tax for pet food
   C. correct to charge sales tax for a newspaper
   D. correct to charge sales tax for a magazine

7. The Assistant Manager of the store is 7.____
   A. Susan B. David
   C. Bob D. Betty Crocker

8. What day was the initial investigation conducted? 8.____
   A. Monday B. Wednesday
   C. Tuesday D. Thursday

9. The list the investigator was shown contained 9.____
   A. a list of sales taxable items
   B. a list of non-taxable items
   C. a list of products on which sales tax was mistakenly charged
   D. the Certificate of Authority

10. According to the above passage, sales tax was to be charged on 10.____
    A. pet food B. cigarettes
    C. gasoline D. toilet paper

11. According to the above passage, the sales tax was _____%. 11.___
    A. seven B. nine C. eight D. ten

12. According to the passage, how often was the sales tax submitted? 12.___
    A. Every month
    B. Quarterly
    C. Twice a year
    D. Once every six months

13. According to the passage, where are the sales tax monies sent? 13.___
    A. River City
    B. Metro City
    C. Metropolis
    D. Hillswood

14. According to the passage, which of the following is TRUE? Bob's business, called Bob's 14.___
    A. News and Variety, has been open for five years
    B. Department Store, has been open for six years
    C. Variety, has been open for six years
    D. News, has been open for five years

15. The only question the investigator had about Bob's books was why receipts for _____ than in other years. 15.___
    A. 2005 were so much lower
    B. 2004 were so much lower
    C. 2005 were so much higher
    D. 2004 were so much higher

KEY (CORRECT ANSWERS)

1. D	6. A	11. C
2. D	7. A	12. B
3. C	8. B	13. B
4. C	9. B	14. D
5. A	10. D	15. B

EXAMINATION SECTION

Questions 1-4.

Questions 1 to 4 measure your ability to recognize objects, people, events, parts of maps, or crime, accident, or other scenes to which you have been exposed.

Below and on the following pages are twenty illustrations. Study them carefully. In the test, you will be shown pairs of drawings. For each pair, you will be asked which is or are from the twenty illustrations in this part.

COMMUNITY
CENTER

U.S.
MAIL
U.S.
MAIL
U.S.
MAIL

CONSTRUCTION
CO.

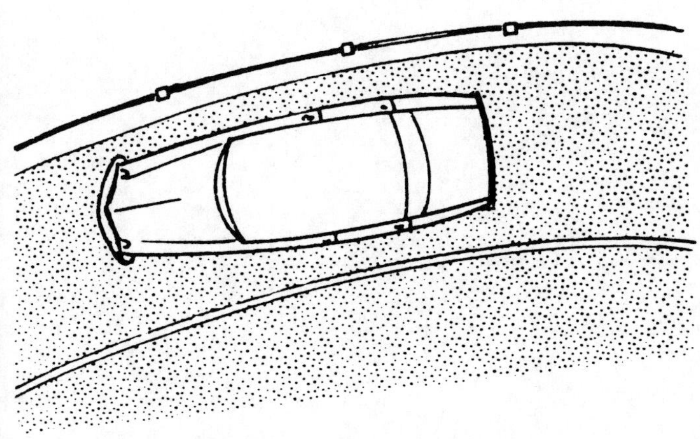

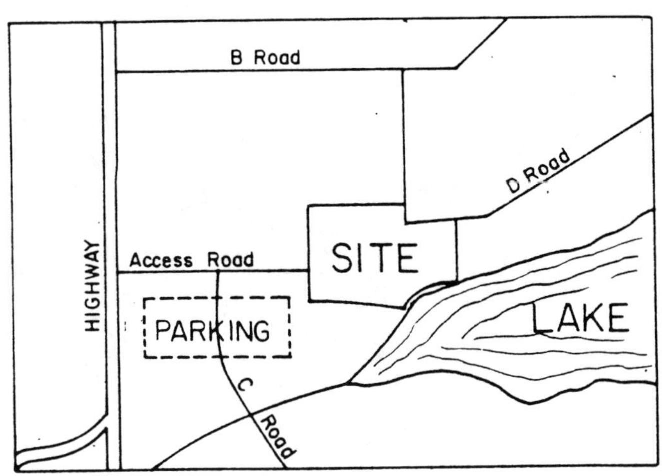
B Road
D Road
HIGHWAY
Access Road
SITE
PARKING
LAKE
C
Road

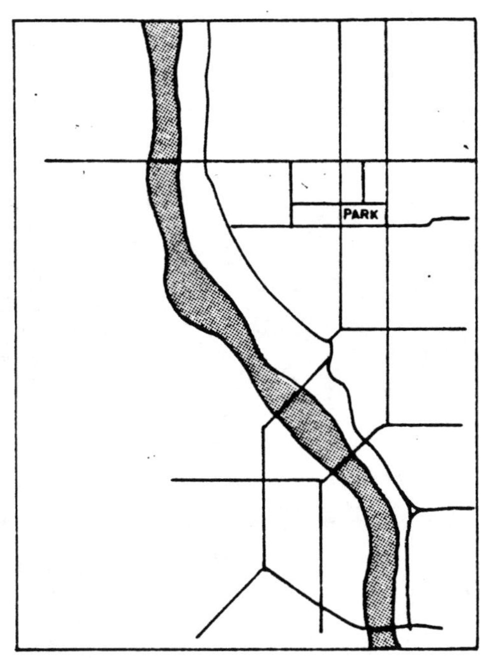
PARK

Questions 1-4.

DIRECTIONS: In Questions 1 to 4, select the choice that corresponds to the scene(s) that is(are) from the illustrations for this section. *PRINT THE LETTER OF THE CORRECT ANSWER IN THE SPACE AT THE RIGHT.*

1. 1.____

I

II.

A. I *only*
B. II *only*
C. Both I and II
D. Neither I nor II

2. 2.____

I.

II.

A. I *only*
B. II *only*
C. Both I and II
D. Neither I nor II

3. 3. ____

I. II.

A. I *only*
B. II *only*
C. Both I and II
D. Neither I nor II

4. 4. ____

I. II.

A. I *only*
B. II *only*
C. Both I and II
D. Neither I nor II

Questions 5-6.

DIRECTIONS: Questions 5 and 6 measure your ability to notice and interpret details accurately. You will be shown a picture, below, and then asked a set of questions about the picture. You do NOT need to memorize this picture. You may look at the picture when answering the questions.

5. Details in the picture lend some support to or do NOT tend to contradict which of the following statements about the person who occupies the room? 5.___
   I. The person is very careless.
   II. The person smokes

   The CORRECT answer is:
   A. I *only* B. II *only*
   C. Both I and II D. Neither I nor II

6. The number on the piece of paper on the desk is *most likely* a 6.___
   A. ZIP code B. street number
   C. social security number D. telephone area code

Questions 7-10.

DIRECTIONS: Questions 7 to 10 measure your ability to recognize objects or people in differing views, contexts, or situations. Each question consists of three pictures; one labeled *I*, and one labeled *II*. In each question, you are to determine whether *A - I only, B - II only, C - Both I and II*, or *D - Neither I nor II* COULD be the Subject.

The Subject is *always* ONE person or ONE object. The Subject-picture shows the object or person as it, he, or she appeared at the time of initial contact. Pictures I and II show objects from a different viewpoint than that of the Subject-picture. For example, if the Subject-picture presents a front view, I and II may present back views, side views, or a back and a side view. Also, art objects may be displayed differently -- may have a different base or frame or method of hanging.

When the Subject is a person, I or II will be a picture of a different person or will be a picture of the same person after some change has taken place: The person may have made a deliberate attempt to alter his or her appearance, such as wearing (or taking off) a wig, growing (or shaving off) a beard or mustache, or dressing as a member of the opposite sex. The change may also be a natural one, such as changing a hair style, changing from work clothes to play clothes or from play clothes to work clothes, or growing older, thinner, or fatter. *None has had cosmetic surgery.*

7. 7.____

Subject

I.

II.

A. I *only*
B. II *only*
C. Both I and II
D. Neither I nor II

8. 8.____

Subject **I.** **II.**

A. I *only* B. II *only*
C. Both I and II D. Neither I nor II

9. 9.____

Subject **I.** **II.**

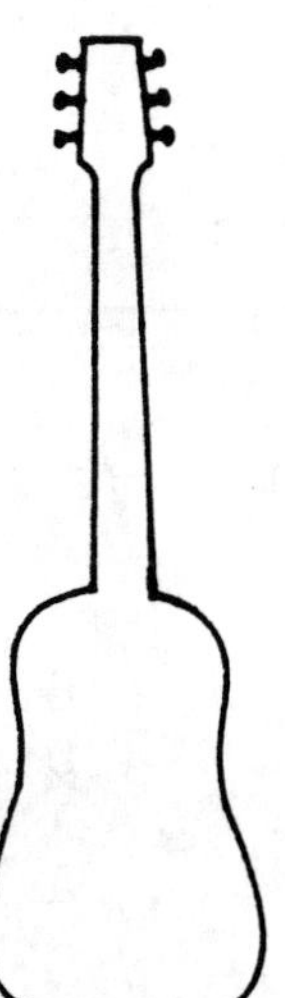

A. I *only* B. II *only*
C. Both I and II D. Neither I nor II

10. 10.____

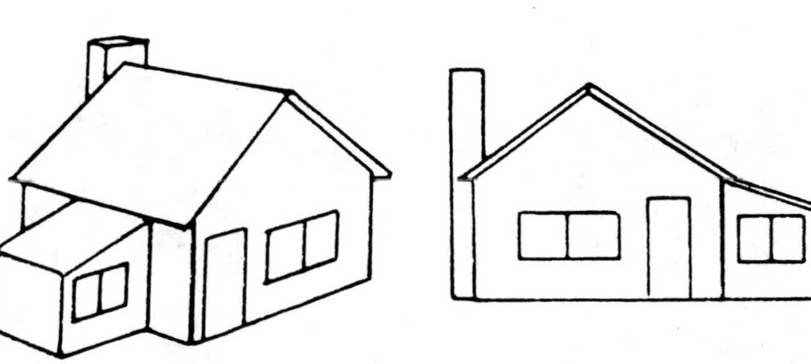

A. I *only*
B. II *only*
C. Both I and II
D. Neither I nor II

KEY (CORRECT ANSWERS)

1. B
2. D
3. A
4. A
5. B
6. B
7. D
8. A
9. D
10. D

VISUAL RECALL

EXAMINATION SECTION

DIRECTIONS: Each question or incomplete statement is followed by several suggested answers or completions. Select the one that BEST answers the question or completes the statement. *PRINT THE LETTER OF THE CORRECT ANSWER IN THE SPACE AT THE RIGHT.*
This test consists of four(4) pictures with questions following each picture. Study each picture for three (3) minutes. Then answer the questions based upon what you remember without looking back at the pictures.

Questions 1-5

DIRECTIONS: Questions 1 through 5 are based on the drawing below showing a view of a waiting area in a public building.

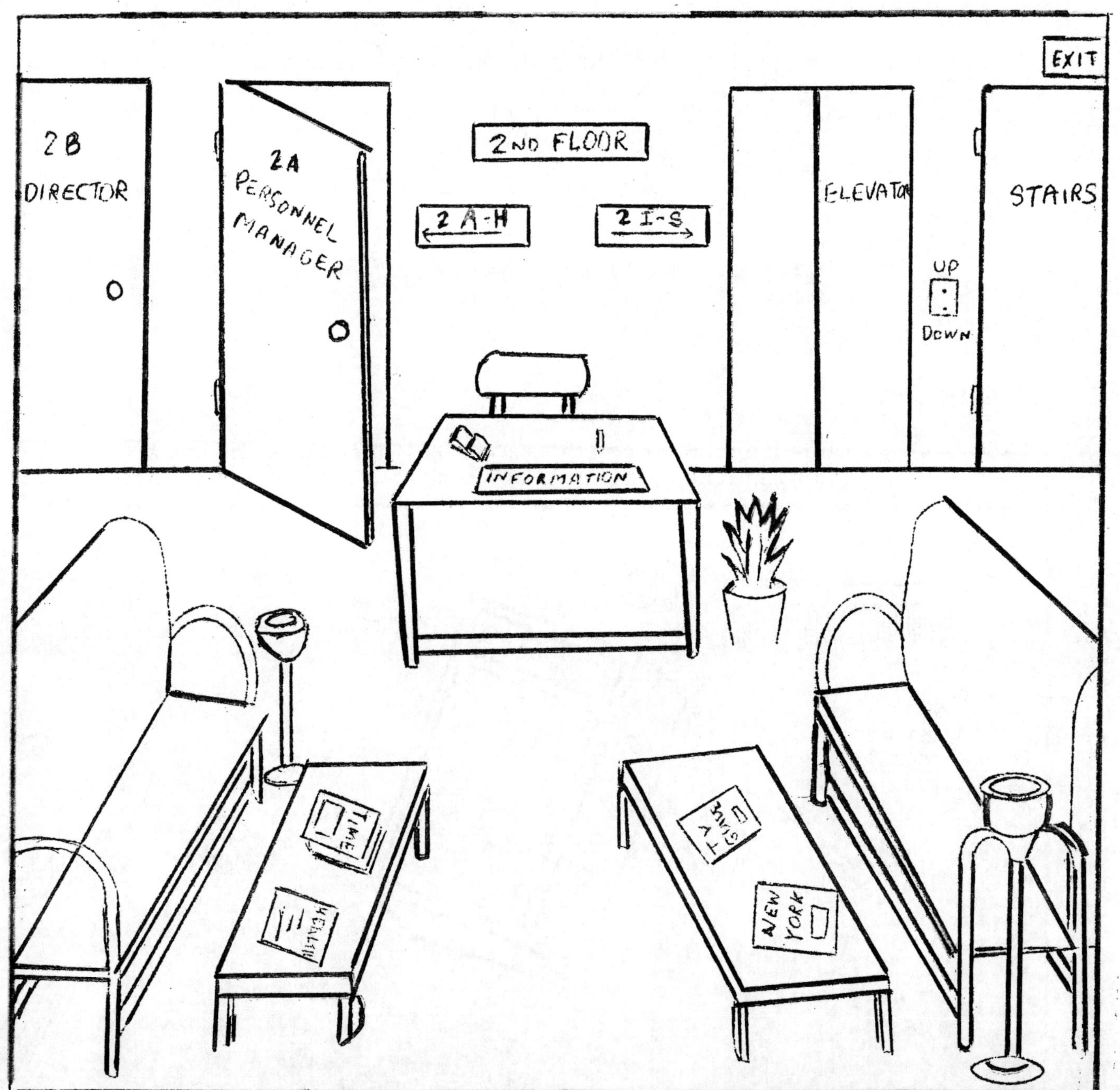

1. A desk is shown in the drawing. Which of the following is on the desk? 1.___
A(n)
   A. plant B. telephone
   C. in-out file D. *Information* sign

2. On which floor is the waiting area? 2.___
   A. Basement B. Main floor
   C. Second floor D. Third floor

3. The door <u>immediately to the right</u> of the desk is a(n) 3.___
   A. door to the Personnel Office
   B. elevator door
   C. door to another corridor
   D. door to the stairs

4. Among the magazines on the tables in the waiting area are 4.___
   A. TIME and NEWSWEEK
   B. READER'S DIGEST and T.V. GUIDE
   C. NEW YORK and READER'S DIGEST
   D. TIME and T.V. GUIDE

5. One door is partly open. 5.___
This is the door to
   A. the Director's office
   B. the Personnel Manager's office
   C. the stairs
   D. an unmarked office

Questions 6-9.

DIRECTIONS: Questions 6 through 9 are based on the drawing below showing the contents of a male suspect's pockets.

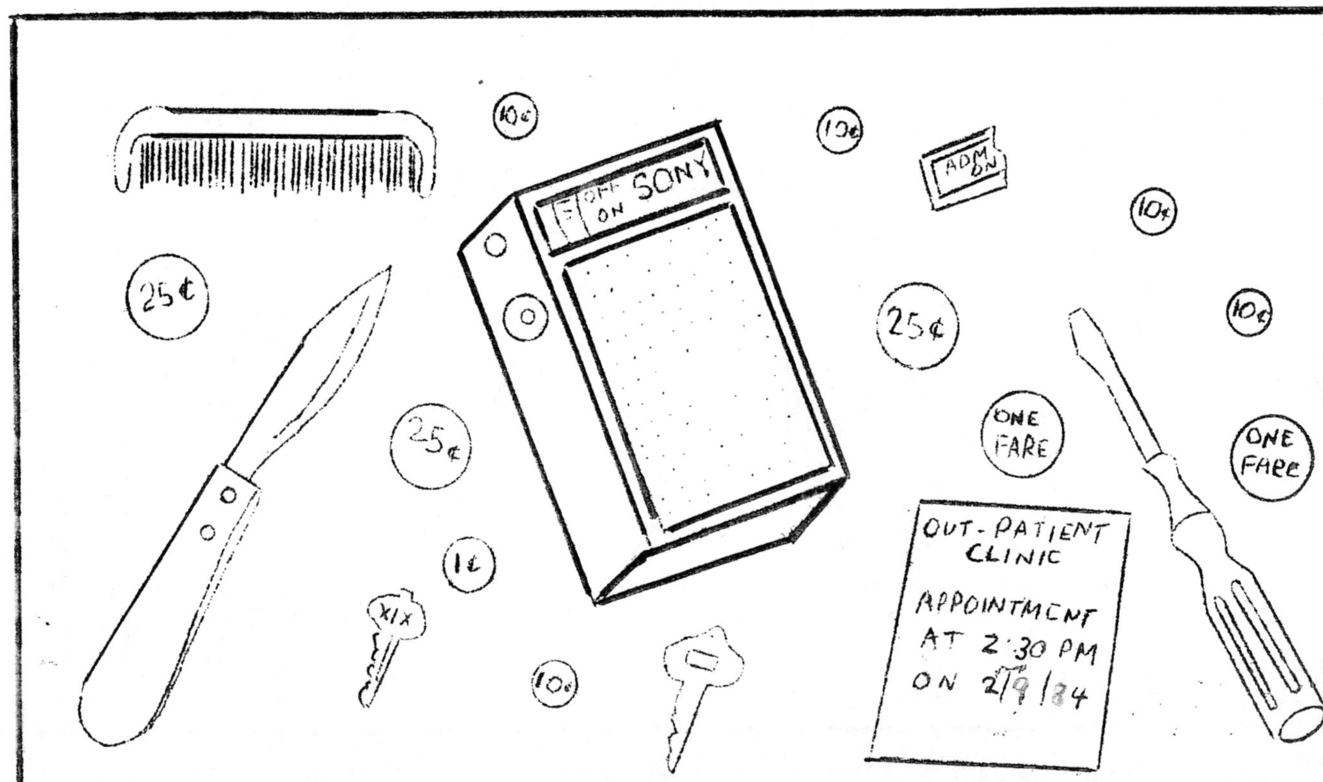

6. The suspect had a slip in his pockets showing an appointment at an out-patient clinic on 6.___
   A. February 9, 1984 B. September 2, 1983
   C. February 19, 1983 D. September 12, 1984

7. The transistor radio that was found on the suspect was made by 7.___
   A. RCA B. GE C. Sony D. Zenith

8. The coins found in the suspect's pockets have a TOTAL value of 8.___
   A. 56¢ B. 77¢ C. $1.05 D. $1.26

9. All except one of the following were found in the suspect's pockets. 9.___
   Which was NOT found?
   A
   A. ticket stub B. comb
   C. subway token D. pen

Questions 10-13.

DIRECTIONS: Questions 10 through 13 are based on the picture showing the contents of a woman's handbag. Assume that all of the contents are shown in the picture.

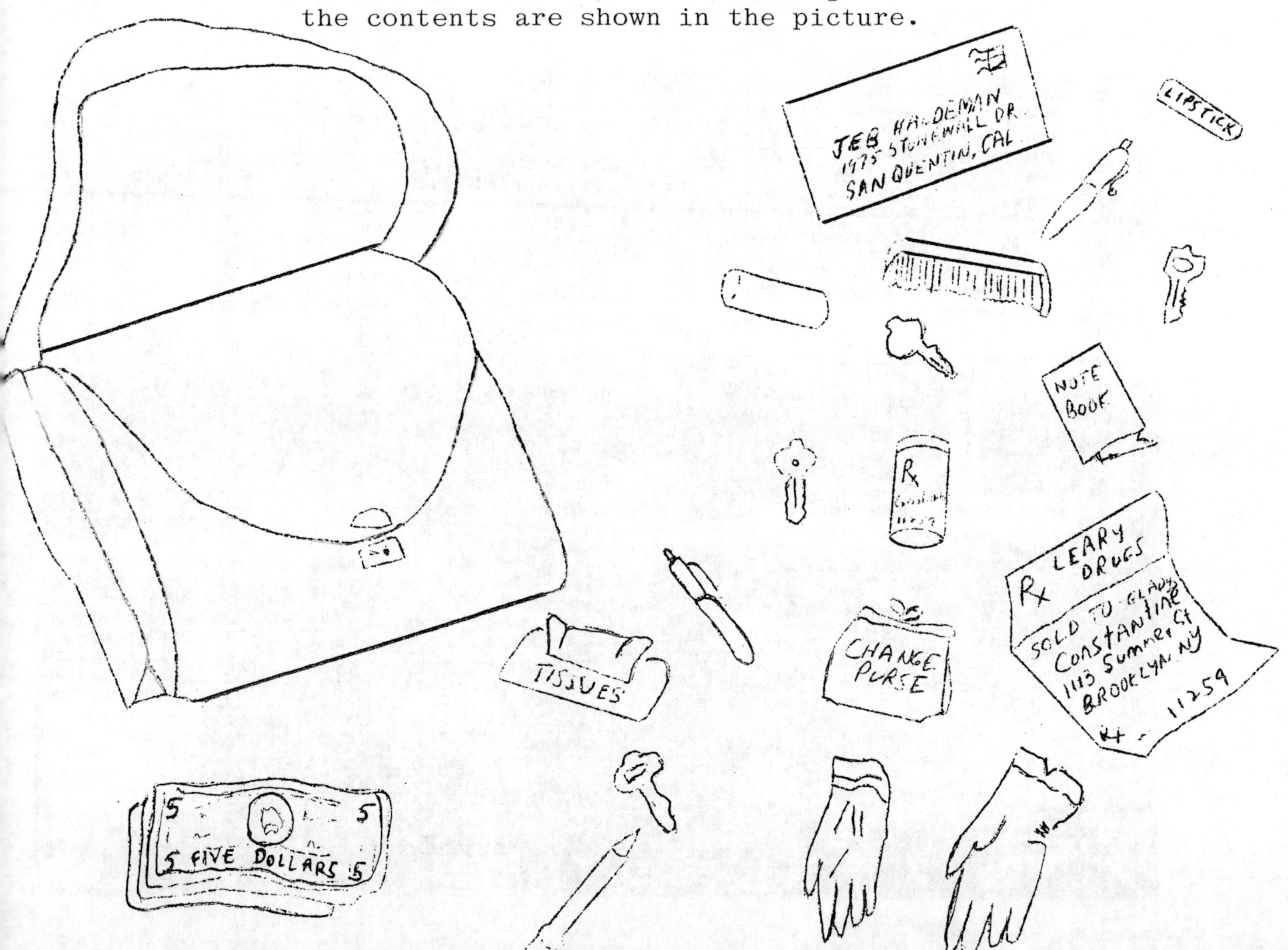

10. Where does Gladys Constantine live? 10.____
_____ Street in _____.
A. Chalmers; Manhattan
B. Summer; Manhattan
C. Summer; Brooklyn
D. Chalmers; Brooklyn

11. How many keys were in the handbag? 11.____
A. 2
B. 3
C. 4
D. 5

12. How much money was in the handbag? 12.____
_____ dollar(s).
A. Exactly five
B. More than five
C. Exactly ten
D. Less than one

13. The sales slip found in the handbag shows the purchase of which of the following? 13.____
A. The handbag
B. Lipstick
C. Tissues
D. Prescription medicine

Questions 14-18.

DIRECTIONS: Questions 14 through 18 are based on the street scene below. A robbery may be in progress at the watch repair shop across the street from where you are standing. Study and memorize the details before answering these questions.

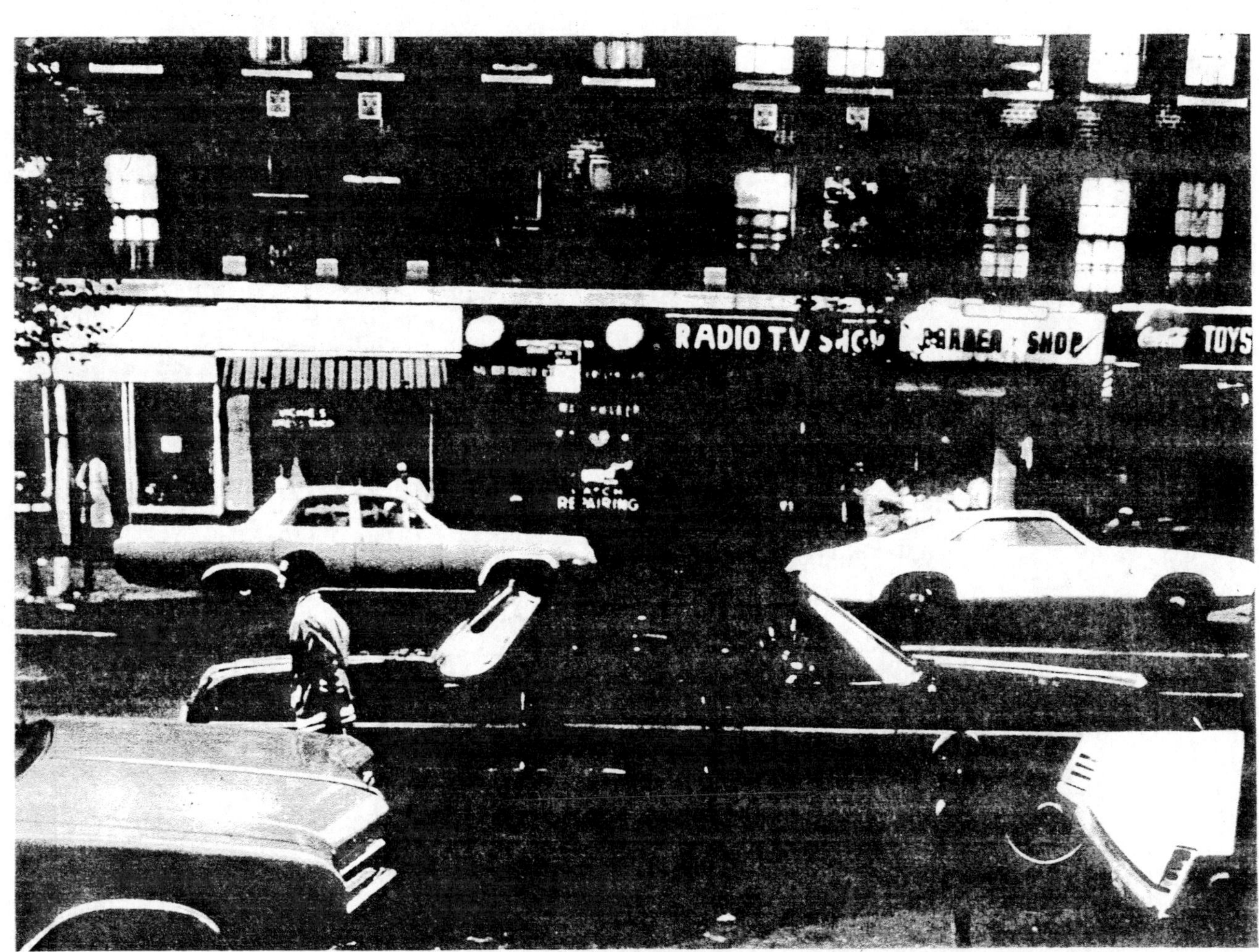

14. The boy by the dark-colored car 14.___
   A. had on dark glasses
   B. was a lookout
   C. had on a jacket
   D. wore an Afro haircut

15. The group of men on the sidewalk were 15.___
   A. facing one another
   B. looking at the watch repair shop
   C. all blacks
   D. talking and laughing

16. Nearest to the watch repair shop was a 16.___
   A. boy standing by a dark-colored car
   B. woman in a doorway
   C. group of men on the sidewalk
   D. man next to a light-colored car

17. The dark-colored car 17.___
   A. was a four-door sedan
   B. carried New York State plates
   C. was headed uptown
   D. had a man in the driver's seat

18. A woman on the sidewalk appeared to be 18.___
   A. looking at the apartment windows directly above her
   B. looking toward the watch repair shop
   C. watching the boy by the dark-colored car
   D. coming out of a store

KEY (CORRECT ANSWERS)

1. D	6. A	11. C	16. D
2. C	7. C	12. B	17. A
3. B	8. D	13. D	18. B
4. D	9. D	14. C	
5. B	10. C	15. A	

EXAMINATION SECTION

DIRECTIONS: Each question or incomplete statement is followed by several suggested answers or completions. Select the one that BEST answers the question or completes the statement. *PRINT THE LETTER OF THE CORRECT ANSWER IN THE SPACE AT THE RIGHT.*

Questions 1-3.

DIRECTIONS: Questions 1 to 3 measure your ability to fill out forms correctly and to remember information and ideas. Below and on the following two pages are directions for completing two kinds of forms, a correctly completed sample of each form, and a section from a procedures manual. You should memorize the sets of directions and the section from the procedures manual.

In the test, you will be (1) asked questions about the information and ideas in the manual and (2) presented with completed forms and asked to identify entries that are INCORRECT (contain wrong information, incomplete information, information in wrong order, etc.).

DIRECTIONS FOR COMPLETING CASE REPORT FORM

A case report form (see completed sample) is to be filled out by each officer at the time of the preliminary investigation. The entry for each numbered box is as follows:

Box 1 - The time the assignment was received.

Box 2 - The day, date, and time of the occurrence, in that order. Names of months and days may be abbreviated.

Box 3 - The manner in which the report was received. Use P = person, TOC = Through Official Channels (911 or other emergency numbers), M = mail, or T = telephone.

Box 4 - Name of the person notifying the department.

Box 5 - The address of the occurrence. Include number, street, and village, and name of establishment, if appropriate. Do NOT abbreviate the name of a street, village, or establishment. If no street address is available, supply directions.

Box 6 - Victim's name, last name first.

Box 7 - Victim's birthdate - month, day, and year. Use the style shown in the completed sample.

Box 8 - Victim's sex and race: F = female, M = male, B = black, W = white, Y = yellow, O = other.

Box 9 - Relationship of victim to the offender (be as specific as possible):
HU = husband, WI = wife, MO = mother, FA = father, SO = son, DA = daughter, BR = brother, SI = sister, AQ = acquaintance, ST = stranger, UN = unknown.

SAMPLE OF COMPLETED CASE REPORT FORM

<table>
<tr><td colspan="2">1. Time Received
5:57 PM</td><td colspan="2">2. Date and Time of Occurrence
Wed., Oct. 17, 1987, 1:00 PM</td></tr>
<tr><td colspan="3">3. Original Complaint Received
TOC</td><td>4. Reported by
Jeffrey Greene</td></tr>
<tr><td colspan="4">5. Place of Occurrence
Sam's Stationery Shop, 130 Main St., Brooketown</td></tr>
<tr><td>6. Victim's Name
Silver, Sam</td><td colspan="2">7. Date of Birth
3/17/42</td><td>8. Sex and Race
M - W</td></tr>
<tr><td colspan="4">7. Relationship to the Offender
ST</td></tr>
</table>

DIRECTIONS FOR COMPLETING
AUTOMOBILE FIELD INTERVIEW FORM

An automobile field interview form (see completed sample on the following page) is to be filled out when a car is stopped under suspicious circumstances, but no arrests are made. The entry for each numbered box is as follows:

Box 1 - Driver's name, last name first.

Box 2 - Village of residence, if within the county

Box 3 - Type of vehicle: S = sedan, C = convertible, SW = station wagon, V = van, T = truck.

Box 4 - Vehicle registration number.

Box 5 - Time and place of interview: location (street address only), time (per 24-hour clock), date, in that order.

Box 6 - Type of area: C = commercial, H = highway, R = residential, I = industrial, S = school

Box 7 - Patrol post number: precinct number is first digit; sector number is last two digits.

Box 8 - Officer's name and shield number, in that order.

SAMPLE OF COMPLETED AUTOMOBILE FIELD INTERVIEW FORM

1. Operator Robbins, Susan		2. Village Shady Brook
3. Type of Vehicle C		4. Registration C 7237
5. Time and Place of Interview Merry Road at Elm Street, 1428, 2/7/87		
6. Type of Area R	7. Post No. 221	8. Officer Sally Dodd, 2212

CASE REPORT MANUAL

Section 1 - Solvability Factors

A solvability factor can be defined as any information about a crime that can provide a means to determine who committed it. In other words, a solvability factor is a useful clue to the identity of the perpetrator.

Based on national-level research, the following twelve universal factors have been identified:

1. Existence of witnesses to the crime
2. Knowledge of a perpetrator's name
3. Knowledge of a perpetrator's whereabouts
4. Description of a perpetrator
5. Identification of a perpetrator
6. Property that has traceable characteristics such as a registration number
7. Existence of a distinctive MO
8. Presence of significant physical evidence such as a set of burglar's tools
9. Description of a perpetrator's automobile
10. Positive results from a crime scene evidence search, such as fingerprints or footprints

11. Belief that a crime may be solved with publicity and/or reasonable investigative effort
12. Opportunity for only one person to have committed the crime

The presence of at least one of these solvability factors is necessary for there to be a reasonable chance for a solution to the crime. When there is no solvability factor, the chance of crime solution is limited. Therefore, the police officer who arrives at the scene of a crime first must make the greatest possible effort to identify solvability factors. This effort should include identification of witnesses and a thorough search of the crime scene.

DIRECTIONS: After you have memorized the directions and manual section, try to answer the following questions without referring to the study materials.

1. Which of the following crimes is *most likely* to have a solvability factor? 1.____
   A. A pickpocket takes several wallets on a crowded bus.
   B. Two muggers take money from a blind man in an alley.
   C. A hospital drug cabinet is broken into during a major emergency.
   D. A kidnapper escapes in a van decorated with pink, yellow, and avocado-green paint.

2. At 7:30 AM on Wednesday, February 6, 1987, Patrol Officer Alex White was assigned to investigate a suspected child-beating. The boy had been brought to the hospital, and Dr. Paul Cohen called the local station house at 7:20 AM. David Pepson, a White boy born on June 27, 1985, was brought from his home by his mother, who claims that her husband had punished David an hour earlier for making loud noises. David resides with his parents at 86 Whitewood Lane in Middletown. 2.____

CASE REPORT FORM

<table>
<tr><td colspan="2">1. Time Received
7:30 AM</td><td colspan="2">2. Date and Time of Occurrence
Wed., February 6, 1987, 5:00 AM</td></tr>
<tr><td colspan="3">3. Original Complaint Received
T</td><td>4. Reported by
Dr. Paul Cohen</td></tr>
<tr><td colspan="4">5. Place of Occurrence
86 Whitewood Lane, Middletown</td></tr>
<tr><td>6. Victim's Name
David Pepson</td><td colspan="2">7. Date of Birth
6/27/85</td><td>8. Sex and Race
M - W</td></tr>
<tr><td colspan="4">9. Relationship to the Offender
FA</td></tr>
</table>

Of the following, the box in the form above which is filled out INCORRECTLY is Box

A. 3 B. 4 C. 8 D. 9

3. Officer Steven Brown, 7234, stopped a station wagon in the business section of Westville. He talked to the driver, John Caseman, on Rocky Road near South Bend and the western boundary of section 16 of precinct 2 at 8:20 PM on 3/8/87. The vehicle, registration number 2729H belongs to Mr. Caseman, who resides in Silverton. 3.___

AUTOMOBILE FIELD INTERVIEW FORM

<table>
<tr><td colspan="2">1. Operator
Caseman, John</td><td>2. Village
Westville</td></tr>
<tr><td colspan="2">3. Type of Vehicle
V</td><td>4. Registration
2729H</td></tr>
<tr><td colspan="3">5. Time and Place of Interview
Rocky Road near South Bend, 2020, 3/8/87</td></tr>
<tr><td>6. Type of Area
C</td><td>7. Post No.
216</td><td>8. Officer
Steven Brown, 7234</td></tr>
</table>

Of the following, the box in the form above which is filled out INCORRECTLY is Box

A. 1 B. 3 C. 5 D. 7

Questions 4-6.

DIRECTIONS: Questions 4 to 6 measure your ability to recall information in a set of bulletins. To do well in the test, you must memorize both the pictorial and the written portions of each of the following eight bulletins.

Date of Issuance 5/13/87

INFORMATION WANTED

by

Police Department, County of Allamin

Hooblertown, Indiana 43102

The Allamin County Police Department homicide squad requests all auto repair shops, dealers and General Motors parts dealers in the precinct be contacted and questioned relative to the below described vehicle which is wanted for a felony - leaving the scene of a fatality. If vehicle is located, contact the homicide squad, (731) 624-1372. Refer to Homicide Case 130.

Place of Occurrence:	Midway State Road, South Strata, Indiana
Time of Occurrence:	0240 hours on March 3, 1987
Vehicle Wanted:	1980 Oldsmobile Cutlass Supreme, color green
Damage:	The Vehicle will have damage to the plastic grill located in the vicinity of the right front headlights. The chrome strip which is affixed to the center of the hood was recovered at the scene.
Parts:	The following parts will be needed to repair the vehicle: 1. Hood - GM Part No. 557547 or 557557 2. Plastic Grill - GM Part No. 22503156

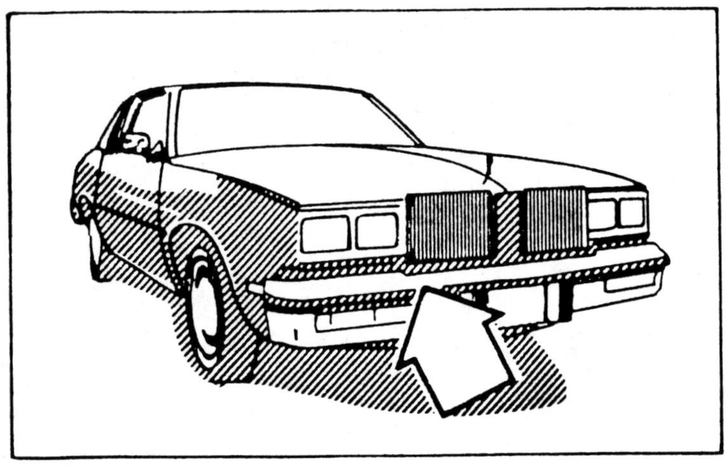

BULLETIN NO.
9- 85

W A N T E D

by

Police Department, County of Paradise

Cobbs Cove, Louisiana 41723

for

M U R D E R

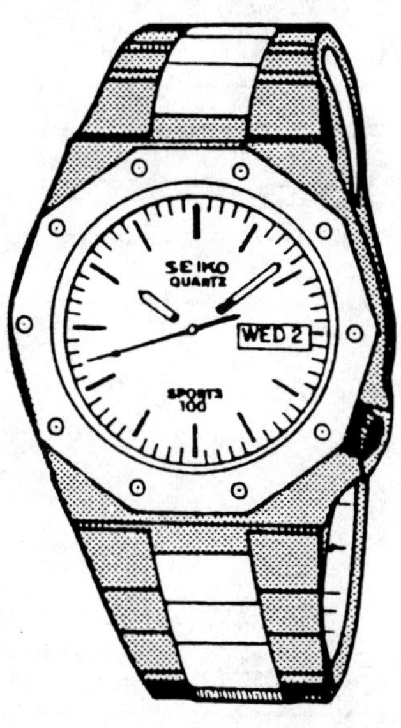

No. FJ110M

Note
Seiko watch with Gold Face and three section band is not a standard import into this area.

Occurrence: Blue Jay Way and Nickel Drive, Yellowbird, 0530 hours on April 12, 1985.

Modus Operandi: The deceased returned to his home at 2 Blue Jay Way, Yellowbird, at about 0530 hours, April 12, 1985. Four male whites were waiting in the vicinity of his garage and robbed him of U.S. currency and the above watch. They ran to the intersection of Blue Jay Way and Nickel Drive and got into a late model, shiny dark color, four door sedan with large tail-lights. The deceased chased them to the corner. One shot was fired causing his death.

Subjects: Four Male Whites, dark hair.

Property: One Seiko Quartz - Sports 100 - wrist watch, yellow metal face and crystal retainer. The band is an expandable three-section, white, yellow, white metal.

Note: Anyone with information is requested to contact the Paradise County Homicide Squad.

BULLETIN NO.
15- 85

W A N T E D

by

Police Department, County of Whitewall
Short Hills, Kentucky 27135

for

M U R D E R

RC-550JW/C

Occurrence: Public street, Brown Avenue, 60 ft. north of Camino Street, South Hill, KY, at 2340 hours, 6/25/85.

Modus Operandi: The victim of the murder was walking south on Brown Avenue when he was accosted by the suspect and shot in the head by the suspect.

Subject: Male, Black, 25-28 years, 5'9"-6' tall, thin build, short dark hair, medium dark skin, wearing a dark waist-length jacket, sneakers - armed with a gun.

Property: The above property, a JVC AM-FM cassette radio, Model RC 550JW/C made of black plastic with chrome trim was stolen during the commission of a murder on Brown Avenue in South Hill. The battery compartment door is missing from the radio.

Note: Anyone with information concerning the murder or the radio is asked to call the Whitewall Homicide Squad.

BULLETIN NO.
6- 85

W A N T E D

by

Police Department, County of Larinda
Blue Ridge, CA 97235

for

B U R G L A R Y

#1

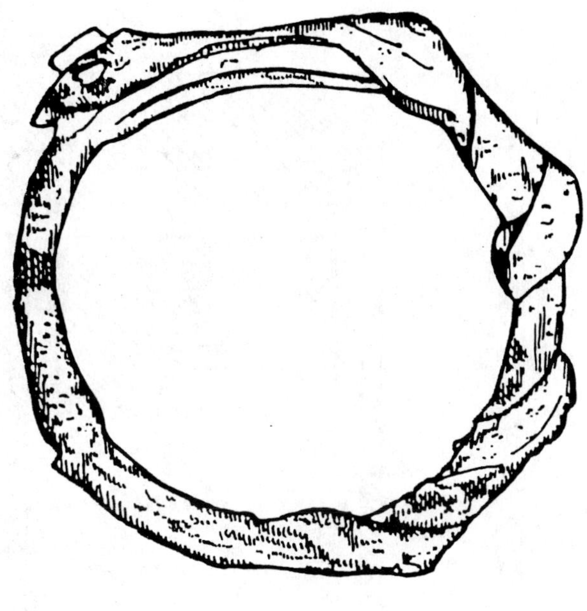

#2

Date of Occurrence: August 17, 1985 - 1930 to 2230 hours.

Place of Occurrence: Private home, 37 Cliffmount Dr., Palasino, CA

Property: Two distinctive, original designer rings taken.

1. Ladies, yellow gold, 18K ring, size 8, an alligator with green emerald eye.
2. Mans, yellow gold ring, a snake with $\frac{1}{4}$ carat white diamond head and white diamond chips for eyes.

Value: 1. $5,000 2. $7,500

Note: Any information - contact Burglary Squad, Refer to DD 4-25.

BULLETIN NO.
12-'85

W A N T E D

by

Police Department, County of Canton
Midship, Texas 84290

for

B U R G L A R Y

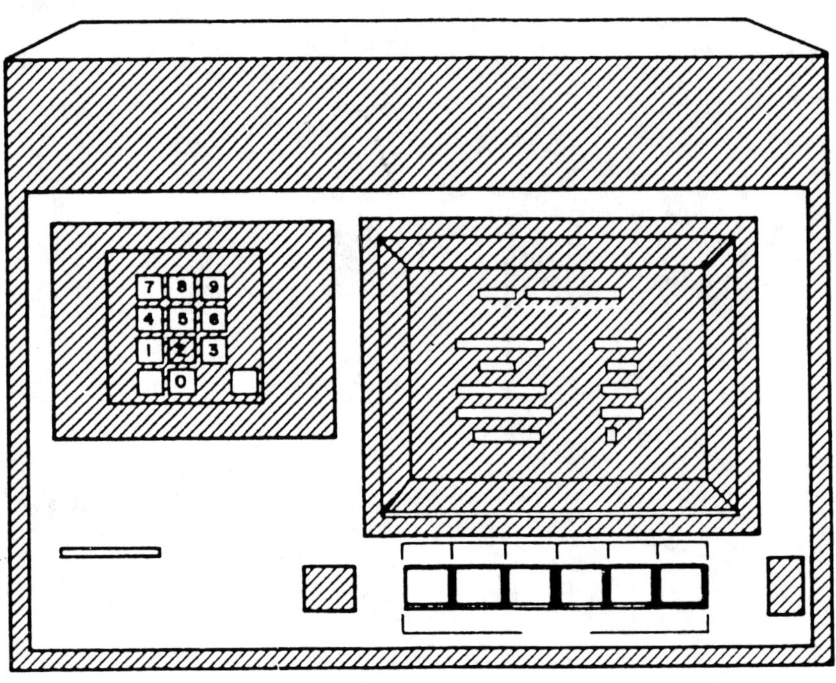

Date of Occurrence: July 31, 1985 - 1640 hours to August 1 - 0720 hou

Place of Occurrence: 606 Hillmont Drive, Alston, TX
Freemont Testing Systems

Property: Three engine analysers, color red, measuring 14" x 20" x 19"

Serial Numbers:
1. AN-0059
2. BP-0079
3. CR-0099

Value: $6,666.00 each.

Note: Request officers on patrol check service stations on post for the above items. Any information contact Detective Bryant, Third Squad, and refer to DD 3-52.

BULLETIN NO.
5-84

W A N T E D

by

Police Department, County of Marina
Waterford, CT 03612

for

R O B B E R Y

1984 PHOTO

Occurrences:	Robberies of gas stations and boutiques in North End precincts of Marina County.
Modus Operandi:	Subject enters store and uses telephone or shops. He then produces sawed-off shotgun or revolver from under his coat and announces robbery.
Subject:	Harry Hamilton, Male, White, DOB 6/22/43, 5'10", 180 lbs., medium complexion, severely pockmarked face.
Further Details:	Contact Robbery Squad at (203) 832-7663. Refer to Robbery Case 782. Robbery Squad has warrant for subject.

IF THIS PERSON ENTERS YOUR STORE DIAL 911 OR THE ABOVE NUMBER

BULLETIN NO.
30-84

W A N T E D

by

Police Department, County of Panfield
Lanser, South Carolina 30012

for

R O B B E R Y

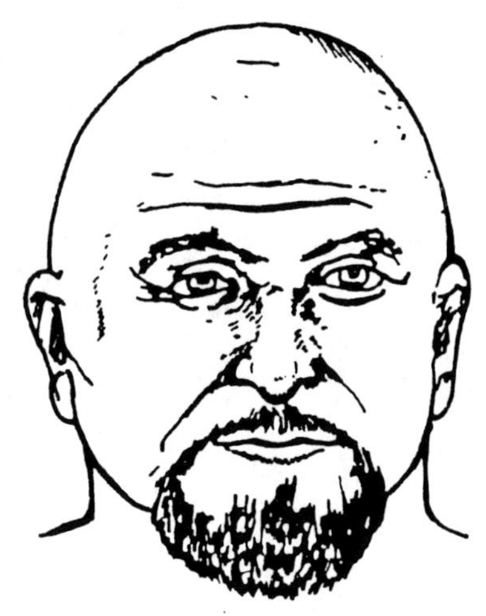

#1

1984 PHOTO
#2

Occurrence: 3 North Avenue, Anita, South Carolina, on 11/26/84 at 2310 hours.

Modus Operandi: The above subjects forced their way into the private residence of a rug dealer, accosted the dealer, his wife, and brother, demanding jewelry, currency, escaped on foot after binding victims.

Subjects: No. 1 - Male, White, 40-45 years, 200 lbs., heavy buil bald shaved head, fair complexion, mustache, goatee, large hooked nose, black leather jacket, armed with a knife.
No. 2 - Male, White, 6'1" tall, medium build, brown hair, subject identified as Mark Nine, DOB 4/16/48, last known address 1275 East 61st Street, Brooklyn, NY in 1981, hard drug user, armed with a hand gun, subjec has been indicted for residence robbery. See Wanted Bulletin 21-82.

Possible 3rd Suspect: Male, Hispanic, 30-35 years, 5'6", thin build, collar-length black wavy hair, eyes close together, with a large Doberman. Subject observed in the area before robbery talking to bald, stocky male. Also seen entering a vehicle containing 3 or 4 males after the robbery.

Loss: U.S. currency and jewelry valued at $3,000 to $4,000.

Further Details: Contact Robbery Squad.

BULLETIN NO.
1-85

W A N T E D

by

Police Department, County of Fantail
Sweet Waters, Vermont 04610

for

H I - J A C K I N G

Occurrence:	Vicinity of Nikon Plaza, off Jewel Avenue & Brook Bubble Road, Sweet Waters, VT at 1820 hours, 2/6/85.
Modus Operandi:	Subjects accosted the driver of a United Parcel tractor/trailer, forcing him into a pale yellow van-type vehicle, make and year unknown. Vehicle contained a black and yellow leopard rug. Driver released after two (2) hours, in the vicinity of West Lake, VT. Tractor/trailer recovered in White River, New Hampshire.
Subjects:	Four (4) male Whites, one possibly named Joe, armed with hand guns. No further description.
Loss:	Photo of above item: one (1) of four (4) broadcasting TV zoom lenses made by Nikon, valued at $7,000. Also included in the Nikon loss were current models of cameras, lenses, calculators, valued at $196,000. Medical supplies, mfg. by True Tell Inc., value $49,000. High quality medical examination scopes, industrial fiberscopes, cassette recorders and cameras, all mgf. by Canon Inc. valued at over $250,000. Sweaters, young mens, vee-neck design, mfg. Milford, Inc., labeled Dimension, Robt. Klein, J.C. Penney. Valued at over $20,450. Above items bearing serial numbers have been entered in NCIC.
Further Details:	Contact Robbery Squad.

DIRECTIONS: After you have memorized both the pictorial and written portions of the bulletins, try to answer the following questions WITHOUT referring to the study materials.

4. Which of the following statements about the contents of the *Information Wanted* bulletin is or are true? 4.___
   I. The subject vehicle is involved in a felony.
   II. The subject vehicle is green-colored.

   The CORRECT answer is:
   A. I *only*
   B. II *only*
   C. Both I and II
   D. Neither I nor II

5. 5.___

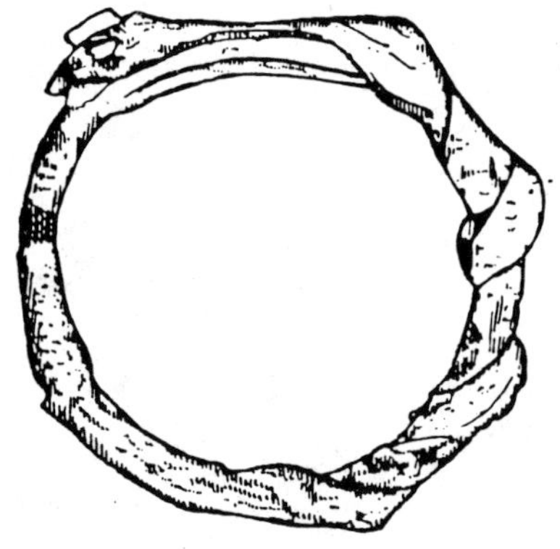

   Which of the following statements about the object above is or are true?
   I. It was taken in the robbery of a residence.
   II. Its value is between $1,000 and $2,000.

   The CORRECT answer is:
   A. I *only*
   B. II *only*
   C. Both I and II
   D. Neither I nor II

6. Which of the following, if any, fits the description of the individual who is wanted for the robbery of several gas stations? 6.___

   A.

   B.

C. 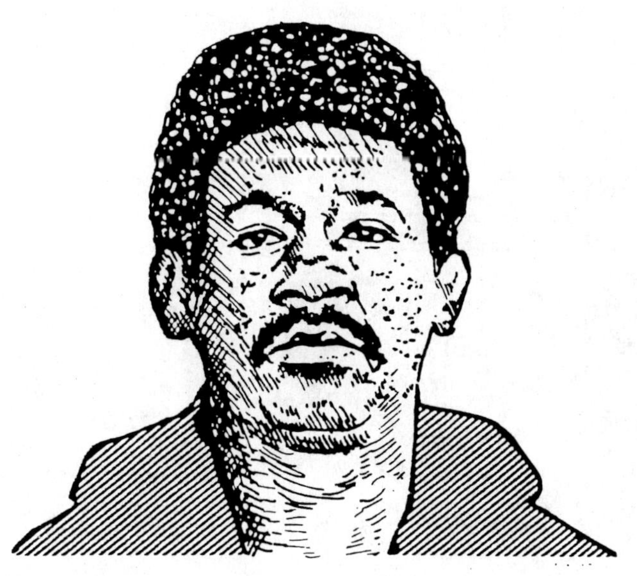

D. None of these

Questions 7-10.

DIRECTIONS: Questions 7 to 10 measure your ability to memorize and recall addresses, identification numbers and codes, and similar data.

In the test, you will be asked questions about the following body of information. You will NOT have the information in front of you when you take the test.

RADIO SIGNALS

01 - Back in Service
02 - Acknowledgement (OK)
06 - On Coffee
08 - Off Meal, Coffee, Personal
27 - Valid License
33 - Clear Channel (Any Emergency Request)
41 - One-Car Assistance Request
63 - Responding to Command
78 - Police Officer in Danger
99 - Possible Emergency Situation, Respond Quietly

TRUCK-TRACTOR IDENTIFICATION NUMBERS

Make	VIN* Plate Location
Autocar	8
Brockway.......	2
Diamond Reo....	9
Ford...........	10
GMC............	4
Kenworth.......	1
Peterbuilt.....	7
White..........	5

*Vehicle Identification Number

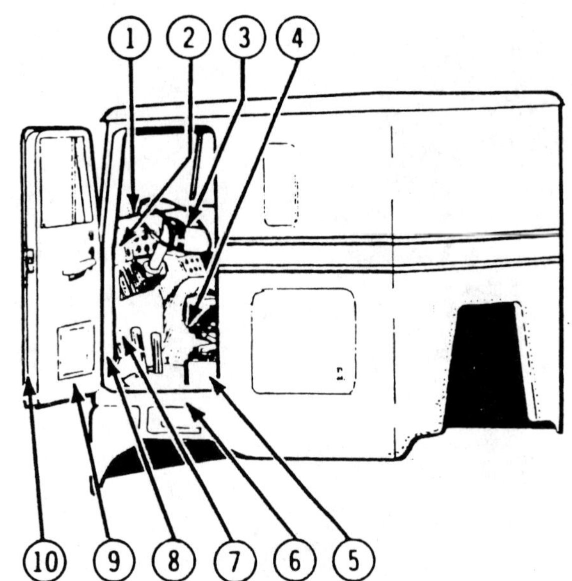

Location of County Precinct Houses

First - In H,* on S side of Merrick Rd., just E of Grand Avenue.
Second - In OB,* 1/8 mi. E of Seaford-Oyster Bay Expressway, 1/8 mi. S. of Jericho Trnpk.
Third - In NH,* 1/8 mi. N of Hillside Ave., 1/8 mi. W of Willis Avenue
Fourth - In H, on E side of Broadway, just N of Rockaway Avenue
Fifth - In H, on S side of Dutch Broadway, 1/4 mi. N of Exit 14 of Southern State Parkway
Six - In NH, just E of Community Drive, and just S of Whitney Pond Park
Seventh - In H, on side of Merrick Rd., just W of Seaford-Oyster Bay Expressway
Eighth - In H, on E side of Wantagh Ave., just N of Hempstead-Farmingdale Trnpk.

Location of Universities, Colleges, and Institutes

Adelphi U. - In H,* 1/4 mi. E of Nassau Blvd., 1/4 mi. S of Stewart Ave
Hofstra U. - In H, at Oak and Fulton Streets.
Molloy College - In H, on Hempstead Ave., just S of Southern State Pkway., and midway between Exits 19 and 20.
C.W. Post College - In OB,* on Northern Blvd., 1½ mi. W of Massapequa-Glen Cove Rd.
Nassau Community College - In H, on Stewart Ave., ½ mi. E of Clinton Rd
Long Island Agri. & Tech. Institute - In OB, ½ mi. E of Round Swamp Rd. between Bethpage State Park and Old Bethpage Village Restoration.
N.Y. Inst. of Technology - In OB, on Northern Blvd., just E of line dividing OB and NH.
U.S. Merchant Marine Acad. - In NH,* at NW end of Elm Point Rd.

*H - Town of Hempstead; NH - Town of North Hempstead; OB - Town of Oyster Bay.

DIRECTIONS: After you have memorized the listed data, try to answer the following questions WITHOUT referring to the list.

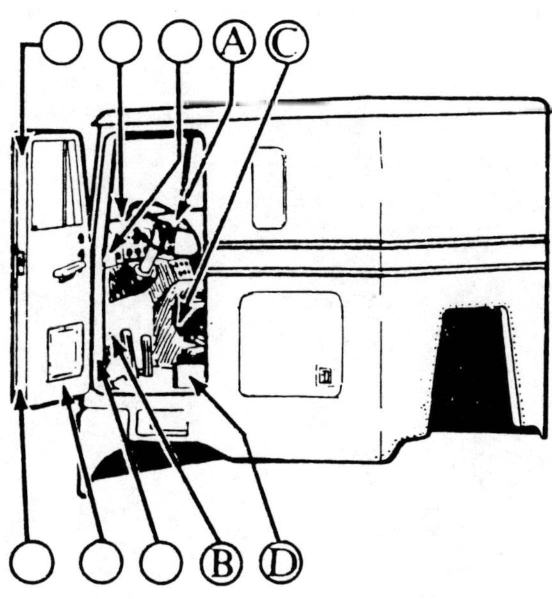

7. On a GMC truck-tractor, above, the VIN is located at 7.____
   A. A B. B C. C D. D

8. The radio signal for *back in service* is 8.____
   A. 01 B. 04 C. 08 D. none of these

9. The Third Precinct House is located in 9.____
   A. NH, 1/8 mi. N of Hillside Ave., 1/8 mi. W of Willis Ave.
   B. NH, 1/4 mi. S of I.U. Willets Rd., 1/4 mi. E of Herricks Rd.
   C. Williston Park, on Willis Ave., 1/4 mi. S of Northern State Parkway
   D. Mineola, on Mineola Blvd., 1/2 mi. N of Jericho Trnpk.

10. The U.S. Merchant Marine Academy is at the NW end of ____ Rd. 10.____
   A. Sands Point B. Mill Neck
   C. Kings Point D. Elm Point

KEY (CORRECT ANSWERS)

1. D
2. D
3. B
4. C
5. A
6. D
7. C
8. A
9. A
10. D

ABILITY TO APPLY STATED LAWS, RULES AND REGULATIONS

EXAMINATION SECTION

DIRECTIONS: For each of the questions below, select the letter that represents the BEST of the four choices. *PRINT THE LETTER OF THE CORRECT ANSWER IN THE SPACE AT THE RIGHT.*

Questions 1-2.

DIRECTIONS: Questions 1 and 2 are to be answered on the basis of the following passage.

Effective January 1, 2005, employees who are entitled to be paid at an overtime minimum wage rate according to the terms of a state minimum wage order must be paid for overtime at a rate at least time and one-half of the appropriate regular minimum wage rate for non-overtime work. For the purpose of this policy statement, the term *appropriate regular minimum wage rate* means $6.00 per hour or a lower minimum wage rate established in accordance with the provisions of a state minimum wage order. OVERTIME MINIMUM WAGES MAY NOT BE OFFSET BY PAYMENTS IN EXCESS OF THE REGULAR MINIMUM RATE FOR NON-OVERTIME WORK.

1. A worker who ordinarily works forty hours a week at an agreed wage of $6.00 an hour is required to work ten hours in excess of forty during a payroll week and is paid for the extra ten hours at his $6.00 per hour rate. 1.___
Using the information contained in the above passage, it is BEST to conclude
   A. this was a correct application of the regulation
   B. this was an incorrect application of the regulation
   C. the employee was not underpaid because he or she agreed upon the wage rate
   D. the employee did not perform his job well

2. According to the information in the above passage, the employee in Question 1 was MOST likely underpaid at least 2.___
   A. $90.00
   B. $17.25
   C. $30.00
   D. not underpaid at all

Question 3.

DIRECTIONS: Question 3 is to be answered on the basis of the following passage.

The following guidelines establish a range of monetary assessments for various types of child labor violations. They are general in nature and may not cover every specific situation. In determining the appropriate monetary amount within the range shown, consideration will be given to the criteria enumerated in the statute, namely *the size of the employer's business, the good faith of the employer, the gravity of the violation, the history of previous violations, and the failure to comply with record keeping or other requirements*. For example, the penalty for a larger firm (25 or more employees) would tend to be in the higher range since such firms should have knowledge of the laws. The gravity of the violation would depend on such factors as the age of the minor, whether required to be in school, and the degree of exposure to the hazards of prohibited occupations. Failure to keep records of the hours of work of the minors would also have a bearing on the size of the penalty.

Violation	Penalty
1. a. No employment certificate - child of employer (Sec. 131 or 132) b. No posted hours of work (Sec. 178)	1. 1st violation - $ 0-$100 2nd violation - $100-$250 3rd violation - $250-$500
2. a. Invalid employment certificate, e.g., *student non-factory* rather than *general* for a 16 year old in non-factory work (Sec. 132) b. Maximum or prohibited hours - less than one half hour beyond limit on any day, occasional, no pattern. (Sec. 130.2e, 131.3f, 170.1, 171.1, 170.2, 172.1, 173.1; Ed.L. 3227, 3228)	2. 1st violation - $ 0-$100 2nd violation - $150-$250 3rd violation - $250-$500
3. a. No employment certificate. (Sec. 130.2e, 131.3f, 131, 132, 138; Ed.L. 3227, 3228; ACAL 35.01, 35.05) b. Maximum or prohibited hours - (1) less than one half hour beyond limit on regular basis, (2) more than one half hour beyond limit either occasional or on a regular basis (Sec. 130.2e, 131.3f, 170.1, 171.1, 170.2, 172.1, 173.1; Ed.L. 3227, 3228)	3. 1st violation - $100-$250 2nd violation - $250-$500 3rd violation - $400-$500
4. Prohibited Occupations - Hazardous Employment (Sec. 130.1, 131.3f, 131.2, 133)	4. 1st violation - $300-$500 2nd violation - $400-$500 3rd violation - $400-$500

<u>COMPLIANCE CONFERENCE PRIOR TO ASSESSMENT OF PENALTY.</u>

After a child labor violation is reported, a compliance conference will be scheduled affording the employer the opportunity to be heard on the reported violation. A determination regarding the assessment of a civil penalty will be made following the conference.

RIGHT TO APPEAL

If the employer is aggrieved by the determination following such conference, the employer has the right to appeal such determination within 60 days of the date of issuance to the Industrial Board of Appeals, 194 Washington Avenue, Albany, New York 12210 as prescribed by its Rules of Procedure.

3. According to the above passage, a firm with its third violation of child labor laws regarding no posted hours of work (Sec. 178) and prohibited occupations-hazardous employment would be fined 3.___
   A. $600-$1,000
   B. $650
   C. $1,000
   D. cannot be determined from the information given

Question 4.

DIRECTIONS: Question 4 is to be answered on the basis of the following passage.

Section 198c. Benefits or Wage Supplements.

1. In addition to any other penalty or punishment otherwise prescribed by law, any employer who is party to an agreement to pay or provide benefits or wage supplements to employees or to a third party or fund for the benefit of employees and who fails, neglects, or refuses to pay the amount or amounts necessary to provide such benefits or furnish such supplements within thirty days after such payments are required to be made, shall be guilty of a misdemeanor, and upon conviction shall be punished as provided in Section One Hundred Ninety-Eight-a of this article. Where such employer is a corporation, the president, secretary, treasurer, or officers exercising corresponding functions shall each be guilty of a misdemeanor.

2. As used in this section, the term *benefits or wage supplements* includes, but is not limited to, reimbursement for expenses; health, welfare, and retirement benefits; and vacation, separation or holiday pay.

4. According to the above passage, an employer who had agreed to furnish an employee with a car and then failed to provide a car is 4.___
   A. not guilty of a misdemeanor
   B. most likely guilty of a misdemeanor
   C. not affected by the above regulation
   D. guilty of a felony

Question 5.

DIRECTIONS: Question 5 is to be answered on the basis of the following passage.

Manual workers must be paid weekly and not later than seven calendar days after the end of the week in which the wages are earned. However, a manual worker employed by a non-profitmaking organization must be paid in accordance with the agreed terms of employment, but not less frequently than semi-monthly. A manual worker means a mechanic, workingman, or laborer. Railroad workers, other than executives, must be paid on or before Thursday of each week the wages earned during the seven-day period ending on Tuesday of the preceding week. Commission sales personnel must be paid in accordance with the agreed terms of employment but not less frequently than once in each month and not later than the last day of the month following the month in which the money is earned. If the monthly payment of wages, salary, drawing account or commissions is substantial, then additional compensation such as incentive earnings may be paid less frequently than once in each month, but in no event later than the time provided in the employment agreement.

5. A non-executive railroad worker has not been paid for the previous week's work. It is Wednesday. 5.____
According to the above passage, which of the following is TRUE?
The above regulation
  A. was not violated since the ending period is the following Tuesday
  B. was violated
  C. was not violated since the employee could be paid on Thursday
  D. does not apply in this case

Question 6.

DIRECTIONS: Question 6 is to be answered on the basis of the following passage.

No deductions may be made from wages except deductions authorized by law, or which are authorized in writing by the employee and are for the employee's benefit. Authorized deductions include payments for insurance premiums, pensions, U.S. bonds, and union dues, as well as similar payments for the benefit of the employee. An employer may not make any payment by separate transaction unless such charge or payment is permitted as a deduction from wages. Examples of illegal deductions or charges include payments by the employee for spoilage, breakage, cash shortages or losses, and cost and maintenance of required uniforms.

6. An employee working on a cash register is short $40 at the end of his shift. The $40 is deducted from his wages. According to the above passage, the deduction is 6.___
   A. legal because it is legal to deduct cash losses
   B. legal because the employee is at fault
   C. illegal because the employee was not told of the deduction in advance
   D. illegal

Questions 7-8.

DIRECTIONS: Questions 7 and 8 are to be answered on the basis of the following passage.

No employee shall be paid a wage at a rate less than the rate at which an employee of the opposite sex in the same establishment is paid for equal work on a job, the performance of which requires equal skill, effort, and responsibility, and which is performed under similar working conditions, except where payment is made pursuant to a differential based on:

a. A system which measures earnings by quantity or quality of production
b. A merit system
c. A seniority system; or
d. Any other factor other than sex.

Any violation of the above is illegal.

7. A woman working in a factory on a piece-rate system as a sewing machine operator received less pay than a male sewing machine operator who finished more items. According to the above regulation, this is 7.___
   A. legal
   B. illegal
   C. legal, but not ethical
   D. no conclusion can be made from the information given

8. A male worker is in the same job title as a female worker. The male worker has been employed by the firm for three years, the female for two. Using the regulation stated above, if the male worker is paid more than the female worker, the action is 8.___
   A. legal
   B. illegal
   C. legal, but not ethical
   D. no conclusion can be made from the information given

Question 9.

DIRECTIONS: Question 9 is to be answered on the basis of the following passage.

Section 162. Time Allowed for Meals.

1. Every person employed in or in connection with a factory shall be allowed at least sixty minutes for the noon day meal.

2. Every person employed in or in connection with a mercantile or other establishment or occupation coming under the provisions of this chapter shall be allowed at least forty-five minutes for the noon day meal, except as in this chapter otherwise provided.

3. Every person employed for a period or shift starting before noon and continuing later than seven o'clock in the evening shall be allowed an additional meal period of at least twenty minutes between five and seven o'clock in the evening.

4. Every person employed for a period or shift of more than six hours starting between the hours of one o'clock in the afternoon and six o'clock in the morning, shall be allowed at least sixty minutes for a meal period when employed in or in connection with a factory, and forty-five minutes for a meal period when employed in or in connection with a mercantile or other establishment or occupation coming under the provision of this chapter, at a time midway between the beginning and end of such employment.

5. The commissioner may permit a shorter time to be fixed for meal periods than hereinbefore provided. The permit therefore shall be in writing and shall be kept conspicuously posted in the main entrance of the establishment. Such permit may be revoked at any time.

In administering this statute, the Department applies the following interpretations and guidelines:

Employee Coverage. Section 162 applies to every *person* in any establishment or occupation covered by the Labor Law. Accordingly, all categories of workers are covered, including white collar management staff.

Shorter Meal Periods. The Department will permit a shorter meal period of not less than 30 minutes as a matter of course, without application by the employer, so long as there is no indication of hardship to employees. A meal period of not less than 20 minutes will be permitted only in special or unusual cases after investigation and issuance of a special permit.

9. An employee is given twenty minutes for lunch. According to the information given in the above passage, the employer 9.____
   A. is in violation
   B. is not in violation
   C. should be fined $250
   D. no conclusion can be made from the information given

Question 10.

DIRECTIONS: Question 10 is to be answered on the basis of the following passage.

An employee shall not be obliged to incur expenses in the arrangement whereby the employee's wages or salary are directly deposited in a bank or financial institution or in the withdrawal of such wages or salary from the bank or financial institution. Some examples of expenses are as follows:

1. A service charge, *per check* charge, or administrative or processing charge
2. Carfare in order to get to the bank or financial institution to withdraw wages

An employee shall not be obliged to lose a substantial amount of uncompensated time in order to withdraw wages from a bank or financial institution. Although the employer is not required to provide employees with paid time in which to withdraw such monies, the Department has held that the employer should provide for the loss of time when the employee requires more than 15 minutes to withdraw wages. Such time includes travel time to and from, as well as actual time spent at the bank or financial institution in withdrawing such monies. The loss of such time without compensation constitutes a difficulty.

The withdrawal of wages may not interfere with an employee's meal period to the extent that it decreases the meal period to less than 30 minutes. Thus, although the time required for withdrawal of wages may be 15 minutes or less, the loss of even 8 or 9 minutes from a thirty minute meal period creates a difficulty.

10. An employee is unable to withdraw wages at any time other than her lunch break. She needs twenty minutes to withdraw wages and has a forty-five minute lunch break. According to the information contained in the above passage, the employer 10.___
   A. is in violation
   B. is not in violation
   C. should be fined $250
   D. no conclusion can be made from the information given

KEY (CORRECT ANSWERS)

1. B	6. D
2. B	7. A
3. D	8. A
4. B	9. D
5. C	10. A

POLICE SCIENCE
EXAMINATION SECTION

DIRECTIONS FOR THIS SECTION :
Each question or incomplete statement is followed by several suggested answers or completions. Select the one that BEST answers the question or completes the statement. *PRINT THE LETTER OF THE CORRECT ANSWER IN THE SPACE AT THE RIGHT.*

TEST 1

1. The scene of a crime is the area within the immediate vicinity of the specific location of the crime in which evidence might be found. This definition serves as an *acceptable* working guide for the discovery of evidence by the police because 1. ...
   A. evidence found outside the crime scene can be just as valuable as evidence found nearby
   B. it assigns the finding of evidence to those responsible for its discovery
   C. it is likely that the most important evidence will be found within the area of the crime scene
   D. evidence found within the area of the crime scene is more readily acceptable
2. It is important that the police give proper attention to the investigation of apparently minor, as well as major, complaints made by citizens. 2. ...
   Of the following, the one which is the MOST valid reason for doing so is that
   A. minor complaints are frequently of great importance to the complainant
   B. minor complaints are more readily disposed of
   C. minor complaints may be an indication of a serious police problem
   D. police efficiency is determined by their attitude towards citizen complaints
3. Hearsay evidence may be defined as testimony by one person that another person told him about a criminal act which that other person had witnessed. 3. ...
   Hearsay evidence is usually NOT admissible in a criminal trial *mainly* because
   A. hearsay evidence is consistently biased and deliberately distorted
   B. hearsay evidence is usually not relevant to the issues of the case
   C. such evidence is usually distorted by both the original witness and the person to whom he stated his observations
   D. the witness to the criminal act is not being cross-examined under oath
4. Arrests should not be given too much weight in the appraisal of a policeman's performance, since a large number of arrests does not necessarily indicate that a man is doing a good police job. 4. ...
   This statement is
   A. *true;* factors other than the total of arrests must also be considered in judging police effectiveness

B. *false;* the basic job of the police is to suppress crime and the surest measure of this is the number of arrests made
C. *true;* arrest figures are not indicative in any way of a patrolman's efficiency
D. *false;* although some policemen are in a better position to make arrests than others, the law of averages should operate to even this out

5. Arson is a particularly troublesome crime for the police. Of the folowing statements, the one which is the MOST important reason why this is so is that 5. ...
A. arsonists usually seek the protection of darkness for their crimes
B. arsons occur so infrequently that the police lack a definite approach
C. important evidence is frequently destroyed by the fire itself
D. witnesses find it difficult to distinguish arsonists from other criminals

6. Undoubtedly the police have an important contribution to make to the welfare of youth. Of the following, the PRINCIPAL reason for this is that 6. ...
A. effectiveness is a result of experience and the police have had the longest experience in youth work
B. no other agency can make use of the criminal aspects of the law as effectively as the police
C. the police are in a strategic position to observe children actually or potentially delinquent and the conditions contributing thereto
D. welfare agencies lack an understanding of the problems of youth

7. Adolescents, whether delinquent or not, are especially sensitive to the attitudes of their own small group and are more responsive to the judgments of their companions than to those of their own family. 7. ...
According to this statement, it would be MOST accurate to conclude that
A. adolescents are concerned more with their gang's opinion of them than with their own families' reaction to their behavior
B. adolescents are more personally sensitive to criticism of their conduct than adults
C. adolescent misbehavior can best be approached through the family
D. adolescent misbehavior is often caused by the lack of parental interest

8. It is safe to say that the significant patterns of behavior conveyed by movies, press, or radio must reach individuals whose behavior resistance is low, in order to be influential. 8. ...
It follows from the above statement that it would be MOST desirable to
A. consider the public press a negative factor in the developmental pattern of individuals
B. encourage youth to imitate significant patterns of behavior which they observe

C. exclude all children from attending movies which portray patterns of behavior of an anti-social nature
D. prevent exposure of potentially delinquent children to unfavorable influences

9. The suggestion has been made that the Police Department issue identification cards to be used by juveniles over 18 who wish to drink alcoholic beverages in bars. 9. ...
The one of the following which is NOT a valid criticism of this proposal is that it might
A. appear to bestow positive social approval on the consumption of alcoholic beverages by youths
B. induce more youngsters to congregate in bars
C. lead to a "black market" in counterfeit identification cards
D. shield youths from exposure to unwholesome situations

10. An apparently senile man informs a patrolman that he is returning from a visit to his daughter and that he is unable to find his way back home because he has forgotten his address. 10. ...
Of the following courses of action, the FIRST one that should be taken by the patrolman is to
A. question the man in an effort to establish his identity
B. request the police missing persons section to describe to you any person recently reported as missing
C. suggest that the man return to his daughter for travel directions to his home
D. telephone a description of the man to the precinct station house

11. Of the following facts about a criminal the one which would be of MOST value in apprehending and identifying the criminal would be that he 11. ...
A. drives a black Chevrolet 1973 sedan with chrome license-plate holders
B. invariably uses a .38 caliber Colt blue-steel revolver with walnut stock and regulation front sight
C. talks with a French accent and frequently stutters
D. usually wears 3-button single-breasted "Ivy League" suits and white oxford cloth button-down-collar shirts

12. A pawnshop dealer has submitted to the police an accurate and complete description of a wrist watch which he recently purchased from a customer. 12. ...
The one of the following factors that would be MOST important in determining whether this wrist watch was stolen is the
A. degree of investigative perseverance demonstrated by the police
B. exactness of police records describing stolen property
C. honesty and neighborhood reputation of the pawnbroker
D. time interval between the purchase of the wrist watch by the pawnbroker and his report to the police

13. A police officer noticed a man fumbling at the controls of an automobile, starting with a lurch, grinding the gears, and then driving on the wrong side of the street. The police officer signaled the car to stop, warned the driver about his driving, and permitted him to depart. 13. ...

This procedure was

A. *right;* it is good public relations for the police to caution rather than punish inadvertent violations of law
B. *wrong;* the police officer should have arrested the driver for driving while in an intoxicated condition
C. *right;* the bad driving probably was due to nervousness caused by the presence of the police officer
D. *wrong;* the police officer should have investigated the possibility that this was a stolen car

14. A police officer at the scene of a serious vehicular accident requests two witnesses to the accident not to speak to each other until he has received from each of them a statement concerning the accident. 14. ...
The MOST likely reason for this request by the police officer is that if the witnesses were allowed to speak to each other at this time they might
A. become involved in a violent quarrel over what actually occurred
B. change their opinion so that identical statements to the police would result
C. discuss the possibility of a bribe offer to either of them by one of the operators involved in the accident
D. have their original views of the accident somewhat altered by hearing each other's view of the accident

15. Police Officer Z is directing traffic when he observes a car approaching him which appears to meet the description of a car stolen several days previously. Police Officer Z signals the driver of this car to stop. The car does not stop or slacken its speed, and proceeds past Police Officer Z. In an effort to stop the car, Police Officer Z fires several shots at the car. 15. ...
The action of Police Officer Z was
A. *improper;* Police Officer Z should know that pistol marksmanship is not always accurate, even at relatively close ranges
B. *proper;* it is legally justifiable to fire at an escaping felon
C. *improper;* it is possible that the driver misunderstood the police officer's signal to stop
D. *proper;* Police Officer Z was on foot duty and there was no other immediately available means of halting the car

16. Assume that a recent study showed a 2% increase in highway fatalities in the first six months of this year over the last six months of last year. 16. ...
Of the following factors, generally the LEAST important one to include in a report evaluating this study is the
A. age and sex distribution of drivers
B. total number of automobiles in use
C. total number of miles automobiles were driven
D. total population

17. Tests have shown that sound waves set up by a siren have a greater intensity ahead than at either side or at the rear of a police car. 17. ...

On the basis of this statement, it would be MOST reasonable for the operator of a police car, when responding to the scene of an emergency and using the siren, to expect that a motorist approaching an intersection from

A. a side street may not stop his vehicle as soon as a more distant motorist directly ahead of the police car
B. directly ahead may not stop his vehicle as soon as a more distant motorist approaching from the rear of the police car
C. directly ahead may not stop his vehicle as soon as a more distant motorist approaching from the side of the police car
D. the rear of the police car may stop his vehicle before the less distant motorist approaching from a side street

18. An alarm broadcast for criminals escaping by car directs policemen to observe occupants of all cars, even occupants in cars not meeting the description of the fleeing car. 18. ...
The MOST likely reason for this is that
A. cars of the same make are not distinctive enough to be of any recognition value
B. the car's appearance may have been greatly altered after the crime was committed
C. the criminals may have disguised themselves after the commission of the crime
D. the escaping criminals may change to a different car after leaving the scene

19. Five minutes after receiving an alarm for a blue 1970 Buick four-door sedan which had been used as a get-away car by bank robbers, a radio patrol team spots and stops a car which seems to fit the description. 19. ...
The one of the following which is MOST likely to indicate the need for further careful investigation is that the
A. car has a cracked rear side window
B. driver does not have a registration certificate for this car
C. rear license plate is rusted
D. occupants of the car consist of three poorly dressed men

20. A police officer, on foot, who is several blocks away observes a woman being dragged into a car, which drives off very rapidly. 20. ...
Of the following, his FIRST action should be to
A. call headquarters from the nearest call-box or public telephone
B. commandeer a bus and pursue the other car
C. shoot in the direction of the scene as a warning
D. step into a hallway and await the approach of the car

21. A citizen requests police assistance in locating his adult son who has not been home for a period of twenty-four hours. Questioning of the citizen reveals no reason for the son's absence. 21. ...
The MOST appropriate of the following actions that the police should take is to

A. advise the citizen to contact all nearby hospitals and then contact the police again if this is not successful
B. conduct a thorough investigation in an attempt to locate the missing son
C. politely inform the citizen that no police action will be taken since the son is an adult
D. suggest that the citizen wait several days and, if his son has not then returned home, they will accept the complaint

22. A police officer is guarding the entrance of an apartment in which a homicide occurred. While awaiting the arrival of the detectives assigned to the case, he is approached by a newspaper reporter who asks to be admitted. The police officer refuses to admit him. 22. ...
The police officer's action was
A. *wrong;* the police should cooperate with the press
B. *right;* the reporter might unintentionally destroy evidence if admitted
C. *wrong;* experienced police reporters can be trusted to act intelligently in this situation
D. *right;* this reporter should not be given an advantage over other newspaper men

23. A police officer, in a radio car, investigating a reported store hold-up, which occurred shortly before his arrival, enters the store. The salesclerk who witnessed the hold-up starts telling the police officer, in a confused and excited manner, what had happened. 23. ...
The BEST course for the patrolman to follow initially is to
A. ask the clerk to write out an account of what had happened
B. let the clerk tell her story without interruption
C. try to confine the clerk to answering relevant questions
D. wait until the clerk calms down before taking her statement

24. A phone call is received at police headquarters indicating that a burglary is now taking place in a large loft building. Several radio motor patrol teams are dispatched to the scene. In order to prevent the escape of the burglars, the two police officers arriving first at the building, knowing that there is at least one entrance on each of the four sides of the building, should FIRST 24. ...
A. station themselves at diagonally opposite corners, outside of the building
B. enter the building and proceed to search for the criminals
C. station themselves at the most likely exit from the building
D. enter the building and remain on the ground floor attempting to keep all stairways under observation

25. The MAJOR purpose of alternate-side-of-the-street parking, in effect in certain areas of the city, is to 25. ...
A. allow for proper cleaning of the streets by the Department of Sanitation

B. reduce the number of parking tickets given out by the police
C. give a greater number of motorists an opportunity to utilize the available parking space
D. insure that fire hydrants will be accessible at all times to the fire department

TEST 2

1. The basic purpose of patrol is to create a public impression of police presence everywhere so that potential offenders will think there is no opportunity for successful misconduct. 1. ...
In the assignment of police personnel, the type of police activity that MOST nearly realizes this purpose is
   A. traffic summons duty B. traffic duty
   C. patrol of all licensed premises
   D. patrol by the detective force
   E. radio motor patrol
2. A police officer, who is asked by a civilian about a legal matter, directs him to the appropriate court. 2. ...
Of the following information given by the police officer, the item which is LEAST likely to be useful to the civilian is
   A. hours during which the court is in session
   B. location of the court
   C. name of the judge sitting in this court
   D. location of the complaint clerk within the court building
   E. transportation directions necessary to get to the court
3. A police officer discovers two teen-aged gangs, numbering about 50 boys, engaged in a free-for-all fight. The BEST immediate course for the police officer to adopt is to 3. ...
   A. call the station house for reinforcements
   B. fire over the heads of the boys and order them to disperse
   C. arrest the ringleaders
   D. call upon adult bystanders to assist him in restoring order
   E. attempt to stop the fight by using his club
4. A radio motor patrol team arrives on the scene a few minutes after a pedestrian has been killed on a busy street by a hit-and-run driver. After obtaining a description of the car, the FIRST action the police officer should take is to 4. ...
   A. radio a description of the fleeing car to precinct headquarters
   B. try to overtake the fleeing car
   C. obtain complete statements from everyone at the scene
   D. call for an ambulance
   E. inspect the site of the accident for clues
5. A police officer is approached by an obviously upset woman who reports that her husband is missing. The FIRST thing the police officer should do is to 5. ...
   A. check with the hospitals and the police station

B. tell the woman to wait a few hours and call the police station if her husband hasn't returned by then
C. obtain a description of the missing man so that an alarm can be broadcast
D. ask the woman why she thinks her husband is missing
E. make certain that the woman lives in his precinct

6. A violin is reported as missing from the home of Mrs. Brown. It would be LEAST important to the police, before making a routine check of pawn shops, to know that this violin 6. ...
A. is of a certain unusual shade of red
B. has dimensions which are different from those of most violins
C. has a well-known manufacturer's label stamped inside the violin
D. has a hidden number given to the police by the owner
E. has one tuning key with a chip mark on it in the shape of a triangle

7. In making his rounds, a police officer should follow the same route and schedule each time. 7. ...
The suggested procedure is
A. *good;* a fixed routing enables the patrolman to proceed methodically and systematically
B. *poor;* criminals can avoid observation by studying the police officer's routine
C. *good;* without a fixed routine a police officer may overlook some of his many duties
D. *poor;* a fixed routine reduces a patrolman's alertness and initiative
E. *good;* residents in the area covered will have more confidence in police efficiency

8. Policemen should call for ambulances to transport injured people to the hospital rather than use patrol cars for this purpose. 8. ...
Of the following, the MOST valid reason for this policy is that
A. there is less danger of aggravating injuries
B. patrol cars cannot be spared from police duty
C. patrol cars are usually not equipped for giving emergency first aid
D. medical assistance reaches the injured person sooner
E. responsibility for treating injured people lies with the Department of Hospitals

9. A business man requests advice concerning good practice in the use of a safe in his business office. 9. ...
The one of the following points which should be stressed MOST in the use of safes is that
A. a safe should not be placed where it can be seen from the street
B. the combination should be written down and carefully hidden in the office
C. a safe located in a dark place is more tempting to a burglar than one which is located in a well-lighted place

D. factors of size and weight alone determine the protection offered by a safe
E. the names of the manufacturer and the owner should be painted on the front of the safe

10. During a quarrel on a crowded city street, one man stabs another and flees. A police officer arriving at the scene a short time later finds the victim unconscious, calls for an ambulance and orders the crowd to leave. 10. ...
His action was
A. *bad;* there may have been witnesses to the assault among the crowd
B. *good;* it is proper first aid procedure to give an injured person room and air
C. *bad;* the assailant is probably among the crowd
D. *good;* a crowd may destroy needed evidence
E. *bad;* it is poor public relations for the police to order people about needlessly

11. A police officer walking his post at 3 A.M. notices heavy smoke coming out of a top floor window of a large apartment house. 11. ...
Of the following, the action he should take FIRST is to
A. make certain that there really is a fire
B. enter the building and warn all the occupants of the apartment house
C. attempt to extinguish the fire before it gets out of control
D. call the Fire Department
E. call precinct headquarters for Fire Department help

12. Two rival youth gangs have been involved in several minor clashes. The youth patrolman working in their area believes that a serious clash will occur if steps are not taken to prevent it. 12. ...
Of the following, the LEAST desirable action for the patrolman to take in his effort to head off trouble is to
A. arrest the leaders of both groups as a warning
B. warn the parents of the dangerous situation
C. obtain the cooperation of religious and civic leaders in the community
D. alert all social agencies working in that neighborhood
E. report the situation to his superior

13. Policemen are instructed to pay particular attention to anyone apparently making repairs on an auto parked on a street. 13. ...
The MOST important reason for this rule is that
A. the auto may be parked illegally
B. the person making the repairs may be obstructing traffic
C. working on autos is prohibited on certain streets
D. many people injure themselves while working on autos
E. the person making the repairs may be stealing the auto

14. After making an arrest of a criminal, the police officer is LEAST likely to request some kind of transportation if the 14. ...
A. prisoner is apparently a violent mental patient
B. distance to be travelled is considerable

C. prisoner is injured
D. prisoner is in an alcoholic stupor
E. prisoner talks of escaping

15. The Police Department, in an effort to prevent losses due to worthless checks, suggests to merchants that they place near the cash register a card stating that the merchant reserves the right to require positive identification and fingerprints from all persons who cash checks. 15. ...
This procedure is
A. *poor;* the merchant's regular customers may be offended by compulsory fingerprinting
B. *poor;* the taking of fingerprints would not deter the professional criminal
C. *good;* the police criminal files may be enlarged by the addition of all fingerprints taken
D. *poor;* this system could not work unless the fingerprinting was made mandatory
E. *good;* the card might serve to discourage persons from attempting to cash worthless checks

16. A factory manager asks a patrolman to escort his payroll clerk to and from the local bank when payroll money is withdrawn. The patrolman knows that it is against departmental policy to provide payroll escort service. 16. ...
The police officer *should*
A. refuse and explain why he cannot do what is requested
B. refer the manager to his precinct commander
C. tell the manager that police officers have more important tasks
D. advise the manager that he will provide this service if other duties do not interfere
E. suggest that pay checks be issued to employees

17. A motorist who has been stopped by a motorcycle patrolman for speeding acts rudely. He hints about his personal connections with high officials in the city government and demands the patrolman's name and shield number. 17. ...
The police officer *should*
A. arrest the motorist for threatening a policeman in the performance of his duty
B. give his name and shield number without comment
C. ignore the question since his name and shield number will be on the summons he is about to issue
D. give his name and shield number but add to the charges against the motorist
E. ask the motorist why he wants the information and give it only if the answer is satisfactory

18. Tire skid-marks provide valuable information to policemen investigating automobile accidents. 18. ...
The MOST important information obtained from this source is the
A. condition of the road at the time of the accident
B. effectiveness of the automobile's brakes
C. condition of the tires
D. point at which the driver first saw the danger
E. speed of the automobile at the time of the accident

19. A police officer observes several youths in the act of looting a peanut-vending machine. The youths flee in several directions as he approaches, ignoring his order to halt. The police officer then shoots at them and they halt and are captured. 19. ...
The police officer's action was
   A. *right;* it was the most effective way of capturing the criminals
   D. *wrong;* extreme measures should not be taken in apprehending petty offenders
   C. *right;* provided that there was no danger of shooting innocent bystanders
   D. *wrong;* this is usually ineffective when more than one offender is involved
   E. *right;* it is particularly important to teach juvenile delinquents respect for the law

20. Before permitting automobiles involved in an accident to depart, a police officer should take certain measures. 20. ...
Of the following, it is LEAST important that the police officer make certain that
   A. both drivers are properly licensed
   B. the automobiles are in safe operating condition
   C. the drivers have exchanged names and license numbers
   D. the drivers are physically fit to drive
   E. he obtains the names and addresses of drivers and witnesses

21. A detective, following a tip that a notorious bank robber is to meet a woman in a certain restaurant, is seated in a booth from which he can observe people entering and leaving. While waiting, he notices a flashily dressed woman get up from a table and slip by the cashier without paying her check. The detective ignored the incident and continued watching for the wanted man. 21. ...
This course of action was
   A. *correct;* the woman probably forgot to pay her bill
   B. *incorrect;* he should have arrested the woman since "a bird in the hand is worth two in the bush"
   C. *correct;* it is not the duty of the police department to protect businessmen from loss due to their own negligence
   D. *incorrect;* he should have followed the woman since she may lead to the bank robber
   E. *correct;* the detective should not risk losing the bank robber by checking on this incident

22. All police officers are required to maintain a record of their daily police activity in a memorandum book. The LEAST likely reason for this requirement is to 22. ...
   A. make it unnecessary for the police officer to remember police incidents
   B. give supervisors information concerning the police officer's daily work
   C. serve as a possible basis to refute unjustified complaints against the patrolman
   D. make a record of information that may have a bearing on a court action
   E. record any action which may later require an explanation

23. Policemen have a duty to take into custody any person who is actually or apparently mentally ill. 23. ...
Of the following cases, the one LEAST likely to fall under this provision of the law is the
   A. quarrelsome person who makes unjustifiable accusations
   B. elderly man who appears confused and unable to dress or feed himself
   C. young man who sits on the sidewalk curb staring into space and, when questioned, gives meaningless answers
   D. man who shouts obscenities at strangers in the streets
   E. woman who accuses waiters of attempting to poison her

24. A police officer should not take notes, while first questioning a suspect. Of the following, the MOST important reason for this procedure is that 24. ...
   A. information obtained at this time will probably not be truthful
   B. unessential facts can be eliminated if statements are written later
   C. the physical reactions of the suspect during interrogation can be better observed
   D. the exact wording is of no importance
   E. the statement will be better organized if written later

25. A police officer should know the occupations and habits of the people on his beat. In heavily populated districts, however, it is too much to ask that the police officer know all the people on his beat. 25. ...
If this statement is correct, the one of the following which would be the MOST practical course for the police officer to follow is to
   A. concentrate on becoming acquainted with the oldest residents of the beat
   B. limit his attention to people who work as well as live in the district
   C. limit his attention to people with criminal records
   D. concentrate on becoming acquainted with key people such as janitors, bartenders and local merchants
   E. concentrate on becoming acquainted with the newest residents of the beat

---

TEST 3

1. A police officer off-duty but in uniform recognizes a stolen car parked outside of a tavern. He notices that the radiator of the car is warm, indicating recent use. 1. ...
Of the following, the MOST practical course for the police officer to follow is to
   A. enter the tavern and ask aloud for the driver of the car
   B. stand in a nearby doorway and watch the car
   C. search for the patrolman on the beat and report the facts to him
   D. telephone the station house as soon as he arrives home
   E. enter the tavern and privately ask the bartender if he knows who owns the car

2. When a person is arrested he is always asked whether he uses narcotics, regardless of the charge against him. Of the following, the MOST important reason for asking this question is that 2. ...
   A. drug addicts can be induced to confess by withholding narcoticsfrom them
   B. the theft of narcoticsis becoming a serious police problem
   C. criminals are usually drug addicts
   D. many drug addicts commit crimes in order to obtain money for the purchase of narcotics
   E. it may be possible to convict the suspect of violation of the narcotics law
3. Of the following types of crimes, increased police vigilance would probably be LEAST successful in preventing 3. ...
   A. murder B. burglary C. prostitution
   D. automobile thefts E. robbery
4. The Police Department has been hiring civilian women to direct traffic at school crossings. The MOST important reason for this policy is 4. ...
   A. to stimulate civic interest in police problems
   B. to dramatize the traffic safety problem
   C. that women are more careful of the safety of children
   D. that young school children have more confidence in women who are mothers of their playmates
   E. to free policemen for regular patrol duty
5. Of the following, the fact that makes it MOST difficult to identify stolen cars is that 5. ...
   A. thieves frequently damage stolen cars
   B. many cars are similar in appearance
   C. thieves frequently disguise stolen cars
   D. owners frequently don't report stolen cars which are covered by insurance
   E. owners frequently delay reporting the theft
6. When testifying in a criminal case, it is MOST important that a policeman endeavor to 6. ...
   A. avoid technical terms which may be unfamiliar to the jury
   B. lean over backwards in order to be fair to the defendant
   C. assist the prosecutor even if some exaggeration is necessary
   D. avoid contradicting other prosecution witnesses
   E. confine his answers to the questions asked
7. When investigating a burglary, a policeman should obtain as complete descriptions as possible of articles of value which were stolen, but should list,without describing, stolen articles which are relatively valueless. 7. ...
   This suggested procedure is
   A. *poor;* what is valueless to one person may be of great value to another
   B. *good;* it enables the police to concentrate on recovering the most valuable articles
   C. *poor;* articles of little value frequently provide the only evidence connecting the suspect to the crime

D. *good;* the listing of the inexpensive items is probably incomplete
E. *poor;* the police should make the same effort to recover all stolen property, regardless of value

8. At 10 A.M. on a regular school day, a police officer notices a boy about 11 years old wandering in the street. When asked the reason he is not in school, he replies that he attends school in the neighborhood, but that he felt sick that morning. The police officer then took the boy to the principal of the school. 8. ...
This method of handling the situation was
A. *bad;* the police officer should have obtained verification of the boy's illness
B. *good;* the school authorities are best equipped to deal with the problem
C. *bad;* the police officer should have obtained the boy's name and address and reported the incident to the attendance officer
D. *good;* seeing the truant boy escorted by a policeman will deter other children from truancy
E. *bad;* the principal of a school should not be saddled with a truancy problem

9. During an investigation of a robbery a policeman caught one of the witnesses contradicting himself on one point. Upon questioning, the witness readily admitted the contradiction. The policeman should conclude that 9. ...
A. the witness was truthful but emotionally disturbed by the experience
B. all of the statements of the witness should be disregarded as untrustworthy
C. the statements of the witness should be investigated carefully
D. the witness was trying to protect the guilty person
E. contradictions of this sort are inevitable

10. A woman was found dead by her estranged husband in the kitchen of a ground floor apartment. The husband stated that, although the apartment was full of gas and tightly closed, all the burners of the kitchen range were shut. The husband had gone to the apartment to get some clothes. When a patrolman arrived, the apartment was still heavy with gas fumes. 10. ...
Of the following, the MOST likely explanation for these circumstances is that
A. gas seeped into the apartment under the door from a defective gas furnace in the basement
B. the husband has given false information to mislead the police
C. the woman changed her mind about committing suicide and opened the jets just before she collapsed
D. a leak in the kitchen range had been repaired
E. the woman had died from some other cause than asphyxiation

11. A police officer on post hears a cry for help from a woman in a car with two men. He approaches the car and is told by the woman that the men are kidnapping her. The men 11. ...

claim to be the woman's husband and doctor, and state that they are taking her to a private mental hospital.
Of the following, the BEST course for the police officer is to
A. take all of them to the station house for further questioning
B. permit the woman to depart and arrest the men
C. call for an ambulance to take the woman to the nearest city mental hospital
D. accompany the car to the private mental hospital
E. permit the car to depart on the basis of the explanation

12. Social security cards are not acceptable proof of identification for police purposes. 12. ...
Of the following, the MOST important reason for this rule is that the social security card
A. is easily obtained
B. states on its face "for social security purposes -- not for identification"
C. is frequently lost
D. does not contain the address of the person
E. does not contain a photograph, description or fingerprints of the person

13. Many well-meaning people have proposed that officers in uniform not be permitted to arrest juveniles. 13. ...
This proposal is
A. *good;* the police are not equipped to handle juvenile offenders
B. *bad;* juvenile offenders would lose respect for all law enforcement agencies
C. *good;* offending juveniles should be segregated from hardened criminals
D. *bad;* frequently it is the uniformed officer who first comes upon the youthful offender
E. *good;* contact with the police would prevent any rehabilitative measures from being taken

14. An off-duty policeman was seated in a restaurant when two men entered, drew guns and robbed the cashier. The policeman made no effort to prevent the robbery or apprehend the criminals. Later he justified his conduct by stating that a policeman when off-duty is a private citizen with the same duties and rights of all private citizens. 14. ...
The policeman's conduct was
A. *wrong;* a policeman must act to prevent crimes and apprehend criminals at all times
B. *right;* he was out of uniform at the time of the robbery
C. *wrong;* he had his gun with him at the time of the robbery
D. *right;* it would have been foolhardy for him to intervene when outnumbered by armed robbers
E. *wrong;* he should have obtained the necessary information and descriptions after the robbers left

15. Drivers with many convictions for Traffic Law violations sometimes try to conceal this record by cutting off the lower part of the operator's license and attaching to it a clean section from a blank application form. A police officer who stops a driver and notices that his operator's license is torn and held together by transparent tape should FIRST 15. ...
   A. verify the driver's explanation of the torn license
   B. examine both parts of the license to see if they match
   C. request additional proof of identity
   D. take the motorist to the station house for further questioning
   E. check the records of the Bureau of Motor Vehicles for unanswered summonses

KEYS (CORRECT ANSWERS)

TEST 1

1.	C	11.	C
2.	C	12.	B
3.	D	13.	D
4.	A	14.	D
5.	C	15.	C
6.	C	16.	D
7.	A	17.	A
8.	D	18.	B
9.	D	19.	B
10.	A	20.	A

21. B
22. B
23. C
24. A
25. A

TEST 2

1.	E	11.	D
2.	C	12.	A
3.	A	13.	E
4.	A	14.	E
5.	D	15.	E
6.	C	16.	A
7.	B	17.	B
8.	A	18.	E
9.	C	19.	B
10.	A	20.	C

21. E
22. A
23. A
24. C
25. D

TEST 3

1. B
2. D
3. A
4. E
5. C
6. E
7. C
8. B
9. C
10. B
11. A
12. E
13. D
14. A
15. B

EXAMINATION SECTION

DIRECTIONS: Each question or incomplete statement is followed by several suggested answers or completions. Select the one that BEST answers the question or completes the statement. *PRINT THE LETTER OF THE CORRECT ANSWER IN THE SPACE AT THE RIGHT.*

1. A sergeant tells a patrolman to perform a certain duty. If the patrolman does not completely understand the order, he should 1.___
   A. carry out the order to the best of his ability and then request further information if necessary
   B. carry out the order to the best of his ability so that he does not give the appearance of being unable to follow orders
   C. inform the sergeant that he does not understand the order
   D. request clarification from a more experienced patrolman

2. While on patrol, you are informed by the manager of a supermarket that an object which appears to be a homemade bomb has been discovered in his market. Your FIRST action should be to 2.___
   A. go to the market and make sure that everyone leaves it immediately
   B. go to the market, examine the bomb, and then decide what action is to be taken
   C. question the manager in detail in an effort to determine whether this is really a bomb
   D. telephone the Bomb Squad for instructions as to how the bomb should be rendered harmless

3. A patrolman on post would be MOST likely to make a regular hourly signal-box call to his precinct, rather than an immediate call, when he 3.___
   A. discovers a traffic signal light which is not functioning properly
   B. discovers what appears to be an abandoned car on his post
   C. notices a street name sign which has been damaged
   D. overhears a conversation relating to a possible disturbance between two groups of teenagers

4. A patrolman is on post, and a citizen sees him *ringing in* on a street police call box to the station house. The citizen asks him what the purpose of the box is. Of the following, the BEST course of action for the officer to follow in this situation is to 4.___
   A. speak to the desk officer over the call box phone and get his permission to answer the question

B. suggest that he write to the Community Relations Office of the Police Department for complete information
C. tactfully suggest to the man it is a police matter and hence confidential
D. tell the man what the call box is and what it is used for

5. The MOST reasonable advice that a patrolman can give to a merchant who asks what he should do if he receives a telephone call from a person he doesn't recognize regarding an alleged emergency at his store after ordinary business hours is that the merchant should go to the store and, if police officers are not at the scene, he should 5.___
A. continue past the store and call the police for assistance
B. continue past the store, and return and enter it if there doesn't appear to be an emergency
C. enter the store and ascertain whether the alleged emergency exists
D. enter the store only if there is no one apparently loitering in the vicinity

6. A patrolman is asked by a citizen the location of a candy store which the patrolman knows is under observation for suspected bookmaking activity. 6.___
In such a situation, the patrolman should
A. give the proper directions to the citizen
B. give the proper directions to the citizen, but tell him the store is under observation
C. state that he does not know the location of the store
D. tell the citizen that he may be arrested if the store is raided

7. *Whenever a crime has been committed, the criminal has disturbed the surroundings in one way or another by his presence.* 7.___
The LEAST valid deduction for the police to make from this statement is that
A. clues are thus present at all crime scenes
B. even the slightest search at crime scenes will turn up conclusive evidence
C. the greater the number of criminals involved in a crime, the greater the number of clues likely to be available
D. the completely clueless crime is rarely encountered in police work

8. It is suggested that a suspect should not be permitted to walk in or about the scene of a crime where fingerprints may be present until a thorough search has been made for such evidence. 8.___
This suggested procedure is
A. *good*; the suspect would, if permitted to walk about the scene, smear all fingerprints that might be found by police investigators

B. *bad*; the return of a suspect to the scene of a crime provides an opportunity to obtain additional fingerprints from the suspect
C. *good*; if the suspect handled any objects at the scene, the value of any original fingerprints, as evidence, might be seriously impaired
D. *bad*; the return of a suspect to the scene of a crime provides an opportunity to identify objects that had been handled during the commission of the crime

9. Of the following, the one which is the purpose of the police fingerprinting procedure is the 9.___
   A. identification of deceased persons
   B. identification of the guilty
   C. protection of the innocent
   D. recognition of first offenders

10. A patrolman is the first one to arrive at the scene of a murder. A suspect offers to make a statement to him concerning the crime. The patrolman refuses to accept the statement. 10.___
The patrolman's action was
   A. *good*; interrogation of suspects should be performed by experienced detectives
   B. *poor*; the suspect may later change his mind and refuse to make any statement
   C. *good*; the patrolman will be too busy maintaining order at the scene to be able to accept the statement
   D. *poor*; a statement made by the suspect would quickly solve the crime

11. The scene of a crime is the area within the immediate vicinity of the specific location of the crime in which evidence might be found. 11.___
This definition serves as an acceptable working guide for the discovery of evidence by the police because
   A. evidence found outside the crime scene can be just as valuable as evidence found nearby
   B. it assigns the finding of evidence to those responsible for its discovery
   C. it is likely that the most important evidence will be found within the area of the crime scene
   D. evidence found within the area of the crime scene is more readily accepted

12. It is important that the police give proper attention to the investigation of apparently minor, as well as major, complaints made by citizens. 12.___
Of the following, the one which is the MOST valid reason for doing so is that
   A. minor complaints are frequently of great importance to the complainant
   B. minor complaints are more readily disposed of

C. minor complaints may be an indication of a serious police problem
D. police efficiency is determined by their attitude towards citizen complaints

13. Hearsay evidence may be defined as testimony by one person that another person told him about a criminal act which that other person had witnessed. 13.___
Hearsay evidence is usually NOT admissible in a criminal trial MAINLY because
A. hearsay evidence is consistently biased and deliberately distorted
B. hearsay evidence is usually not relevant to the issues of the case
C. such evidence is usually distorted by both the original witness and the person to whom he stated his observations
D. the witness to the criminal act is not being cross-examined under oath

14. Arrests should not be given too much weight in the appraisal of a policeman's performance since a large number of arrests does not necessarily indicate that a man is doing a good police job. 14.___
This statement is
A. *true*; factors other than the total of arrests must also be considered in judging police effectiveness
B. *false*; the basic job of the police is to suppress crime and the surest measure of this is the number of arrests made
C. *true*; arrest figures are not indicative in any way of a patrolman's efficiency
D. *false*; although some policemen are in a better position to make arrests than others, the law of averages should operate to even this out

15. Arson is a particularly troublesome crime for the police. 15.___
Of the following statements, the one which is the MOST important reason why this is so is that
A. arsonists usually seek the protection of darkness for their crimes
B. arsons occur so infrequently that the police lack a definite approach
C. important evidence is frequently destroyed by the fire itself
D. witnesses find it difficult to distinguish arsonists from other criminals

16. Undoubtedly, the police have an important contribution to make to the welfare of youth. 16.___
Of the following, the PRINCIPAL reason for this is that
A. effectiveness is a result of experience and the police have had the longest experience in youth work

B. no other agency can make use of the criminal aspects of the law as effectively as the police
C. the police are in a strategic position to observe children actually or potentially delinquent and the conditions contributing thereto
D. welfare agencies lack an understanding of the problems of youth

17. Adolescents, whether delinquent or not, are especially sensitive to the attitudes of their own small group and are more responsive to the judgments of their companions than to those of their own family. 17.___
According to this statement, it would be MOST accurate to conclude that
A. adolescents are concerned more with their gang's opinion of them than with their own families' reaction to their behavior
B. adolescents are more personally sensitive to criticism of their conduct than adults
C. adolescent misbehavior can best be approached through the family
D. adolescent misbehavior is often caused by the lack of parental interest

18. It is safe to say that the significant patterns of behavior conveyed by movies, press, or radio must reach individuals whose behavior resistance is low, in order to be influential. 18.___
It follows from the above statement that it would be MOST desirable to
A. consider the public press a negative factor in the developmental pattern of individuals
B. encourage youth to imitate significant patterns of behavior which they observe
C. exclude all children from attending movies which portray patterns of behavior of an anti-social nature
D. prevent exposure of potentially delinquent children to unfavorable influences

19. The suggestion has been made that the Police Department issue identification cards to be used by juveniles over 21 who wish to drink alcoholic beverages in bars. 19.___
The one of the following which is NOT a valid criticism of this proposal is that it might
A. appear to bestow positive social approval on the consumption of alcoholic beverages by youths
B. induce more youngsters to congregate in bars
C. lead to a *black market* in counterfeit identification cards
D. shield youths from exposure to unwholesome situations

20. An apparently senile man informs a patrolman that he is returning from a visit to his daughter and that he is unable to find his way back home because he has forgotten his address. 20.___
Of the following courses of action, the FIRST one that should be taken by the patrolman is to
   A. question the man in an effort to establish his identity
   B. request the police missing persons section to describe to you any person recently reported as missing
   C. suggest that the man return to his daughter for travel directions to his home
   D. telephone a description of the man to the precinct station house

21. Of the following facts about a criminal, the one which would be of MOST value in apprehending and identifying the criminal would be that he 21.___
   A. drives a black Cadillac 1988 sedan with chrome license plate holders
   B. invariably uses a .38 caliber Colt blue-steel revolver with walnut stock and regulation front sight
   C. talks with a French accent and frequently stutters
   D. usually wears 3-button single-breasted *Ivy League* suits and white oxford cloth button-down-collar shirts

22. A pawnshop dealer has submitted to the police an accurate and complete description of a wristwatch which he recently purchased from a customer. 22.___
The one of the following factors that would be MOST important in determining whether this wristwatch was stolen is the
   A. degree of investigative perseverance demonstrated by the police
   B. exactness of police records describing stolen property
   C. honesty and neighborhood reputation of the pawnbroker
   D. time interval between the purchase of the wristwatch by the pawnbroker and his report to the police

23. A patrolman noticed a man fumbling at the controls of an automobile, starting with a lurch, grinding the gears, and then driving on the wrong side of the street. The patrolman signaled the car to stop, warned the driver about his driving, and permitted him to depart. 23.___
This procedure was
   A. *right*; it is good public relations for the police to caution rather than punish inadvertent violations of law
   B. *wrong*; the patrolman should have arrested the driver for driving while in an intoxicated condition
   C. *right*; the bad driving probably was due to nervousness caused by the presence of the patrolman
   D. *wrong*; the patrolman should have investigated the possibility that this was a stolen car

24. A patrolman at the scene of a serious vehicular accident requests two witnesses to the accident not to speak to each other until he has received from each of them a statement concerning the accident. 24.___
The MOST likely reason for this request by the patrolman is that if the witnesses were allowed to speak to each other at this time, they might
   A. become involved in a violent quarrel over what actually occurred
   B. change their opinion so that identical statements to the police would result
   C. discuss the possibility of a bribe offer to either of them by one of the operators involved in the accident
   D. have their original views of the accident somewhat altered by hearing each other's view of the accident

25. Patrolman Z is directing traffic when he observes a car approaching him which appears to meet the description of a car stolen several days previously. Patrolman Z signals the driver of this car to stop. The car does not stop or slacken its speed and proceeds past Patrolman Z. In an effort to stop the car, Patrolman Z fires several shots at the car. 25.___
The action of Patrolman Z was
   A. *improper*; Patrolman Z should know that pistol marksmanship is not always accurate, even at relatively close ranges
   B. *proper*; it is legally justifiable to fire at an escaping felon
   C. *improper*; it is possible that the driver misunderstood the patrolman's signal to stop
   D. *proper*; Patrolman Z was on foot duty and there was no other immediately available means of halting the car

26. Assume that a recent study showed a 2% increase in highway fatalities in the first six months of 2007 over the last six months of 2006. 26.___
Of the following factors, generally the LEAST important one to include in a report evaluating this study is the
   A. age and sex distribution of drivers
   B. total number of automobiles in use
   C. total number of miles automobiles were driven
   D. total population

27. Tests have shown that sound waves set up by a siren have a greater intensity ahead than at either side or at the rear of a police car. 27.___
On the basis of this statement, it would be MOST reasonable for the operator of a police car, when responding to the scene of an emergency and using the siren, to expect that a motorist approaching an intersection from
   A. a side street may not stop his vehicle as soon as a more distant motorist directly ahead of the police car

B. directly ahead may not stop his vehicle as soon as a more distant motorist approaching from the rear of the police car
C. directly ahead may not stop his vehicle as soon as a more distant motorist approaching from the side of the police car
D. the rear of the police car may stop his vehicle before the less distant motorist approaching from the street

28. An alarm broadcast for criminals escaping by car directs policemen to observe occupants of all cars, even occupants in cars not meeting the description of the fleeing car. 28.___
The MOST likely reason for this is that
A. cars of the same make are not distinctive enough to be of any recognition value
B. the car's appearance may have been greatly altered after the crime was committed
C. the criminals may have disguised themselves after the commission of the crime
D. the escaping criminals may change to a different car after leaving the scene

29. Five minutes after receiving an alarm for a blue 1980 Buick four-door sedan which had been used as a get-away car by bank robbers, a radio patrol team spots and stops a car which seems to fit the description. 29.___
The one of the following which is MOST likely to indicate the need for further careful investigation is that the
A. car has a cracked rear side window
B. driver does not have a registration certificate for this car
C. rear license plate is rusted
D. occupants of the car consist of three poorly dressed men

30. A foot patrolman who is several blocks away observes a woman being dragged into a car, which drives off very rapidly. 30.___
Of the following, his FIRST action should be to
A. call headquarters from the nearest call box or public telephone
B. commandeer a bus and pursue the other car
C. shoot in the direction of the scene as a warning
D. step into a hallway and await the approach of the car

31. A citizen requests police assistance in locating his adult son who has not been home for a period of twenty-four hours. Questioning of the citizen reveals no reason for the son's absence. 31.___
The MOST appropriate of the following actions that the police should take is to
A. advise the citizen to contact all nearby hospitals and then contact the police again if this is not successful

B. conduct a thorough investigation in an attempt to locate the missing son
C. politely inform the citizen that no police action will be taken since the son is an adult
D. suggest that the citizen wait several days; and if his son has not then returned home, they will accept the complaint

32. A patrolman is guarding the entrance of an apartment in which a homicide occurred. While awaiting the arrival of the detectives assigned to the case, he is approached by a newspaper reporter who asks to be admitted. The patrolman refuses to admit him. 32.____
The patrolman's action was
A. *wrong*; the police should cooperate with the press
B. *right*; the reporter might unintentionally destroy evidence if admitted
C. *wrong*; experienced police reporters can be trusted to act intelligently in this situation
D. *right*; this reporter should not be given an advantage over other newspaper men

33. A radio patrolman investigating a reported store hold-up, which occurred shortly before his arrival, enters the store. The salesclerk who witnessed the hold-up starts telling the patrolman, in a confused and excited manner, what had happened. 33.____
The BEST course for the patrolman to follow initially is to
A. ask the clerk to write out an account of what had happened
B. let the clerk tell her story without interruption
C. try to confine the clerk to answering relevant questions
D. wait until the clerk calms down before taking her statement

34. A phone call is received at police headquarters indicating that a burglary is now taking place in a large loft building. Several radio motor patrol teams are dispatched to the scene. 34.____
In order to prevent the escape of the burglars, the two patrolmen arriving first at the building, knowing that there is at least one entrance on each of the four sides of the building, should FIRST
A. station themselves at diagonally opposite corners, outside of the building
B. enter the building and proceed to search for the criminals
C. station themselves at the most likely exit from the building
D. enter the building and remain on the ground floor, attempting to keep all stairways under observation

Questions 35-56.

DIRECTIONS: In each of Questions 35 through 56, select the lettered word which means MOST NEARLY the same as the capitalized word. Place the letter which corresponds to your choice in the space at the right.

35. AVARICE 35.___
A. flight B. greed C. pride D. thrift

36. PREDATORY 36.___
A. offensive B. plundering
C. previous D. timeless

37. VINDICATE 37.___
A. clear B. conquer C. correct D. illustrate

38. INVETERATE 38.___
A. backward B. erect C. habitual D. lucky

39. DISCERN 39.___
A. describe B. fabricate C. recognize D. seek

40. COMPLACENT 40.___
A. indulgent B. listless
C. overjoyed D. satisfied

41. ILLICIT 41.___
A. insecure B. unclear C. unlawful D. unlimited

42. PROCRASTINATE 42.___
A. declare B. multiply C. postpone D. steal

43. IMPASSIVE 43.___
A. calm B. frustrated
C. thoughtful D. unhappy

44. AMICABLE 44.___
A. cheerful B. flexible C. friendly D. poised

45. FEASIBLE 45.___
A. breakable B. easy
C. likeable D. practicable

46. INNOCUOUS 46.___
A. harmless B. insecure
C. insincere D. unfavorable

47. OSTENSIBLE 47.___
A. apparent B. hesitant C. reluctant D. showy

48. INDOMITABLE 48.___
A. excessive B. unconquerable
C. unreasonable D. unthinkable

49. CRAVEN 49.___
A. cowardly B. hidden C. miserly D. needed

50. ALLAY 50.___
A. discuss B. quiet C. refine D. remove

51. ALLUDE 51.___
A. denounce B. refer C. state D. support

52. NEGLIGENCE 52.___
A. carelessness B. denial
C. objection D. refusal

53. AMEND 53.___
A. correct B. destroy C. end D. list

54. RELEVANT 54.___
A. conclusive B. careful
C. obvious D. related

55. VERIFY 55.___
A. challenge B. change C. confirm D. reveal

56. INSIGNIFICANT 56.___
A. incorrect B. limited
C. unimportant D. undesirable

Questions 57-61.

DIRECTIONS: Questions 57 through 61 are to be answered on the basis of the graphs shown on the following page.

CLEARANCE RATES FOR CRIMES AGAINST THE PERSON

2004

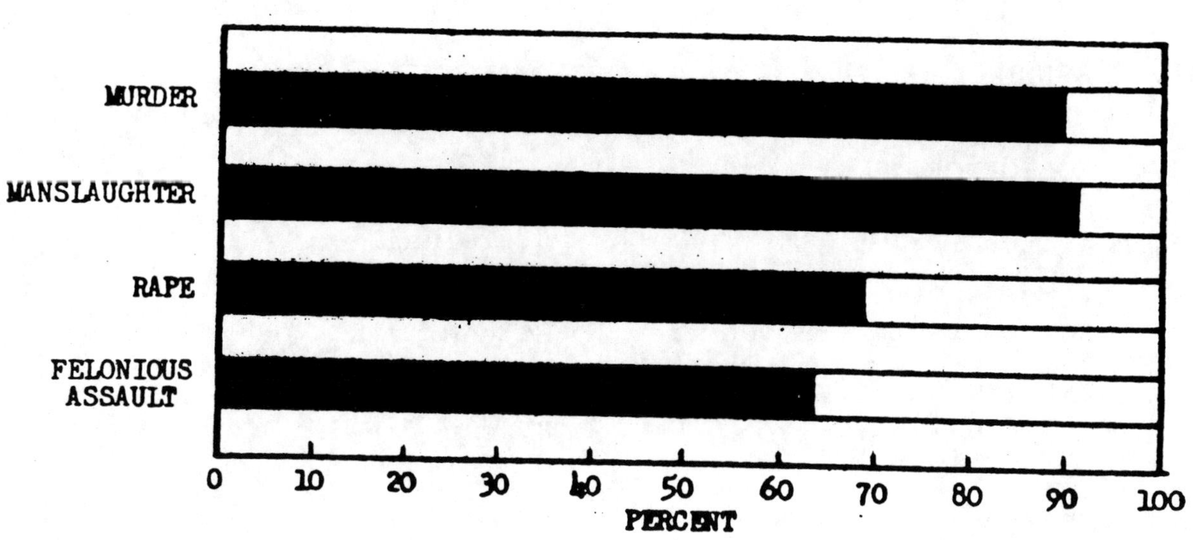

2005

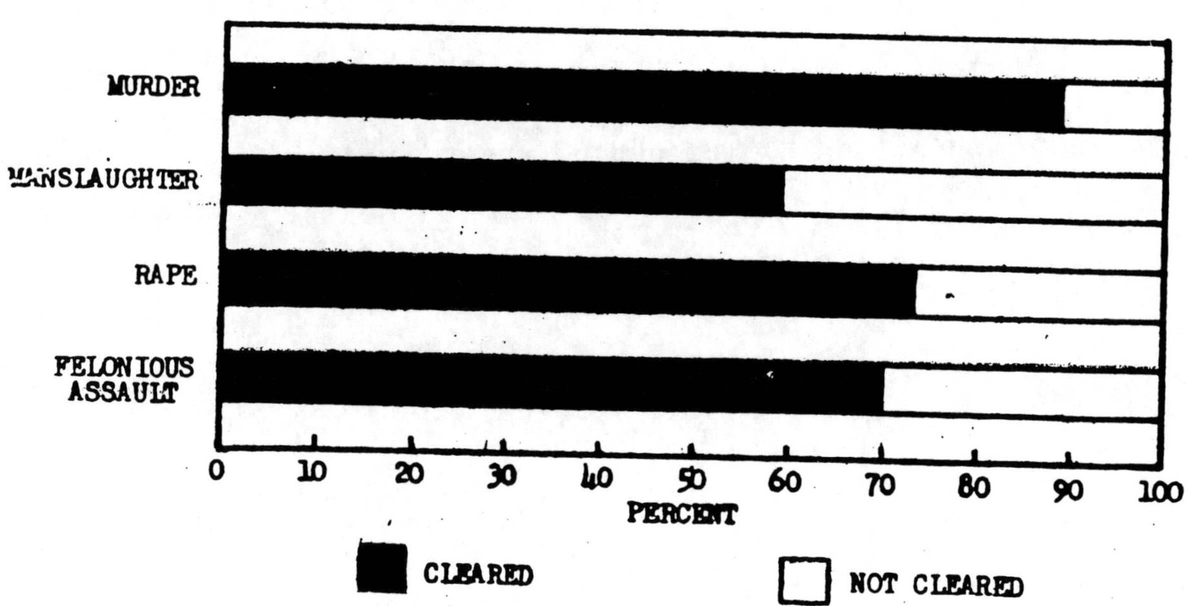

CLEARED NOT CLEARED

NOTE: The clearance rate is defined as the percentage of reported cases which were closed by the police through arrests or other means.

57. According to the above graphs, the AVERAGE clearance rate for all four crimes for 2005 57.___
   A. was greater than in 2004
   B. was less than in 2004
   C. was the same as in 2004
   D. cannot properly be compared to the 2004 figures

58. According to the above graphs, the crimes which did NOT show an increasing clearance rate from 2004 to 2005 were 58.___
   A. manslaughter and murder
   B. rape and felonious assault
   C. manslaughter and felonious assault
   D. rape and murder

59. According to the above graphs, the average clearance rate for the two year period 2004-2005 was SMALLEST for the crime of 59.___
   A. murder
   B. manslaughter
   C. rape
   D. felonious assault

60. If, in 2005, 63 cases of reported felonious assault remained *not cleared*, then the total number of felonious assault cases reported that year was MOST NEARLY 60.___
   A. 90 B. 150 C. 210 D. 900

61. In comparing the graphs for 2004 and 2005, it would be MOST accurate to state that 61.___
   A. it is not possible to compare the total number of crimes cleared in 2004 with the total number cleared in 2005
   B. the total number of crimes reported in 2004 is greater than the number in 2005
   C. there were fewer manslaughter cases cleared during 2004 than in 2005
   D. there were more rape cases cleared during 2005 than manslaughter cases cleared in the same year

62. A radio motor patrol car finds it necessary to travel at 90 miles per hour for a period of 1 minute and 40 seconds. The number of miles which the car travels during this period is 62.___
   A. 1 5/6 B. 2 C. 2½ D. 3 3/4

63. A radio motor patrol car has to travel a distance of 15 miles in an emergency. 63.___
If it does the first two-thirds of the distance at 40 m.p.h. and the last third at 60 m.p.h., the total number of minutes required for the entire run is MOST NEARLY
   A. 15 B. 20 C. 22½ D. 25

64. A patrol car had 11½ gallons of gasoline at the beginning of a trip of 196 miles and 5½ gallons at the end of the trip. During the trip, gasoline was bought for $10.85 at a cost of $1.55 per gallon. 64.____
The average number of miles driven per gallon of gasoline is MOST NEARLY
A. 14 B. 14.5 C. 15 D. 15.5

65. There are 15 patrolmen assigned to a certain operation. One-third earn $42,000 per year, three earn $44,100 per year, one earns $49,350 per year, and the rest earn $55,810 per year. 65.____
The average annual salary of these patrolmen is MOST NEARLY
A. $47,500 B. $48,000 C. $48,500 D. $49,000

66. In 2006, the cost of patrol car maintenance and repair was $2,500 more than in 2005, representing an increase of 10%. 66.____
The cost of patrol car maintenance and repair in 2006 was MOST NEARLY
A. $2,750 B. $22,500 C. $25,000 D. $27,500

67. A police precinct has an assigned strength of 180 men. Of this number, 25% are not available for duty due to illness, vacations, and other reasons. Of those who are available for duty, 1/3 are assigned outside of the precinct for special emergency duty. 67.____
The ACTUAL available strength of the precinct, in terms of men immediately available for precinct duty, is
A. 45 B. 60 C. 90 D. 135

68. Five police officers are taking target practice. 68.____
The number of rounds fired by each and the percentage of perfect shots is as follows:

Officer	Rounds Fired	Perfect Shots
R	80	30%
S	70	40%
T	75	60%
U	92	25%
V	96	66 2/3%

The average number of perfect shots fired by them is MOST NEARLY
A. 30 B. 36 C. 42 D. 80

69. A dozen 5-gallon cans of paint weigh 494 pounds. Each can, when empty, weighs 3 pounds. 69.____
The weight of one gallon of paint is MOST NEARLY _____ lbs.
A. 5 B. 6½ C. 7½ D. 8

Questions 70-71.

DIRECTIONS: Questions 70 and 71 are to be answered SOLELY on the basis of the following paragraph.

The medical examiner may contribute valuable data to the investigator of fires which cause fatalities. By careful examination of the bodies of any victims, he not only establishes cause of death, but may also furnish, in many instances, answers to questions relating to the identity of the victim and the source and origin of the fire. The medical examiner is of greatest value to law enforcement agencies because he is able to determine the exact cause of death through an examination of tissue of apparent arson victims. Thorough study of a burned body or even of parts of a burned body will frequently yield information which illuminates the problems confronting the arson investigator and the police.

70. According to the above paragraph, the MOST important task of the medical examiner in the investigation of arson is to obtain information concerning the 70.___
   A. identity of arsonists   B. cause of death
   C. identity of victims   D. source and origin of fires

71. The CENTRAL thought of the above paragraph is that the medical examiner aids in the solution of crimes of arson when 71.___
   A. a person is burnt to death
   B. identity of the arsonist is unknown
   C. the cause of the fire is known
   D. trained investigators are not available

Questions 72-75.

DIRECTIONS: Questions 72 through 75 are to be answered SOLELY on the basis of the following paragraph.

A foundling is an abandoned child whose identity is unknown. Desk officers shall direct the delivery, by a policewoman if available, of foundlings actually or apparently under two years of age to the American Foundling Hospital, or if actually or apparently two years of age or over, to the Children's Center. In all other cases of dependent or neglected children, other than foundlings, requiring shelter, desk officers shall provide for obtaining such shelter as follows: between 9 A.M. and 5 P.M., Monday through Friday, by telephone direct to the Bureau of Child Welfare, in order to ascertain the shelter to which the child shall be sent; at all other times, direct the delivery of a child actually or apparently under two years of age to the American Foundling Hospital, or if the child is actually or apparently two years of age or over to the Children's Center.

72. According to the above paragraph, it would be MOST correct to state that 72.___
   A. a foundling as well as a neglected child may be delivered to the American Foundling Hospital
   B. a foundling but not a neglected child may be delivered to the Children's Center
   C. a neglected child requiring shelter, regardless of age, may be delivered to the Bureau of Child Welfare
   D. the Bureau of Child Welfare may determine the shelter to which a foundling may be delivered

73. According to the above paragraph, the desk officer shall provide for obtaining shelter for a neglected child, apparently under two years of age, by 73.___
   A. directing its delivery to Children's Center if occurrence is on a Monday between 9 A.M. and 5 P.M.
   B. telephoning the Bureau of Child Welfare if occurrence is on a Sunday
   C. directing its delivery to the American Foundling Hospital if occurrence is on a Wednesday at 4 P.M.
   D. telephoning the Bureau of Child Welfare if occurrence is at 10 A.M. on a Friday

74. According to the above paragraph, the desk officer should direct delivery to the American Foundling Hospital of any child who is 74.___
   A. actually under 2 years of age and requires shelter
   B. apparently under two years of age and is neglected or dependent
   C. actually 2 years of age and is a foundling
   D. apparently under 2 years of age and has been abandoned

75. A 12-year-old neglected child requiring shelter is brought to a police station on Thursday at 2 P.M. 75.___
Such a child should be sent to
   A. a shelter selected by the Bureau of Child Welfare
   B. a shelter selected by the desk officer
   C. the Children's Center
   D. the American Foundling Hospital when a brother or sister, under 2 years of age, also requires shelter

Questions 76-78.

DIRECTIONS: Questions 76 through 78 are to be answered SOLELY on the basis of the following paragraph.

In addition to making the preliminary investigation of crimes, patrolmen should serve as eyes, ears, and legs for the detective division. The patrol division may be used for surveillance, to serve warrants and bring in suspects and witnesses, and to perform a number of routine tasks for the detectives which will increase the time available for tasks that require their special skills and facilities. It is to the advantage of individual detectives, as well as of the detective division, to have patrolmen working in this manner; more cases are cleared by arrest and a greater proportion of stolen property is recovered when, in addition to the detective regularly assigned, a number of patrolmen also work on the case. Detectives may stimulate the interest and participation of patrolmen by keeping them currently informed of the presence, identity, or description, hangouts, associates, vehicles and method of operation of each criminal known to be in the community.

76. According to the above paragraph, a patrolman should 76.___
   A. assist the detective in certain of his routine functions
   B. be considered for assignment as a detective on the basis of his patrol performance
   C. leave the scene once a detective arrives
   D. perform as much of the detective's duties as time permits

77. According to the above paragraph, patrolmen should aid detectives by 77.___
   A. accepting assignments from detectives which give promise of recovering stolen property
   B. making arrests of witnesses for the detective's interrogation
   C. performing all special investigative work for detectives
   D. producing for questioning individuals who may aid the detective in his investigation

78. According to the above paragraph, detectives can keep patrolmen interested by 78.___
   A. ascertaining that patrolmen are doing investigative work properly
   B. having patrolmen directly under his supervision during an investigation
   C. informing patrolmen of the value of their efforts in crime prevention
   D. supplying the patrolmen with information regarding known criminals in the community

Questions 79-80.

DIRECTIONS: Questions 79 and 80 are to be answered SOLELY on the basis of the following paragraph.

State motor vehicle registration departments should and do play a vital role in the prevention and detection of automobile thefts. The combatting of theft is, in fact, one of the primary purposes of the registration of motor vehicles. In 2003, there were approximately 61,309,000 motor vehicles registered in the United States. That same year, some 200,000 of them were stolen. All but 6 percent have been or will be recovered. This is a very high recovery ratio compared to the percentage of recovery of other stolen personal property. The reason for this is that automobiles are carefully identified by the manufacturers and carefully registered by many of the states.

79. The CENTRAL thought of the above paragraph is that there is a close relationship between the 79.___
   A. number of automobiles registered in the United States and the number stolen
   B. prevention of automobile thefts and the effectiveness of police departments in the United States
   C. recovery of stolen automobiles and automobile registration
   D. recovery of stolen automobiles and of other stolen property

80. According to the above paragraph, the high recovery ratio for stolen automobiles is due to 80.___
   A. state registration and manufacturer identification of motor vehicles
   B. successful prevention of automobile thefts by state motor vehicle departments
   C. the fact that only 6% of stolen vehicles are not properly registered
   D. the high number of motor vehicles registered in the United States

Questions 81-84.

DIRECTIONS: Questions 81 through 84 are to be answered SOLELY on the basis of the following paragraph.

It is not always understood that the term *physical evidence* embraces any and all objects, living or inanimate. A knife, gun, signature, or burglar tool is immediately recognized as physical evidence. Less often is it considered that dust, microscopic fragments of all types, even an odor, may equally be physical evidence and often the most important of all. It is well established that the most useful types of physical evidence are generally microscopic in dimensions, that is, not noticeable by the eye and, therefore, most likely to be overlooked by the criminal and by the investigator. For this reason, microscopic evidence persists for months or years after all other evidence has been removed and found inconclusive. Naturally, there are limitations to the time of collecting microscopic evidence as it may be lost or decayed. The exercise of judgment as to the possibility or profit of delayed action in collecting the evidence is a field in which the expert investigator should judge.

81. The one of the following which the above paragraph does NOT consider to be physical evidence is a 81.___
   A. criminal thought
   B. minute speck of dust
   C. raw onion smell
   D. typewritten note

82. According to the above paragraph, the rechecking of the scene of a crime 82.___
   A. is useless when performed years after the occurrence of the crime
   B. is advisable chiefly in crimes involving physical violence

C. may turn up microscopic evidence of value
D. should be delayed if the microscopic evidence is not subject to decay or loss

83. According to the above paragraph, the criminal investigator should 83.___
A. give most of his attention to weapons used in the commission of the crime
B. ignore microscopic evidence until a request is received from the laboratory
C. immediately search for microscopic evidence and ignore the more visible objects
D. realize that microscopic evidence can be easily overlooked

84. According to the above paragraph, 84.___
A. a delay in collecting evidence must definitely diminish its value to the investigator
B. microscopic evidence exists for longer periods of time than other physical evidence
C. microscopic evidence is generally the most useful type of physical evidence
D. physical evidence is likely to be overlooked by the criminal and by the investigator

Questions 85-87.

DIRECTIONS: Questions 85 through 87 are to be answered SOLELY on the basis of the following paragraph.

Sometimes, but not always, firing a gun leaves a residue of nitrate particles on the hands. This fact is utilized in the paraffin test which consists of applying melted paraffin and gauze to the fingers, hands, and wrists of a suspect until a cast of approximately 1/8 of an inch is built up. The heat of the paraffin causes the pores of the skin to open and release any particles embedded in them. The paraffin cast is then removed and tested chemically for nitrate particles. In addition to gunpowder, fertilizers, tobacco ashes, matches, and soot are also common sources of nitrates on the hands.

85. Assume that the paraffin test has been given to a person suspected of firing a gun and that nitrate particles have been found. 85.___
It would be CORRECT to conclude that the suspect
A. is guilty
B. is innocent
C. may be guilty or innocent
D. is probably guilty

86. In testing for the presence of gunpowder particles on human hands, the characteristic of paraffin which makes it MOST serviceable is that it 86.___
A. causes the nitrate residue left by a fired gun to adhere to the gauze

B. is waterproof
C. melts at a high temperature
D. helps to distinguish between gunpowder nitrates and other types

87. According to the above paragraph, in the paraffin test, the nitrate particles are removed from the pores because the paraffin 87.___
A. enlarges the pores
B. contracts the pores
C. reacts chemically with nitrates
D. dissolves the particles

Questions 88-90.

DIRECTIONS: Questions 88 through 90 are to be answered SOLELY on the basis of the following paragraph.

Pickpockets operate most effectively when there are prospective victims in either heavily congested areas or in lonely places. In heavily populated areas, the large number of people about them covers the activities of these thieves. In lonely spots, they have the advantage of working unobserved. The main factor in the pickpocket's success is the selection of the *right* victim. A pickpocket's victim must, at the time of the crime, be inattentive, distracted, or unconscious. If any of these conditions exist, and if the pickpocket is skilled in his operations, the stage is set for a successful larceny. With the coming of winter, the crowds move southward -- and so do most of the pickpockets. However, some pickpockets will remain in certain areas all year around. They will concentrate on theater districts, bus and railroad terminals, hotels, or large shopping centers. A complete knowledge of the methods of this type of criminal and the ability to recognize them come only from long years of experience in performing patient surveillance and trailing of them. This knowledge is essential for the effective control and apprehension of this type of thief.

88. According to this paragraph, the pickpocket is LEAST likely to operate in a 88.___
A. baseball park with a full capacity attendance
B. subway station in an outlying area late at night
C. moderately crowded dance hall
D. over-crowded department store

89. According to the above paragraph, the one of the following factors which is NOT necessary for the successful operation of the pickpocket is that 89.___
A. he be proficient in the operations required to pick-pockets
B. the *right* potential victims be those who have been the subject of such a theft previously
C. his operations be hidden from the view of others
D. the potential victim be unaware of the actions of the pickpocket

90. According to the above paragraph, it would be MOST correct to conclude that police officers who are successful in apprehending pickpockets 90.____

A. are generally those who have had lengthy experience in recognizing all types of criminals
B. must, by intuition, be able to recognize potential *right* victims
C. must follow tho pickpockets in their southward movement
D. must have acquired specific knowledge and skills in this field

---

KEY (CORRECT ANSWERS)

1. C	26. D	51. B	76. A
2. A	27. A	52. A	77. D
3. C	28. B	53. A	78. D
4. D	29. B	54. D	79. C
5. A	30. A	55. C	80. A
6. A	31. B	56. C	81. A
7. B	32. B	57. B	82. C
8. C	33. C	58. A	83. D
9. B	34. A	59. D	84. C
10. B	35. B	60. C	85. C
11. C	36. B	61. A	86. A
12. C	37. A	62. C	87. A
13. D	38. C	63. B	88. C
14. A	39. C	64. C	89. B
15. C	40. D	65. C	90. D
16. C	41. C	66. D	
17. A	42. C	67. C	
18. D	43. A	68. B	
19. D	44. C	69. C	
20. A	45. D	70. B	
21. C	46. A	71. A	
22. B	47. A	72. A	
23. D	48. B	73. D	
24. D	49. A	74. D	
25. C	50. B	75. A	

EXAMINATION SECTION

DIRECTIONS: Each question or incomplete statement is followed by several suggested answers or completions. Select the one that BEST answers the question or completes the statement. *PRINT THE LETTER OF THE CORRECT ANSWER IN THE SPACE AT THE RIGHT.*

1. Upon arriving at the scene of an accident in which a pedestrian was struck and killed by an automobile, an officer's FIRST action was to clear the scene of spectators. 1.____
   Of the following, the PRINCIPAL reason for this action is that
   A. important evidence may be inadvertently destroyed by the crowd
   B. this is a fundamental procedure in first aid work
   C. the operator of the vehicle may escape in the crowd
   D. witnesses will speak more freely if other persons are not present

2. In questioning witnesses, an officer is instructed to avoid leading questions or questions that will suggest the answer. Accordingly, when questioning a witness about the appearance of a suspect, it would be BEST for him to ask: 2.____
   A. What kind of hat did he wear?
   B. Did he wear a felt hat?
   C. What did he wear?
   D. Didn't he wear a hat?

3. The only personal description the police have of a particular criminal was made several years ago. Of the following, the item in the description that will be MOST useful in identifying him at the present time is the 3.____
   A. color of his eyes
   B. color of his hair
   C. number of teeth
   D. weight

4. Crime statistics indicate that property crimes such as larceny, burglary and robbery, are more numerous during winter months than in summer. 4.____
   The one of the following explanations that MOST adequately accounts for this situation is that
   A. human needs, such as clothing, food, heat and shelter, are greater in winter
   B. criminal tendencies are aggravated by climatic changes
   C. there are more hours of darkness in winter and such crimes are usually committed under cover of darkness
   D. urban areas are more densely populated during winter months, affording greater opportunity for such crimes

5. When automobile tire tracks are to be used as evidence, a plaster cast is made of them. Before the cast is made, however, a photograph of the tracks is taken. 5.____
Of the following, the MOST probable reason for taking a photograph is that
   A. photographs can be duplicated more easily than castings
   B. less skill is required for photographing than casting
   C. the tracks may be damaged in the casting process
   D. photographs are more easily transported than castings

6. It is generally recommended that an officer, in lifting a revolver that is to be sent to the police laboratory for ballistics tests and fingerprint examination, do so by inserting a pencil through the trigger guard rather than into the barrel of the weapon. 6.____
The reason for preferring this procedure is that
   A. every precaution must be taken not to eliminate fingerprints on the weapon
   B. there is a danger of accidentally discharging the weapon by placing the pencil in the barrel
   C. the pencil may make scratches inside the barrel that will interfere with the ballistics tests
   D. a weapon can more easily be lifted by the trigger guard

7. PHYSICIAN is to PATIENT as ATTORNEY is to 7.____
   A. court B. client
   C. counsel D. judge

8. JUDGE is to SENTENCE as JURY is to 8.____
   A. court B. foreman
   C. defendant D. verdict

9. REVERSAL is to AFFIRMANCE as CONVICTION is to 9.____
   A. appeal B. acquittal
   C. error D. mistrial

10. GENUINE is to TRUE as SPURIOUS is to 10.____
   A. correct B. conceived
   C. false D. speculative

11. ALLEGIANCE is to LOYALTY as TREASON IS TO 11.____
   A. felony B. faithful
   C. obedience D. rebellion

12. CONCUR is to AGREE as DIFFER is to 12.____
   A. coincide B. dispute
   C. join D. repeal

13. A person who has an uncontrollable desire to steal without need is called a 13.____
   A. dipsomaniac B. kleptomaniac
   C. monomaniac D. pyromaniac

14. In the sentence, "The placing of any inflammable substance in any building or the placing of any device or contrivence capable of producing fire, for the purpose of causing a fire is an attempt to burn," the MISSPELLED word is 14.____
A. inflammable
B. substance
C. device
D. contrivence

15. In the sentence, "The word 'break' also means obtaining an entrance into a building by any artifice used for that purpose, or by colussion with any person therein," the MISSPELLED word is 15.____
A. obtaining
B. entrance
C. artifice
D. colussion

16. In the sentence, "Any person who with intent to provoke a breech of the peace causes a disturbance or is offensive to others may be deemed to have committed disorderly conduct," the MISSPELLED word is 16.____
A. breech
B. disturbance
C. offensive
D. committed

17. In the sentence, "When the offender inflicts a grevious harm upon the person from whose possession, or in whose presence, property is taken, he is guilty of robbery," the MISSPELLED word is 17.____
A. offender
B. grevious
C. possession
D. presence

18. In the sentence, "A person who willfully encourages or advises another person in attempting to take the latter's life is guilty of a felony," the MISSPELLED word is 18.____
A. willfully
B. encourages
C. advises
D. attempting

19. The treatment to be given the offender cannot alter the fact of his offense; but we can take measures to reduce the chances of similar acts in the future. We should banish the criminal, not in order to exact revenge nor directly to encourage reform, but to deter him and others from further illegal attacks on society. 19.____
According to this paragraph, the PRINCIPAL reason for punishing criminals is to
A. prevent the commission of future crimes
B. remove them safely from society
C. avenge society
D. teach them that crime does not pay

20. Even the most comprehensive and best substantiated summaries of the total volume of criminal acts would not contribute greatly to an understanding of the varied social and biological factors which are sometimes assumed to enter into crime causation, nor would they indicate with any degree of precision the needs of police forces in combating crime. 20.____

According to this statement,

A. crime statistics alone do not determine the needs of police forces in combating crime

B. crime statistics are essential to a proper understanding of the social factors of crime

C. social and biological factors which enter the crime causation have little bearing on police needs

D. a knowledge of the social and biological factors of crime is essential to a proper understanding of crime statistics

21. The policeman's art consists in applying and enforcing a multitude of laws and ordinances in such degree or proportion and in such manner that the greatest degree of social protection will be secured. The degree of enforcement and the method of application will vary with each neighborhood and community. 21.____

According to the foregoing paragraph,

A. each neighborhood or community must judge for itself to what extent the law is to be enforced

B. a policeman should only enforce those laws which are designed to give the greatest degree of social protection

C. the manner and intensity of law enforcement is not necessarily the same in all communities

D. all laws and ordinances must be enforced in a community with the same degree of intensity

22. Police control in the sense of regulating the details of police operations involves such matters as the technical means for so organizing the available personnel that competent police leadership, when secured, can operate effectively. It is concerned not so much with the extent to which popular controls can be trusted to guide and direct the course of police protection as with the administrative relationships which should exist between the component parts of the police organism. 22.____

According to the foregoing statement, police control is

A. solely a matter of proper personnel assignment

B. the means employed to guide and direct the course of police protection

C. principally concerned with the administrative relationships between units of a police organization

D. the sum total of means employed in rendering police protection

23. Two patrol cars hurry to the scene of an accident from different directions. The first proceeds at the rate of 45 miles per hour and arrives in four minutes. Although the second car travels over a route which is three-fourths of a mile longer, it arrives at the scene only a half minute later. The speed of the second car, expressed in miles per hour, is 23.____

A. 50 B. 55 C. 60 D. 65

24. A motorcycle policeman issued 72 traffic summonses in January, 60 in February and 83 in March. In order to average 75 summonses per month for the four months of January, February, March and April, during April he will have to issue ________ summonses. 24.____
A. 80 B. 85 C. 90 D. 95

25. In a unit of the Police Department to which 40 patrolmen are assigned, the sick report record during 1983 was as follows: 25.____

1 was absent 8 days
4 were absent 5 days each
8 were absent 4 days each
5 were absent 3 days each
10 were absent 2 days each
5 were absent 1 day each

The *average* number of days on sick report for all the members of this unit is *most nearly*
A. 1/2 B. 1 C. 2 1/2 D. 3

QUESTIONS 26-30.
Column I lists various statements of fact. Column II is a list of crimes. Next to the numbers corresponding to the number preceding the statements of fact in Column I, place the letter preceding the crime listed in Column II with which Jones should be charged. In answering these questions, the following definitions of crimes should be applied, bearing mind that ALL elements contained in the definitions must be present in order to charge a person with that crime.

BURGLARY is breaking and entering a building with intent to commit some crime therein.

EMBEZZLEMENT is the appropriation to one's own use of another's property which has been entrusted to one's care or which has come lawfully into one's possession.

EXTORTION is taking or obtaining property from another with his consent, induced by a wrongful use of force or fear.

LARCENY is taking and carrying away the personal property of another with intent to deprive or defraud the true owner of the use and benefit of such property.

ROBBERY is the unlawful taking of the personal property of another from his person or in his presence by force or violence, or fear of injury.

Column I

26. Jones, believing Smith had induced his wife to leave him, went to Smith's home armed with a knife with which he intended to assault Smith. When his knock was unanswered, he forced open the door of Smith's home and entered but, finding the house empty, he threw away the knife and left. 26.____

Column II

A. burglary
B. embezzlement
C. extortion
D. larceny
E. robbery
F. no crime

27. Jones was employed as a collection agent by Smith. When Smith refused to reimburse him for certain expenses he claimed to have incurred in connection with his work, Jones deducted this amount from sums he had collected for Smith. 27.____

28. Jones spent the night in a hotel. During the night he left his room, went downstairs to the desk, stole money and returned to his room. 28.____

29. Jones, a building inspector, found that the elevators in Smith's building were being operated without a permit. He threatened to report the matter and have the elevators shut down unless Smith paid him a sum of money. Smith paid the amount demanded. 29.____

30. Jones held-up Smith on the street and, pointing a revolver at him, demanded his money. Smith, without resisting, handed Jones his money. When Jones was apprehended it was discovered that the revolver was a toy. 30.____

QUESTIONS 31-40.

Questions 31-40 consist of statements from which a term is missing. Each of these statements can be completed correctly with one of the terms in the following list. In the space opposite the number corresponding to the number of the question, place the LETTER preceding the term in the following list, which most accurately completes the statement.

A. affidavit
B. appeal
C. arraignment
D. arrest
E. bench warrant
F. habeas corpus
G. indictment
H. injunction
J. sentence
K. subpoena

31. A ________ is a writ calling witnesses to court. 31.____

32. ________ is a method used to obtain a review of a case in court of superior jurisdiction. 32.____

33. A judgment passed by a court on a person on trial as a criminal offender is called a ________. 33.____

34. ________ is a writ or order requiring a person to refrain from a particular act. 34.____

35. ________ is the name given to a writ commanding the bringing of the body of a certain person before a certain court. 35.____

36. A ________ is a court order directing that an offender be brought into court. 36.____

37. The calling of a defendant before the court to answer an accusation is called ________. 37.____

38. The accusation in writing, presented by the grand jury to a competent court charging a person with a public offense is an ________. 38.____

39. A sworm declaration in writing is an ________. 39.____

40. ________ is the taking of a person into custody for the purpose of holding him to answer a criminal charge. 40.____

QUESTIONS 41-55.
Questions 41-55 consist of statements from which a term is missing. Each of these statements can be completed correctly with one of the terms in the following list. In the space opposite the number corresponding to the number of the question, place the LETTER preceding the term in the following list, which MOST accurately completes the statement.

A. accessory
B. accomplice
C. alibi
D. autopsy
E. ballistics
F. capital
G. confidence man
H. commission
J. conspiracy
K. corroborated
L. grand jury
M. homicide
N. misdemeanors
O. penology
P. perjury

41. ________ is the dissection of a dead human body to determine the cause of death. 41.____

42. The general term which means the killing of one person by another is ________. 42.____

43. ________ is the science of the punishment of crime. 43.____

44. False swearing constitutes the crime of ________. 44.____

45. A combination of two or more persons to accomplish a criminal or unlawful act is called ________. 45.____

46. By ________ is meant evidence showing that a defendant was in another place when the crime was committed. 46.____

47. ________ is a term frequently used to describe a person engaged in a kind of swindling operation. 47.____

48. A ________ offense is one for which a life sentence or dealth penalty is prescribed by law. 48.____

49. A violation of a law may be either an act of omission or an act of ________. 49.____

50. An ________ is a person who is liable to prosecution for the identical offense charged against a defendant on trial. 50.____

51. A person would be an ________ who after the commission of a crime aided in the escape of one he knew to be an offender. 51.____

52. An official body called to hear complaints and to determine whether there is ground for criminal prosecution is known as the ________. 52.____

53. Crimes are generally divided into two classes, namely felonies and ________. 53.____

54. ________ is the science of the motion of projectiles. 54.____

55. Testimony of a witness which is confirmed by another witness is ________. 55.____

QUESTIONS 56-60.
Next to the question number which corresponds with the number of each item in Column I, place the letter preceding the adjective in Column II which BEST describes the persons in Column I.

Column I	Column II	
56. a talkative woman	A. abstemious	56.____
	B. pompous	
57. a person on a reducing diet	C. erudite	57.____
	D. benevolent	
58. a scholarly professor	E. docile	58.____
	F. loquacious	
59. a man who seldom speaks	G. indefatigable	59.____
	H. taciturn	
60. a charitable person		60.____

QUESTIONS 61-65.
Next to the question number which corresponds with the number preceding each profession in Column I, place the letter preceding the word in Column II which BEST explains the subject matter of that profession.

Column I	Column II	
61. geologist	A. animals	61.____
62. oculist	B. eyes	62.____
63. podiatrist	C. feet	63.____
64. palmist	D. fortune-telling	64.____
65. zoologist	E. language	65.____
	F. rocks	
	G. stamps	
	H. woman	

QUESTIONS 66-70.
Next to the question number corresponding to the number of each of the words in Column I, place the letter preceding the word in Column II that is most nearly OPPOSITE to it in meaning.

Column I	Column II	
66. comely	A. beautiful	66.____
67. eminent	B. cowardly	67.____
68. frugal	C. kind	68.____
69. gullible	D. sedate	69.____
70. valiant	E. shrewd	70.____
	F. ugly	
	G. unknown	
	H. wasteful	

KEY (CORRECT ANSWERS)

1. A
2. C
3. A
4. C
5. C

6. C
7. B
8. D
9. B
10. C

11. D
12. B
13. B
14. D
15. D

16. A
17. B
18. A
19. A
20. A

21. C
22. C
23. A
24. B
25. C

26. A
27. B
28. D
29. C
30. E

31. K
32. B
33. J
34. H
35. F

36. E
37. C
38. G
39. A
40. D

41. D
42. M
43. O
44. P
45. J

46. C
47. G
48. F
49. H
50. B

51. A
52. L
53. N
54. E
55. K

56. F
57. A
58. C
59. H
60. D

61. F
62. B
63. C
64. D
65. A

66. F
67. G
68. H
69. E
70. B

EXAMINATION SECTION
TEST 1

DIRECTIONS: Each question or incomplete statement is followed by several suggested answers or completions. Select the one that BEST answers the question or completes the statement. *PRINT THE LETTER OF THE CORRECT ANSWER IN THE SPACE AT THE RIGHT.*

1. An indictment is a 1.___
   A. formal charge
   B. overdue payment
   C. bill of particulars relating to a dispute
   D. felony

2. In a trial, a hostile witness is a(n) _____ witness. 2.___
   A. controversial
   B. unfriendly
   C. combative
   D. evasive

3. Which of the following was an event from 1999 that may reduce the number of guns in this country? 3.___
   A. The passage of a strict gun law in Congress
   B. Gun shows were restricted by Congress
   C. The Colt Corporation restricted the sale of its guns
   D. An embargo was placed on guns coming into this country

4. In the state, headlights should be used when visibility is equal to a minimum or less than _____ feet. 4.___
   A. 500
   B. 750
   C. 1,000
   D. 1,250

5. You are required to dim your headlights when an approaching vehicle is within _____ feet of your vehicle. 5.___
   A. 500
   B. 400
   C. 300
   D. 200

6. *Some features of the arrangement of contents in the following pages may perplex some readers.* 6.___
   The word *perplex*, as used in the above sentence, means MOST NEARLY
   A. interest
   B. enlighten
   C. turnoff
   D. confuse

7. Hearsay evidence means 7.___
   A. false evidence
   B. evidence that needs to be verified
   C. it is generally not admissible in court
   D. the person testifying is unsure of its truth

Questions 8-9.

DIRECTIONS: Questions 8 and 9 refer to the following paragraph.

The variations in report writing range from such picayune details as using A.M. or a.m. to more substantive issues as the inclusion or omission of a report summary in the first paragraph.

8. In the above paragraph, the word *picayune* means MOST NEARLY 7.___
   A. grammatic B. debatable
   C. trivial D. tendentious

9. In the above paragraph, the word *substantive* means MOST NEARLY 8.___
   A. cursory B. meaningless
   C. critical D. substantial

10. In accordance with the driver's manual issued by the state, you must report an accident when damage is _____ or more. 9.___
    A. $500 B. $1,000 C. $1,500 D. $2,000

11. It is easier to pass a heavy truck on a highway 10.___
    A. when the roadway is level
    B. when going uphill
    C. when going downhill
    D. on a concrete pavement

12. In most states, motorcyclists are required to use 12.___
    A. headlights and taillights only after sundown
    B. headlights and taillights at all times
    C. taillights only during daylight hours
    D. headlights only during daylight hours

13. DNA refers to 13.___
    A. a person who dies upon arriving at a hospital
    B. genetic material
    C. a chemical reaction
    D. a powerful drug

14. An odometer measures the _____ an automobile. 14.___
    A. speed of
    B. velocity of
    C. distance traveled by
    D. revolutions per second of the engine of

15. *Profiling has recently become a controversial issue in police work.* 15.___
    Profiling, as used in the above sentence, relates to paying special attention to
    A. a recognizable class of people
    B. people of low income
    C. people who exceed the speed limits
    D. the class of people who drive expensive cars

16. Most highways have a minimum speed of _____ MPH. 16.___
A. 40 B. 35 C. 30 D. 25

17. The lowest automobile accident rate occurs in the _____ year age group. 17.___
A. 20 to 35 B. 35 to 50 C. 50 to 65 D. 65 to 80

18. *Writing is characterized as narrative description, exposition, and argument.* 18.___
Exposition, as used in the above sentence, means MOST NEARLY
A. describing the circumstances of the situation
B. the explanation of a piece of information
C. explaining your conclusions
D. giving the pros and cons of a conclusion

19. A report states that the latent prints have been sent to the laboratory. The word *latent*, as used in the above statement, means MOST NEARLY 19.___
A. missing B. visible C. hidden D. damaged

20. After being *acquitted* in the first trial, O.J. Simpson faced a second trial. The second trial was not double jeopardy because 20.___
A. evidence was withheld from the jury
B. he was tried on different criminal charges
C. the second trial was a civil trial
D. the first trial was against the weight of the evidence

21. To *loiter* means MOST NEARLY to 21.___
A. gather in a group of five or more
B. create suspicion of wrongdoing while hanging around
C. obstruct pedestrian movement
D. linger in an aimless way

22. The minimum automobile insurance required for property damage in New York State is 22.___
A. $3,000 B. $5,000 C. $10,000 D. $20,000

23. The maximum speed limit in a village or town is usually _____ MPH. 23.___
A. 20 B. 25 C. 30 D. 40

24. The purpose of the *two second rule* in driving is to 24.___
A. give you enough time to stop if there is a traffic signal ahead
B. give you enough clearance to cut into another lane when passing a car
C. keep enough room between your vehicle and the one ahead
D. provide enough room when entering a highway

25. In most states, you may be arrested for driving with a blood alcohol content of _____ percent or more. 25._

A. .05 B. .10 C. .15 D. .20

KEY (CORRECT ANSWERS)

1. A
2. B
3. C
4. C
5. A

6. D
7. C
8. C
9. D
10. B

11. B
12. B
13. B
14. C
15. A

16. A
17. B
18. B
19. C
20. C

21. D
22. B
23. C
24. C
25. B

TEST 2

DIRECTIONS: Each question or incomplete statement is followed by several suggested answers or completions. Select the one that BEST answers the question or completes the statement. *PRINT THE LETTER OF THE CORRECT ANSWER IN THE SPACE AT THE RIGHT.*

1. A yellow sign showing two children in black indicates a school crossing. The shape of the sign is a 1.___
   A. square B. rectangle C. hexagon D. pentagon

2. Personal vehicles driven by volunteer firefighters responding to alarms are allowed to display _____ lights. 2.___
   A. blue B. green C. red D. amber

3. The color amber is closest to 3.___
   A. green B. yellow C. purple D. blue

4. Larceny in the legal sense means 4.___
   A. the unlawful taking away of another person's property without his consent
   B. overcharging another person who is making a purchase
   C. deceiving another person as to the value of an item he wishes to purchase
   D. adding a service charge to an agreed price to an item that is purchased

5. A misdemeanor in law refers to 5.___
   A. a financial dispute between two litigants
   B. a minor offense
   C. a burglary where a small amount of goods was stolen
   D. unruly behavior in public

6. An overt act means MOST NEARLY a(n) 6.___
   A. foolish act B. act done publicly
   C. illegal act D. outrageous act

7. A defense lawyer works for a client *pro bono*. This means he 7.___
   A. gets paid only if he wins the case
   B. gets paid a fixed fee
   C. works for free
   D. represents his client at half his usual fee

8. Corpus delicti refers to the 8.___
   A. missing person B. murderer
   C. scene of the crime D. dead victim

9. The shape of a stop sign is 9.___
   A. triangular B. square
   C. six-sided D. eight-sided

10. Service signs are _____ with white letters and symbols. 10.
A. blue B. green C. yellow D. red

11. Destination signs are _____ with white letters and symbols. 11.
A. blue B. green C. yellow D. red

12. According to the driver's manual, you are prohibited from passing if you cannot safely return to the right lane before any approaching vehicle comes within _____ feet of your car. 12.
A. 100 B. 150 C. 200 D. 250

13. When parking near a hydrant, you must be clear of the hydrant a minimum distance of _____ feet. 13.
A. 5 B. 10 C. 15 D. 20

14. When parking your vehicle between two parked vehicles, you must park a maximum of _____ inches from the curb. 14.
A. 12 B. 15 C. 18 D. 21

15. In order to insure approval, the framers of the Constitution agreed to add a series of amendments after approval to protect people's rights.
The number of amendments that were added is 15.
A. six B. eight C. ten D. twelve

16. The amendment number that insures a person's right to bear arms is 16.
A. one B. two C. three D. five

17. The amendment number that prevents a person from incriminating himself is 17.
A. one B. three C. five D. seven

18. The right of a person to be secure in his house, and against unreasonable search is amendment number 18.
A. two B. four C. six D. eight

19. The right of people to assemble peaceably is amendment number 19.
A. one B. two C. three D. four

20. 90 kilometers per hour is equivalent to _____ MPH. 20.
A. 40 B. 45 C. 50 D. 55

21. A commercial driver's license is required if the vehicle being driven has a gross weight rating of equal to or more than _____ pounds. 21.
A. 24,000 B. 26,000 C. 28,000 D. 30,000

22. One kilogram is equivalent to _____ pounds. 22.
A. 2.2 B. 2.4 C. 2.6 D. 2.8

23. Failing to stop for a school bus in New York State is worth _____ points on your license. 23.___
   A. 3   B. 4   C. 5   D. 6

24. In the state, the minimum liability insurance required against the death of one person is 24.___
   A. $30,000   B. $50,000   C. $100,000   D. $150,000

25. Before a person is arrested, he is read a statement by the arresting officer. The name associated with this procedure is 25.___
   A. Megan   B. Zenger   C. Scott   D. Miranda

KEY (CORRECT ANSWERS)

1. D
2. A
3. B
4. A
5. B

6. B
7. C
8. D
9. D
10. A

11. B
12. C
13. C
14. A
15. C

16. B
17. C
18. B
19. A
20. D

21. B
22. A
23. C
24. B
25. D

TEST 3

DIRECTIONS: Each question or incomplete statement is followed by several suggested answers or completions. Select the one that BEST answers the question or completes the statement. *PRINT THE LETTER OF THE CORRECT ANSWER IN THE SPACE AT THE RIGHT.*

1. In legal terms, a deposition is 1._
   A. a statement made by a person in open court
   B. a statement under oath, but not in open court
   C. the testimony made by a defendant under oath in open court
   D. a statement under oath that is mainly hearsay

2. In an automobile accident, first check to see if the injured person is breathing. If not, apply 2._
   A. MPR B. IBR C. FHR D. CPR

3. Hazard vehicles, such as snow plows and tow trucks, display _____-colored lights. 3._
   A. blue B. green C. amber D. red

4. The hand signal shown at the right indicates 4._
   A. caution because there is an obstruction ahead
   B. a right turn
   C. a left turn
   D. a stop

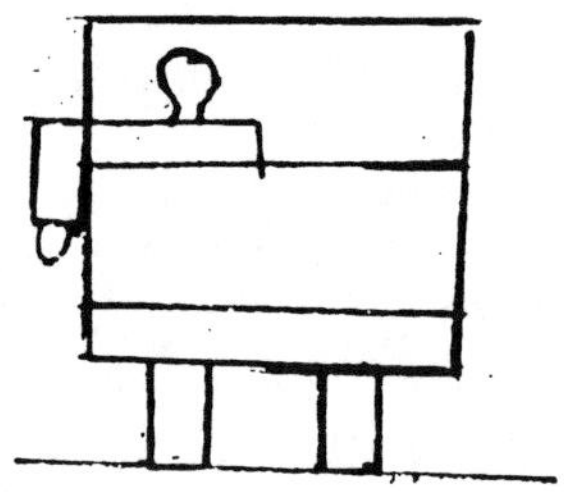

5. A felony is a 5._
   A. crime only where someone is murdered
   B. major crime
   C. crime only where someone is injured
   D. crime only where major physical damage occurs

6. *Embezzlement* means MOST NEARLY 6._
   A. deceiving B. the hiding of funds
   C. stealing D. investing illegally

7. *The writer should be wary of using an entire paragraph for information, while necessary is not really of great importance.* 7._
   The word *wary* in the above sentence means MOST NEARLY
   A. uncertain B. cautious
   C. certain D. serious

8. Hearsay evidence is evidence that 8._
   A. is usually admissible in court
   B. can be inferred from preceding evidence
   C. is based on what another person said out of court
   D. is implied in the testimony of a witness

9. *Excessive bail shall not be required* is amendment number 9.___
A. two B. four C. six D. eight

10. The writ of habeas corpus is used to 10.___
A. insure a defendant receives a fair trial
B. insure a defendant's Fifth Amendment rights
C. reduce or eliminate bail
D. prevent a person from being detained illegally

11. The number of justices in the United States Supreme Court is 11.___
A. 6 B. 7 C. 8 D. 9

12. The *blue wall* refers to law enforcement officers who 12.___
A. do not publicly condemn fellow officers regardless of facts
B. set up roadblocks
C. support their superiors
D. do their utmost to improve their image

13. The difference between burglary and robbery is 13.___
A. burglary is breaking into a building to commit theft, while robbery is the use of violence in taking property from a person
B. the money value taken in a burglary is less than $10,000, whereas in a robbery the money value taken is more than $10,000
C. burglary takes place at night, whereas robbery takes place in the daytime
D. burglary takes place indoors, whereas robbery takes place outdoors

14. The Federal government announced new guidelines relating to automobiles. These standards relate to 14.___
A. automobile weight B. gas mileage requirements
C. car infant seats D. bumper heights

15. General Motors was involved in a famous lawsuit relating to the Chevy Corvair based on 15.___
A. its crashworthiness
B. faulty design of the brake system
C. failure of the transmissions
D. location of the gas tanks

16. State legislatures are considering restrictions on the use of cellular phones while driving an automobile. The main argument for the restrictions is that 16.___
A. driving with one hand is hazardous
B. conversations on the phone are a distraction
C. cellular phones interfere with the ignition system
D. the driver is unlikely to hear sirens or hornblowing

17. *Much of their business involves the unpredictable and the bizarre.* 17.___
The word *bizarre*, as used in the above statement, means MOST NEARLY
A. weird B. routine
C. complicated D. life-threatening

18. *The federal government seized 145 metric tons of cocaine coming into the United States from South America.* 18.___
A metric ton is equal to _____ pounds.
A. 1,800 B. 2,000 C. 2,200 D. 2,400

19. A kilogram is most nearly _____ pounds. 19.___
A. 2.0 B. 2.2 C. 2.4 D. 2.6

20. A narcotic drug used in medicine, but less habit-forming than morphine, is 20.___
A. cocaine B. methadone C. LSD D. heroin

21. Of the following, the one that is a hazard for the large recreational vehicles is 21.___
A. their inability to meet the emission requirements
B. their bumper height above the ground does not match the height of the bumpers on the smaller-sized vehicles
C. because the driver is high above the ground, his ability to see his surroundings is impaired
D. because of the high center of gravity of the recreational vehicles, they become unstable at high speeds

22. State inspection procedures on emissions focus on 22.___
A. hydrocarbons and CO_2 B. CO and CO_2
C. SO_2 and CO D. hydrocarbons and CO

23. *In order to bring a case before a Grand Jury, the prosecutor must present a prima facie case of guilt before the Grand Jury.* 23.___
Prima facie in the above statement means MOST NEARLY
A. overwhelming evidence to convict
B. sufficient to convict unless rebutted by the defense
C. possibly sufficient to convict by an objective jury
D. with additional evidence would be sufficient to convict

24. The KKK was denied a permit to hold a parade in New York City. The Klan sued in court claiming a violation of their rights under the _____ Amendment. 24.___
A. First B. Third C. Fifth D. Eighth

25. In a jury trial for a felony, a jury of twelve must have 25.___
A. a majority decision
B. 9 members finding the defendant guilty
C. 11 members finding the defendant guilty
D. a unanimous finding of guilt

KEY (CORRECT ANSWERS)

1. B
2. D
3. C
4. D
5. B
6. C
7. B
8. C
9. D
10. D
11. D
12. A
13. A
14. C
15. D
16. B
17. A
18. C
19. B
20. B
21. B
22. D
23. B
24. A
25. D

TEST 4

DIRECTIONS: Each question or incomplete statement is followed by several suggested answers or completions. Select the one that BEST answers the question or completes the statement. *PRINT THE LETTER OF THE CORRECT ANSWER IN THE SPACE AT THE RIGHT.*

1. State law defines a juvenile as _____ years of age or less. 1.___
   A. 15 B. 16 C. 17 D. 18

2. A writ of habeas corpus is an order to 2.___
   A. dismiss charges against a detained person
   B. reduce the charges against a detained person
   C. have a detained person confront his accusors
   D. have a detained person brought before a court

3. A person is brought into a police station to face charges. The person brought in when interrogated refuses to tell more than his name and address. 3.___
   In the face of his silence, the proper course to be followed by the interviewer is to
   A. remind the detainee that he is guilty of obstruction of justice
   B. stop the interrogation
   C. remind the detainee that his unwillingness to cooperate will result in high bail
   D. tell the interviewee he is required to cooperate with the police

4. *The implication in most discussions on police discretion is that it is the police administrator who should undertake to spell out policies and rules.* 4.___
   In the above statement, the word *discretion* means MOST NEARLY
   A. the power to judge or act
   B. behavior
   C. competence
   D. ability to reach a conclusion

5. A nickname for amphetamine is 5.___
   A. ice B. pot C. downer D. grass

6. A nickname for cocaine is 6.___
   A. speed B. red devils
   C. snow D. Mary Jane

7. A nickname for marijuana is 7.___
   A. ice B. downer C. snow D. grass

8. A nickname for barbiturates is 8.___
A. angel dust B. quaaludes
C. meth D. downers

9. Of the following, the most widely used drug is 9.___
A. LSD B. crack C. marijuana D. cocaine

10. Crack is related to 10.___
A. angel dust B. quaaludes
C. LSD D. cocaine

11. The police department is changing the type of ammunition they use. The new bullets will have a softer head. The main reason for this change is that 11.___
A. it will not ricochet if it hits a wall
B. it will cause less injury to a person struck by the bullet
C. the bullet is less expensive
D. it will be easier to recover

12. Of the following weapons, the one that is of the semi-automatic type is the 12.___
A. Colt revolver B. 45
C. AK-47 D. Springfield rifle

13. A *Saturday Night Special* is a 13.___
A. semi-automatic gun B. small, cheaply made weapon
C. gun used for hunting D. difficult gun to conceal

14. One inch is equal to _____ centimeters. 14.___
A. 2.54 B. 2.64 C. 2.74 D. 2.84

15. A gun control bill was passed in Congress that was named after President Reagan's press secretary who was shot in an attack on the President. The name of the bill was the _____ bill. 15.___
A. McClure B. Brady
C. Volkmer D. Everett Koop

16. In New York City, if you are caught carrying a concealed gun for which you do not have a permit, you can be jailed for a maximum of _____ months. 16.___
A. 3 B. 6 C. 9 D. 12

17. The Federal Firearm License Law is designed to ensure that individuals who obtain licenses have a legitimate reason for doing so and to deny guns to 17.___
A. people who carry large amounts of money on their person
B. people who have a criminal record
C. senior citizens
D. people under 22 years old

18. According to government studies, the number of guns in the United States is over _____ million. 18.___
A. one hundred B. one hundred and twenty
C. one hundred and fifty D. two hundred

19. According to statistics, when a woman is killed with a gun, it is LEAST likely to be by 19.___
A. her husband B. a relative
C. a stranger D. a friend

20. Federal law states that a person is prohibited from buying a gun who is under the age of 20.___
A. sixteen B. eighteen
C. twenty D. twenty-two

21. Of the following countries in South America, the one that is the largest exporter of drugs into the United States is 21.___
A. Columbia B. Venezuela
C. Chile D. Argentina

22. Of the following, the state in the United States that allows citizens to carry concealed guns is 22.___
A. Arizona B. New Mexico
C. Texas D. Oklahoma

23. A bullet has a diameter of 9 mm. Its diameter, in inches, is MOST NEARLY _____ inch. 23.___
A. 1/4 B. 3/8 C. 1/2 D. 5/8

24. The repeal of the amendment to the Constitution barring the manufacture and selling of whiskey occurred under the administration of President 24.___
A. Roosevelt B. Hoover C. Truman D. Coolidge

25. The shrub from which cocaine is derived is 25.___
A. cacao B. hemp C. liana D. coca

KEY (CORRECT ANSWERS)

1. D	6. C	11. A	16. D	21. A
2. D	7. D	12. C	17. B	22. C
3. B	8. D	13. B	18. D	23. B
4. A	9. C	14. A	19. C	24. A
5. A	10. D	15. B	20. B	25. D

READING COMPREHENSION
UNDERSTANDING AND INTERPRETING WRITTEN MATERIAL

COMMENTARY

The ability to read, understand, and interpret written materials - texts, publications, newspapers, orders, directions, expositions, legal passages - is a skill basic to a functioning democracy and to an efficient business or viable government.

That is why almost all examinations - for beginning, middle, and senior levels - test reading comprehension, directly or indirectly.

The reading test measures how well you understand what you read. This is how it is done: You read a paragraph and several statements based on a question. From the statements, you choose the *one* statement, or answer, that is *BEST* supported by, or *BEST* matches, what is said in the paragraph.

SAMPLE QUESTIONS

DIRECTIONS: Each question has five suggested answers, lettered A, B, C, D, and E. Decide which one is the *BEST* answer. *PRINT THE LETTER OF THE CORRECT ANSWER IN THE SPACE AT THE RIGHT.*

1. The prevention of accidents makes it necessary not only that safety devices be used to guard exposed machinery but also that mechanics be instructed in safety rules which they must follow for their own protection and that the light in the plant be adequate.
The paragraph BEST supports the statement that industrial accidents
A. are always avoidable
B. may be due to ignorance
C. usually result from inadequate machinery
D. cannot be entirely overcome
E. result in damage to machinery

ANALYSIS

Remember what you have to do -
First - Read the paragraph.
Second - Decide what the paragraph means.
Third - Read the five suggested answers.
Fourth - Select the one answer which *BEST* matches what the paragraph says or is *BEST* supported by something in the paragraph. (Sometimes you may have to read the paragraph again in order to be sure which suggested answer is best.)

This paragraph is talking about three steps that should be taken to prevent industrial accidents -
1. use safety devices on machines
2. instruct mechanics in safety rules
3. provide adequate lighting.

SELECTION

With this in mind, let's look at each suggested answer. Each one starts with "Industrial accidents ..."

SUGGESTED ANSWER A.

Industrial accidents (A) are always avoidable.

(The paragraph talks about how to avoid accidents but does not say that accidents are always avoidable.)

SUGGESTED ANSWER B.

Industrial accidents (B) may be due to ignorance.

(One of the steps given in the paragraph to prevent accidents is to instruct mechanics on safety rules. This suggests that lack of knowledge or ignorance of safety rules causes accidents. This suggested answer sounds like a good possibility for being the right answer

SUGGESTED ANSWER C.

Industrial accidents (C) usually result from inadequate machinery.

(The paragraph does suggest that exposed machines cause accidents, but it doesn't say that it is the usual cause of accidents. The word *usually* makes this a wrong answer.)

SUGGESTED ANSWER D.

Industrial accidents (D) cannot be entirely overcome.

(You may know from your own experience that this is a true statement But that is not what the paragraph is talking about. Therefore, it is NOT the correct answer.)

SUGGESTED ANSWER E.

Industrial accidents (E) result in damage to machinery.

(This is a statement that may or may not be true, but, in any case, it is NOT covered by the paragraph.)

Looking back, you see that the one suggested answer of the five give that *BEST* matches what the paragraph says is -

Industrial accidents (B) may be due to ignorance.

The *CORRECT* answer then is B.

Be sure you read *ALL* the possible answers before you make your choic You may think that none of the five answers is really good, but choose the *BEST* one of the five.

---

2. Probably few people realize, as they drive on a concrete road, that steel is used to keep the surface flat in spite of the weight of the busses and trucks. Steel bars, deeply embedded in the concrete, provide sinews to take the stresses so that the stresses cannot crack the slab or make it wavy.

   The paragraph BEST supports the statement THAT a concrete road

   A. is expensive to build
   B. usually cracks under heavy weights
   C. looks like any other road
   D. is used only for heavy traffic
   E. is reinforced with other material

ANALYSIS

This paragraph is commenting on the fact that -

1. few people realize, as they drive on a concrete road, that steel is deeply embedded
2. steel keeps the surface flat
3. steel bars enable the road to take the stresses without cracking or becoming wavy.

SELECTION

Now read and think about the possible answers:

A. A concrete road is expensive to build.
   (Maybe so but that is not what the paragraph is about.)
B. A concrete road usually cracks under heavy weights.
   (The paragraph talks about using steel bars to prevent heavy

weights from cracking concrete roads. It says nothing about how usual it is for the roads to crack. The word *usually* makes this suggested answer wrong.)

C. A concrete road looks like any other road.
(This may or may not be true. The important thing to note is that it has nothing to do with what the paragraph is about.)

D. A concrete road is used only for heavy traffic.
(This answer at least has something to do with the paragraph - concrete roads are used with heavy traffic but it does not say "used only.")

E. A concrete road is reinforced with other material.
(This choice seems to be the correct one on two counts: *First,* the paragraph does suggest that concrete roads are made stronger by embedding steel bars in them. This is another way of saying "concrete roads are reinforced with steel bars." *Second,* by the process of elimination, the other four choices are ruled out as correct answers simply because they do not apply.)

You can be sure that not all the reading questions will be so easy as these.

SUGGESTIONS FOR ANSWERING READING QUESTIONS

1. Read the paragraph carefully. Then read each suggested answer carefully. Read every word, because often one word can make the difference between a right and a wrong answer.
2. Choose that answer which is supported in the paragraph itself. Do not choose an answer which is a correct statement unless it is based on information in the paragraph.
3. Even though a suggested answer has many of the words used in the paragraph, it may still be wrong.
4. Look out for words - such as *always, never, entirely, or only* - which tend to make a suggested answer wrong.
5. Answer first those questions which you can answer most easily. Then work on the other questions.
6. If you can't figure out the answer to the question, guess.

EXAMINATION SECTION

DIRECTIONS FOR THIS SECTION:

The following questions are intended to test your ability to read with comprehension and to understand and interpret written materials, particularly legal passages.

Each question has several suggested answers. *PRINT THE LETTER OF THE CORRECT ANSWER IN THE SPACE AT THE RIGHT.*

It will be necessary for you to read each paragraph carefully because the questions are based only on the material contained therein.

TEST 1

Questions 1-3.

DIRECTIONS: Answer Questions 1 to 3 *SOLELY* on the basis of the following statement:

Foot patrol has some advantages over all other methods of patrol. Maximum opportunity is provided for observation within range of the senses and for close contact with people and things that enable the patrolman to provide a maximum service as an information source and counselor to the public and as the eyes and ears of the police department. A foot patrolman loses no time in alighting from a vehicle, and the performance of police tasks is not hampered by responsibility for his vehicle while afoot. Foot patrol, however, does not have many of the advantages of a patrol car. Lack of both mobility and immediate communication with headquarters lessens the officer's value in an emergency. The area that he can cover effectively is limited and, therefore, this method of patrol is costly.

1. According to this paragraph, the foot patrolman is the eyes and ears of the police department because he is — 1. ...
   A. in direct contact with the station house
   B. not responsible for a patrol vehicle
   C. able to observe closely conditions on his patrol post
   D. a readily available information source to the public
2. The *MOST* accurate of the following statements concerning the various methods of patrol, according to this paragraph, is that — 2. ...
   A. foot patrol should sometimes be combined with motor patrol
   B. foot patrol is better than motor patrol
   C. helicopter patrol has the same advantages as motor patrol
   D. motor patrol is more readily able to communicate with superior officers in an emergency
3. According to this paragraph, it is *CORRECT* to state that foot patrol is — 3. ...
   A. *economical* since increased mobility makes more rapid action possible
   B. *expensive* since the area that can be patrolled is relatively small
   C. *economical* since vehicle costs need not be considered
   D. *expensive* since giving information to the public is time-consuming

Questions 4-6.

DIRECTIONS: Answer Questions 4 to 6 *SOLELY* on the basis of the following statement:

All applicants for an original license to operate a catering establishment shall be fingerprinted. This shall include the officers, employees, and stockholders of the company and the members of a partnership. In case of a change, by addition or substitution, occurring during the existence of a license, the person added or substituted shall be fingerprinted. However, in the case of a hotel containing more than 200 rooms, only the officer or manager filing the application is required to be fingerprinted. The police commissioner may also at his discretion exempt the employees and stockholders of any company. The fingerprints shall be taken on one copy of form C.E. 20 and on two copies of C.E. 21. One copy of form C.E. 21 shall accompany the application. Fingerprints are not required with a renewal application.

4. According to this paragraph, an employee added to the payroll of a licensed catering establishment which is not in a hotel, must — 4. ...
   A. always be fingerprinted
   B. be fingerprinted unless he has been previously fingerprinted for another license

C. be fingerprinted unless exempted by the police commissioner
D. be fingerprinted only if he is the manager or an officer of the company

5. According to this paragraph, it would be *MOST* accurate to state that 5. ...
A. form C.E. 20 must accompany a renewal application
B. form C.E. 21 must accompany all applications
C. form C.E. 21 must accompany an original application
D. both forms C.E. 20 and C.E. 21 must accompany all applications

6. A hotel of 270 rooms has applied for a license to operate a catering establishment on the premises. According to the instructions for fingerprinting given in this paragraph, the 6. ...
A. officers, employees, and stockholders shall be fingerprinted
B. officers and manager shall be fingerprinted
C. employees shall be fingerprinted
D. officer filing the application shall be fingerprinted

Questions 7-9.

DIRECTIONS: Answer Questions 7 to 9 *SOLELY* on the basis of the following statement:

It is difficult to instill in young people inner controls on aggressive behavior in a world marked by aggression. The slum child's environment, full of hostility, stimulates him to delinquency; he does that which he sees about him. The time to act against delinquency is before it is committed. It is clear that juvenile delinquency, especially when it is committed in groups or gangs, leads almost inevitably to an adult criminal life unless it is checked at once. The first signs of vandalism and disregard for the comfort, health, and property of the community should be considered as storm warnings which cannot be ignored. The delinquent's first crime has the underlying element of testing the law and its ability to hit back.

7. A *suitable* title for this entire paragraph based on the material it contains is: 7. ...
A. The Need for Early Prevention of Juvenile Delinquency
B. Juvenile Delinquency as a Cause of Slums
C. How Aggressive Behavior Prevents Juvenile Delinquency
D. The Role of Gangs in Crime

8. According to this paragraph, an *INITIAL* act of juvenile crime *usually* involves a(n) 8. ...
A. group or gang activity B. theft of valuable property
C. test of the strength of legal authority
D. act of physical violence

9. According to this paragraph, acts of juvenile delinquency are *most likely* to lead to a criminal career when they are 9. ...
A. acts of vandalism
B. carried out by groups or gangs
C. committed in a slum environment
D. such as to impair the health of the neighborhood

Questions 10-12.

DIRECTIONS: Answer Questions 10 to 12 *SOLELY* on the basis of the following statement:

The police laboratory performs a valuable service in crime investigation by assisting in the reconstruction of criminal action and by aiding in the identification of persons and things. When studied by a technician, physical things found at crime scenes often reveal facts useful in identifying the criminal and in determining what has occurred. The nature of substances to be examined and the character of the examinations to be made vary so widely that the services of a large variety of skilled scientific persons are needed in crime investigations. To employ such a complete staff and to provide them with equipment and standards needed for all possible analyses and comparisons is beyond the means and the needs of any but the largest police departments. The search of crime scenes for physical evidence also calls for the services of specialists supplied with essential equipment and assigned to each tour of duty so as to provide service at any hour.

10. If a police department employs a large staff of technicians of various types in its laboratory, it will affect crime investigation to the extent that — 10. ...
    - A. most crimes will be speedily solved
    - B. identification of criminals will be aided
    - C. search of crime scenes for physical evidence will become of less importance
    - D. investigation by police officers will not usually be required
11. According to this paragraph, the *MOST* complete study of objects found at the scenes of crimes is — 11. ...
    - A. always done in all large police departments
    - B. based on assigning one technician to each tour of duty
    - C. probably done only in large police departments
    - D. probably done in police departments of communities with low crime rates
12. According to this paragraph, a large variety of skilled technicians is useful in criminal investigations because — 12. ...
    - A. crimes cannot be solved without their assistance as a part of the police team
    - B. large police departments need large staffs
    - C. many different kinds of tests on various substances can be made
    - D. the police cannot predict what methods may be tried by wily criminals

Questions 13-14.

DIRECTIONS: Answer Questions 13 and 14 *SOLELY* on the basis of the following statement:

The emotionally unstable person is always potentially a dangerous criminal, who causes untold misery to other persons and is a source of considerable trouble and annoyance to law enforcement officials. Like his fellow criminals he will be a menace to society as long as he is permitted to be at large. Police activities against him serve to sharpen his wits, and imprisonment gives him the opportunity to learn from others how to commit more serious crimes when he is released. This criminal's mental structure makes it impossible for him to profit by his experience with the police officials, by punishment of any kind or by sympathetic understanding and treatment by well-intentioned persons, professional and otherwise.

13. According to the above paragraph, the *MOST* accurate of the following statements concerning the relationship between emotional instability and crime is that 13. ...
   A. emotional instability is proof of criminal activities
   B. the emotionally unstable person can become a criminal
   C. all dangerous criminals are emotionally unstable
   D. sympathetic understanding will prevent the emotionally unstable person from becoming a criminal

14. According to the above paragraph, the effect of police activities on the emotionally unstable criminal is that 14. ...
   A. police activities aid this type of criminal to reform
   B. imprisonment tends to deter this type of criminal from committing future crimes
   C. contact with the police serves to assist sympathetic understanding and medical treatment
   D. police methods against this type of criminal develop him for further unlawful acts

Questions 15-17.

DIRECTIONS: Answer Questions 15 to 17 *SOLELY* on the basis of the following statement:

Proposals to license gambling operations are based on the belief that the human desire to gamble cannot be suppressed and, therefore, it should be licensed and legalized with the people sharing in the profits, instead of allowing the underworld to benefit. If these proposals are sincere, then it is clear that only one is worthwhile at all. Legalized gambling should be completely controlled and operated by the state with all the profits used for its citizens. A state agency should be set up to operate and control the gambling business. It should be as completely removed from politics as possible. In view of the inherent nature of the gambling business, with its close relationship to lawlessness and crime, only a man of the highest integrity should be eligible to become head of this agency. However, state gambling would encourage mass gambling with its attending social and economic evils in the same manner as other forms of legal gambling; but there is no justification whatever for the business of gambling to be legalized and then permitted to operate for private profit or for the benefit of any political organization.

15. The *CENTRAL* thought of this paragraph may be *correctly* expressed as the 15. ...
   A. need to legalize gambling in the state
   B. state operation of gambling for the benefit of the people
   C. need to license private gambling establishments
   D. evils of gambling

16. According to this paragraph, a problem of legalized gambling which will *still* occur if the state operates the gambling business is 16. ...
   A. the diversion of profits from gambling to private use
   B. that the amount of gambling will tend to diminish
   C. the evil effects of any form of mass gambling
   D. the use of gambling revenues for illegal purposes

17. According to this paragraph, to legalize the business of gambling would be 17. ...
   A. *justified* because gambling would be operated only by a man of the highest integrity

B. *justified* because this would eliminate politics

C. *unjustified* under any conditions because the human desire to gamble cannot be suppressed

D. *unjustified* if operated for private or political profit

Questions 18-20.

DIRECTIONS: Answer Questions 18 to 20 *SOLELY* on the basis of the following statement:

Whenever, in the course of the performance of their duties in an emergency, members of the force operate the emergency power switch at any location on the transit system and thereby remove power from portions of the track, or they are on the scene where this has been done, they will bear in mind that, although power is removed, further dangers exist; namely, that a train may coast into the area even though the power is off, or that the rails may be energized by a train which may be in a position to transfer electricity from a live portion of the third rail through its shoe beams. Employees must look in each direction before stepping upon, crossing, or standing close to tracks, being particularly careful not to come into contact with the third rail.

18. According to this paragraph, whenever an emergency occurs which has resulted in operating the emergency power switch, it is *MOST* accurate to state that 18. ...

A. power is shut off and employees may perform their duties in complete safety

B. there may still be power in a portion of the third rail

C. the switch will not operate if a portion of the track has been broken

D. trains are not permitted to stop in the area of the emergency

19. An *important* precaution which this paragraph urges employees to follow after operating the emergency power switch, is to 19. ...

A. look carefully in both directions before stepping near the rails

B. inspect the nearest train which has stopped to see if the power is on

C. examine the third rail to see if the power is on

D. check the emergency power switch to make sure it has operated properly

20. A trackman reports to you, a patrolman, that a dead body is lying on the road bed. You operate the emergency power switch. A train which has been approaching comes to a stop near the scene. 20. ...
In order to act in accordance with the instructions in the above paragraph, you *should*

A. climb down to the road bed and remove the body

B. direct the train motorman to back up to the point where his train will not be in position to transfer electricity through its shoe beams

C. carefully cross over the road bed to the body, avoiding the third rail and watching for train movements

D. have the train motorman check to see if power is on before crossing to the tracks

21. The treatment to be given the offender cannot alter the fact of his offense; but we can take measures to reduce the chances of similar acts in the future. We should banish the criminal, not in order to exact revenge nor directly to encourage reform, but to deter him and others from further illegal attacks on society. 21. ...
According to this paragraph, the *PRINCIPAL* reason for punishing criminals is to
   A. prevent the commission of future crimes
   B. remove them from society C. avenge society
   D. teach them that crime does not pay

22. Even the most comprehensive and best substantiated summaries of the total volume of criminal acts would not contribute greatly to an understanding of the varied social and biological factors which are sometimes assumed to enter into crime causation, nor would they indicate with any degree of precision the needs of police forces in combating crime. 22. ...
According to this statement,
   A. crime statistics alone do not determine the needs of police forces in combating crime
   B. crime statistics are essential to a proper understanding of the social factors of crime
   C. social and biological factors which enter into crime causation have little bearing on police needs
   D. a knowledge of the social and biological factors of crime is essential to a proper understanding of crime statistics

23. The policeman's art consists of applying and enforcing a multitude of laws and ordinances in such degree or proportion and in such manner that the greatest degree of social protection will be secured. The degree of enforcement and the method of application will vary with each neighborhood and community. 23. ...
According to the foregoing paragraph,
   A. each neighborhood or community must judge for itself to what extent the law is to be enforced
   B. a policeman should only enforce those laws which are designed to give the greatest degree of social protection
   C. the manner and intensity of law enforcement is not necessarily the same in all communities
   D. all laws and ordinances must be enforced in a community with the same degree of intensity

24. Police control in the sense of regulating the details of police operations, involves such matters as the technical means for so organizing the available personnel that competent police leadership, when secured, can operate effectively. It is concerned not so much with the extent to which popular controls can be trusted to guide and direct the course of police protection as with the administrative relationships which should exist between the component parts of the polie organism. 24. ...
According to the foregoing statement, police control is
   A. solely a matter of proper personnel assignment
   B. the means employed to guide and direct the course of police protection
   C. principally concerned with the administrative relationships between units of a police organization
   D. the sum total of means employed in rendering police protection

25. Police Department Rule 5 states that a Deputy Commissioner acting as Police Commissioner shall carry out the orders of the Police Commissioner, previously given, and such orders shall not, except in cases of extreme emergency, be countermanded. 25. ...
This means, most nearly, that, except in cases of extreme emergency,
   A. the orders given by a Deputy Commissioner acting as Police Commissioner may not be revoked
   B. a Deputy Commissioner acting as Police Commissioner should not revoke orders previously given by the Police Commissioner
   C. a Deputy Commissioner acting as Police Commissioner is vested with the same authority to issue orders as the Police Commissioner himself
   D. only a Deputy Commissioner acting as Police Commissioner may issue orders in the absence of the Police Commissioner himself

TEST 2

Questions 1-2.
DIRECTIONS: Answer Questions 1 and 2 *SOLELY* on the basis of the following statement:

The medical examiner may contribute valuable data to the investigator of fires which cause fatalities. By careful examination of the bodies of any victims, he not only establishes cause of death, but may also furnish, in many instances, answers to questions relating to the identity of the victim and the source and origin of the fire. The medical examiner is of greatest value to law enforcement agencies because he is able to determine the exact cause of death through an examination of tissue of apparent arson victims. Thorough study of a burned body or even of parts of a burned body will frequently yield information which illuminates the problems confronting the arson investigator and the police.

1. According to the above paragraph, the *MOST* important task of the medical examiner in the investigation of arson is to obtain information concerning the 1. ...
   A. identity of arsonists   B. cause of death
   C. identity of victims   D. source and origin of fires
2. The *CENTRAL* thought of the above paragraph is that the medical examiner aids in the solution of crimes of arson when 2. ...
   A. a person is burnt to death
   B. identity of the arsonist is unknown
   C. the cause of the fire is known
   D. trained investigators are not available

Questions 3-6.
DIRECTIONS: Answer Questions 3 to 6 *SOLELY* on the basis of the following statement:

A foundling is an abandoned child whose identity is unknown. Desk officers shall direct the delivery, by a policewoman, if available, of foundlings actually or apparently under two years of age, to the Foundling Hospital, or if actually or apparently two years of age or over, to the Children's Center. In all other cases of dependent or neglected children, other than foundlings, requiring shelter, desk officers shall provide for obtaining such shelter as follows: between 9 a.m. and 5 p.m., Monday through Friday, by telephone direct to the Bureau of Child Welfare, in order to ascertain the shelter to which the child shall be sent; at all other times, direct the delivery of a child actually or apparently under two years of age to the Foundling Hospital, or, if the child is actually or apparently two years of age or over, to the Children's Center.

3. According to this paragraph, it would be *MOST* correct to state that 3. ...
   A. a foundling as well as a neglected child may be delivered to the Foundling Hospital
   B. a foundling but not a neglected child may be delivered to the Children's Center
   C. a neglected child requiring shelter, regardless of age, may be delivered to the Bureau of Child Welfare
   D. the Bureau of Child Welfare may determine the shelter to which a foundling may be delivered
4. According to this paragraph, the desk officer shall provide for obtaining shelter for a neglected child, apparently under two years of age, by 4. ...
   A. directing its delivery to the Children's Center if occurrence is on a Monday between 9 a.m. and 5 p.m.
   B. telephoning the Bureau of Child Welfare if occurrence is on a Sunday
   C. directing its delivery to the Foundling Hospital if occurrence is on a Wednesday at 4 p.m.
   D. telephoning the Bureau of Child Welfare if occurrence is at 10 a.m. on a Friday
5. According to this paragraph, the desk officer should direct delivery to the Foundling Hospital of any child who is 5. ...
   A. actually under 2 years of age and requires shelter
   B. apparently under two years of age and is neglected or dependent
   C. actually 2 years of age and is a foundling
   D. apparently under 2 years of age and has been abandoned
6. A 12-year-old neglected child requiring shelter is brought to a police station on Thursday at 2 p.m. Such a child should be sent to 6. ...
   A. a shelter selected by the Bureau of Child Welfare
   B. a shelter selected by the desk officer
   C. the Children's Center
   D. the Foundling Hospital when a brother or sister, under 2 years of age, also requires shelter

Questions 7-9.

DIRECTIONS: Answer Questions 7 to 9 *SOLELY* on the basis of the following statement:

In addition to making the preliminary investigation of crimes, patrolmen should serve as eyes, ears, and legs for the detective division. The patrol division may be used for surveillance, to serve warrants and bring in suspects and witnesses, and to perform a number of routine tasks for the detectives which will increase the time available for tasks that require their special skills and facilities. It is to the advantage of individual detectives, as well as of the detective division, to have patrolmen working in this manner; more cases are cleared by arrest and a greater proportion of stolen property is recovered when, in addition to the detective regularly assigned, a number of patrolmen also work on the case. Detectives may stimulate the interest and participation of patrolmen by keeping them currently informed of the presence, identity, or description, hangouts, associates, vehicles, and method of operation of each criminal known to be in the community.

7. According to this paragraph, a patrolman should 7. ...
   A. assist the detective in certain of his routine functions
   B. be considered for assignment as a detective on the basis of his patrol performance
   C. leave the scene once a detective arrives
   D. perform as much of the detective's duties as time permits
8. According to this paragraph, patrolmen should aid detectives by 8. ...
   A. accepting assignments from detectives which give promise of recovering stolen property
   B. making arrests of witnesses for the detective's interrogation
   C. performing all special investigative work for detectives
   D. producing for questioning individuals who may aid the detective in his investigation
9. According to this paragraph, detectives can keep patrolmen interested by 9. ...
   A. ascertaining that patrolmen are doing investigative work properly
   B. having patrolmen directly under his supervision during an investigation
   C. informing patrolmen of the value of their efforts in crime prevention
   D. supplying the patrolmen with information regarding known criminals in the community

Questions 10-11.

DIRECTIONS: Answer Questions 10 and 11 *SOLELY* on the basis of the following statement:

State motor vehicle registration departments should and do play a vital role in the prevention and detection of automobile thefts. The combatting of theft is, in fact, one of the primary purposes of the registration of motor vehicles. As of recent date, there were approximately 61,309,000 motor vehicles registered in the United States. That same year some 200,000 of them were stolen. All but 6 percent have been or will be recovered. This is a very high recovery ratio compared to the percentage of recovery of other stolen personal property. The reason for this is that automobiles are carefully identified by the manufacturers and carefully registered by many of the states.

10. The *CENTRAL* thought of this paragraph is that there is a close relationship between the 10. ...
    A. number of automobiles registered in the United States *and* the number stolen
    B. prevention of automobile thefts *and* the effectiveness of police departments in the United States
    C. recovery of stolen automobiles *and* automobile registration
    D. recovery of stolen automobiles *and* of other stolen property
11. According to this paragraph, the high recovery ratio for stolen automobiles is due to 11. ...
    A. state registration and manufacturer identification of motor vehicles
    B. successful prevention of automobile thefts by state motor vehicle departments
    C. the fact that only 6% of stolen vehicles are not properly registered

D. the high number of motor vehicles registered in the United States

Questions 12-15.

DIRECTIONS: Answer Questions 12 to 15 *SOLELY* on the basis of the following statement:

It is not always understood that the term "physical evidence" embraces any and all objects, living or inanimate. A knife, gun, signature, or burglar tool is immediately recognized as physical evidence. Less often is it considered that dust, microscopic fragments of all types, even an odor, may equally be physical evidence and often the most important of all. It is well established that the most useful types of physical evidence are generally microscopic in dimensions, that is, not noticeable by the eye and, therefore, most likely to be overlooked by the criminal and by the investigator. For this reason, microscopic evidence persists for months or years after all other evidence has been removed and found inconclusive. Naturally, there are limitations to the time of collecting microscopic evidence as it may be lost or decayed. The exercise of judgment as to the possibility or profit of delayed action in collecting the evidence is a field in which the expert investigator should judge.

12. The *one* of the following which the above paragraph does *NOT* consider to be physical evidence is a 12. ...
   A. criminal thought
   B. minute speck of dust
   C. raw onion smell
   D. typewritten note

13. According to the above paragraph, the re-checking of the scene of a crime 13. ...
   A. is *useless* when performed years after the occurrence of the crime
   B. is *advisable* chiefly in crimes involving physical violence
   C. *may turn up* microscopic evidence of value
   D. *should be delayed* if the microscopic evidence is not subject to decay or loss

14. According to the above paragraph, the criminal investigator *should* 14. ...
   A. give most of his attention to weapons used in the commission of the crime
   B. ignore microscopic evidence until a requiest is received from the laboratory
   C. immediately search for microscopic evidence and ignore the more visible objects
   D. realize that microscopic evidence can be easily overlooked

15. According to the above paragraph, 15. ...
   A. a delay in collecting evidence must definitely diminish its value to the investigator
   B. microscopic evidence exists for longer periods of time than other physical evidence
   C. microscopic evidence is generally the most useful type of physical evidence
   D. physical evidence is likely to be overlooked by the criminal and by the investigator

Questions 16-18.
DIRECTIONS: Answer Questions 16 to 18 *SOLELY* on the basis of the following statement:

Sometimes, but not always, firing a gun leaves a residue of nitrate particles on the hands. This fact is utilized in the paraffin test which consists of applying melted paraffin and gauze to the fingers, hands, and wrists of a suspect until a cast of approximately 1/8 of an inch is built up. The heat of the paraffin causes the pores of the skin to open and release any particles embedded in them. The paraffin cast is then removed and tested chemically for nitrate particles. In addition to gunpowder, fertilizers, tobacco ashes, matches, and soot are also common sources of nitrates on the hands.

16. Assume that the paraffin test has been given to a person suspected of firing a gun and that nitrate particles have been found. It would be *CORRECT* to conclude that the suspect 16. ...
    A. is guilty B. is innocent
    C. may be guilty or innocent D. is probably guilty
17. In testing for the presence of gunpowder particles on human hands, the characteristic of paraffin which makes it *MOST* serviceable is that it 17. ...
    A. causes the nitrate residue left by a fired gun to adhere to the gauze
    B. is waterproof C. melts at a low temperature
    D. helps to distinguish between gunpowder nitrates and other types
18. According to the above paragraph, in the paraffin test, the nitrate particles are removed from the pores because the paraffin 18. ...
    A. enlarges the pores B. contracts the pores
    C. reacts chemically with nitrates
    D. dissolves the particles

Questions 19-21.
DIRECTIONS: Answer Questions 19 to 21 *SOLELY* on the basis of the following statement:

Pickpockets operate most effectively when there are prospective victims in either heavily congested areas or in lonely places. In heavily populated areas, the large number of people about them covers the activities of these thieves. In lonely spots, they have the advantage of working unobserved. The main factor in the pickpocket's success is the selection of the "right" victim. A pickpocket's victim must, at the time of the crime, be inattentive, distracted, or unconscious. If any of these conditions exist, and if the pickpocket is skilled in his operations, the stage is set for a successful larceny. With the coming of winter, the crowds move southward - and so do most of the pickpockets. However, some pickpockets will remain in certain areas all year around. They will concentrate on theater districts, bus and railroad terminals, hotels or large shopping centers. A complete knowledge of the methods of this type of criminal and the ability to recognize them come only from long years of experience in performing patient surveillance and trailing of them. This knowledge is essential for the effective control and apprehension of this type of thief.

19. According to this paragraph, the pickpocket is *LEAST* likely to operate in a 19. ...
    A. baseball park with a full capacity attendance
    B. station in an outlying area late at night

C. moderately crowded dance hall
D. over-crowded department store

20. According to this paragraph, the *one* of the following factors which is *NOT* necessary for the successful operation of the pickpocket is that 20. ...
A. he be proficient in the operations required to pick pockets
B. the "right" potential victims be those who have been the subject of such a theft previously
C. his operations be hidden from the view of others
D. the potential victim be unaware of the actions of the pickpocket

21. According to this paragraph, it would be *MOST* correct to conclude that police officers who are successful in apprehending pickpockets 21. ...
A. are generalling those who have had lengthy experience in recognizing all types of criminals
B. must, by intuition, be able to recognize potential "right" victims
C. must follow the pickpockets in their southward movement
D. must have acquired specific knowledge and skills in this field

Questions 22-23.

DIRECTIONS: Answer Questions 22 and 23 *SOLELY* on the basis of the following statement:

For many years, slums had been recognized as breeding disease, juvenile delinquency,and crime which not only threatened the health and welfare of the people who lived there, but also weakened the structure of society as a whole. As far back as 1834, a sanitary inspection report in the city pointed out the connection between insanitary, overcrowded housing and the spread of epidemics. Down through the years, evidence of slum-produced evils accumulated as the slums themselves continued to spread. This spread of slums was nationwide. Its symptoms and its ill effects were peculiar to no locality, but were characteristic of the country as a whole and imperiled the national welfare.

22. According to this paragraph, people who live in slum dwellings 22. ...
A. cause slums to become worse
B. are threatened by disease and crime
C. create bad housing
D. are the chief source of crime in the country

23. According to this paragraph, the effects of juvenile delinquency and crime in slum areas were 23. ...
A. to destroy the structure of society
B. noticeable in all parts of the country
C. a chief cause of the spread of slums
D. to spread insanitary conditions in the city

Questions 24-25.

DIRECTIONS: Questions 24 and 25 pertain to the following section of the Penal Law:

Section 1942. A person who, after having been three times convicted within this state, of felonies or attempts to commit felonies, or under the law of any other state, government or country, of crimes which if committed within this state would be felonious, commits a felony, other than murder, first or second degree, or treason, within this state, shall be sentenced upon conviction of such fourth, or subsequent, offense to imprisonment in a state prison for an indeterminate term the minimum of which shall be not less than the maximum term provided for first offenders for the crime for which the individual has been convicted, but, in any event, the minimum term upon conviction for a felony as the fourth ,or subsequent, offense, shall be not less than fifteen years, and the maximum thereof shall be his natural life.

24. Under the terms of the above stated portion of Section 1942 of the Penal Law, a person must receive the increased punishment therein provided *if* 24. ...
    A. he is convicted of a felony and has been three times previously convicted of felonies
    B. he has been three times previously convicted of felonies, regardless of the nature of his present conviction
    C. his fourth conviction is for murder, first or second degree, or treason
    D. he has previously been convicted three times of murder, first or second degree, or treason

25. Under the terms of the above stated portion of Section 1942 of the Penal Law, a person convicted of a felony for which the penalty is imprisonment for a term not to exceed ten years, and who has been three times previously convicted of felonies in this state, shall be sentenced to a term the *minimum* of which shall be 25. ...
    A. ten years B. fifteen years
    C. indeterminate D. his natural life

KEYS (CORRECT ANSWERS)

TEST 1

1.	C	11.	C
2.	D	12.	C
3.	B	13.	B
4.	C	14.	D
5.	C	15.	B
6.	D	16.	C
7.	A	17.	D
8.	C	18.	B
9.	B	19.	A
10.	B	20.	C
		21.	A
		22.	A
		23.	C
		24.	C
		25.	B

TEST 2

1.	B	11.	A
2.	A	12.	A
3.	A	13.	C
4.	D	14.	D
5.	D	15.	C
6.	A	16.	C
7.	A	17.	A
8.	D	18.	A
9.	D	19.	C
10.	C	20.	B
		21.	D
		22.	B
		23.	B
		24.	A
		25.	B

REPORT WRITING

EXAMINATION SECTION

DIRECTIONS FOR THIS SECTION:
Each question or incomplete statement is followed by several suggested answers or completions. Select the one that *BEST* answers the question or completes the statement. *PRINT THE LETTER OF THE CORRECT ANSWER IN THE SPACE AT THE RIGHT.*

TEST 1

1. Following are six steps that should be taken in the course of report preparation: 1. ...
   I. Outlining the material for presentation in the report
   II. Analyzing and interpreting the facts
   III. Analyzing the problem
   IV. Reaching conclusions
   V. Writing, revising, and rewriting the final copy
   VI. Collecting data
   According to the principles of good report writing, the *CORRECT order* in which these steps should be taken is:
   A. VI, III, II, I, IV, V B. III, VI, II, IV, I, V
   C. III, VI, II, I, IV, V D. VI, II, III, IV, I, V
2. Following are three statements concerning written reports: 2. ...
   I. Clarity is generally more essential in oral reports than in written reports.
   II. Short sentences composed of simple words are generally preferred to complex sentences and difficult words.
   III. Abbreviations may be used whenever they are customary and will not distract the attention of the reader.
   Which of the following choices *CORRECTLY* classifies the above statements into whose which are valid and those which are not valid?
   A. I and II are valid, but III is not valid.
   B. I is valid, but II and III are not valid.
   C. II and III are valid, but I is not valid.
   D. III is valid, but I and II are not valid.
3. In order to produce a report written in a style that is both understandable and effective, an investigator should apply the principles of unit, coherence, and emphasis. 3. ...
   The *one* of the following which is the *BEST* example of the principle of coherence is
   A. interlinking sentences so that thoughts flow smoothly
   B. having each sentence express a single idea to facilitate comprehension
   C. arranging important points in prominent positions so they are not overlooked
   D. developing the main idea fully to insure complete consideration
4. Assume that a supervisor is preparing a report recommending that a standard work procedure be changed. Of the following, the *MOST* important information that he should include in this report is 4. ...
   A. a complete description of the present procedure
   B. the details and advantages of the recommended procedure
   C. the type and amount of retraining needed
   D. the percentage of men who favor the change

5. When you include in your report on an inspection some information which you have obtained from other individuals, it is *MOST* important that 5. ...
   A. this information have no bearing on the work these other people are performing
   B. you do not report as fact the opinions of other individuals
   C. you keep the source of the information confidential
   D. you do not tell the other individuals that their statements will be included in your report
6. Before turning in a report of an investigation of an accident, you discover some additional information you did not know about when you wrote the report. 6. ...
   Whether or not you re-write your report to include this additional information should depend *MAINLY* on the
   A. source of this additional information
   B. established policy covering the subject matter of the report
   C. length of the report and the time it would take you to re-write it
   D. bearing this additional information will have on the conclusions in the report
7. The *most desirable FIRST* step in the planning of a written report is to 7. ...
   A. ascertain what necessary information is readily available in the files
   B. outline the methods you will employ to get the necessary information
   C. determine the objectives and uses of the report
   D. estimate the time and cost required to complete the report
8. In writing a report, the practice of taking up the *least* important points *first* and the *most* important points *last* is a 8. ...
   A. *good* technique since the final points made in a report will make the greatest impression on the reader
   B. *good* technique since the material is presented in a more logical manner and will lead directly to the conclusions
   C. *poor* technique since the reader's time is wasted by having to review irrelevant information before finishing the report
   D. *poor* technique since it may cause the reader to lose interest in the report and arrive at incorrect conclusions about the report
9. *Which one* of the following serves as the *BEST* guideline for you to follow for effective written reports? Keep sentences 9. ...
   A. *short* and limit sentences to *one* thought
   B. *short* and use *as many* thoughts as possible
   C. *long* and limit sentences to *one* thought
   D. *long* and use *as many* thoughts as possible
10. One method by which a supervisor might prepare written reports to management is to begin with the conclusions, results, or summary, and to follow this with the supporting data. 10. ...

The *BEST* reason why management may *prefer* this form of report is that
- A. management lacks the specific training to understand the data
- B. the data completely supports the conclusions
- C. time is saved by getting to the conclusions of the report first
- D. the data contains all the information that is required for making the conclusions

11. When making written reports, it is *MOST* important that they be 11. ...
    - A. well-worded
    - B. accurate as to the facts
    - C. brief
    - D. submitted immediately

12. Of the following, the *MOST* important reason for a supervisor to prepare good written reports is that 12. ...
    - A. a supervisor is rated on the quality of his reports
    - B. decisions are often made on the basis of the reports
    - C. such reports take less time for superiors to review
    - D. such reports demonstrate efficiency of department operations

13. Of the following, the *BEST* test of a good report is whether it 13. ...
    - A. provides the information needed
    - B. shows the good sense of the writer
    - C. is prepared according to a proper format
    - D. is grammatical and neat

14. When a supervisor writes a report, he can *BEST* show that he has an understanding of the subject of the report by 14. ...
    - A. including necessary facts and omitting nonessential details
    - B. using statistical data
    - C. giving his conclusions but not the data on which they are based
    - D. using a technical vocabulary

15. Suppose you and another supervisor on the same level are assigned to work together on a report. You disagree strongly with one of the recommendations the other supervisor wants to include in the report but you cannot change his views. 15. ...
    Of the following, it would be *BEST* that
    - A. you refuse to accept responsibility for the report
    - B. you ask that someone else be assigned to this project to replace you
    - C. each of you state his own ideas about this recommendation in the report
    - D. you give in to the other supervisor's opinion for the sake of harmony

16. Standardized forms are often provided for submitting reports. 16. ...
    Of the following, the *MOST* important advantage of using standardized forms for reports is that
    - A. they take less time to prepare than individually written reports
    - B. the person making the report can omit information he considers unimportant

C. the responsibility for preparing these reports can be turned over to subordinates
D. necessary information is less likely to be omitted

17. A report which may *BEST* be classed as a *periodic* report is one which 17. ...
A. requires the same type of information at regular intervals
B. contains detailed information which is to be retained in permanent records
C. is prepared whenever a special situation occurs
D. lists information in graphic form

18. In the writing of reports or letters, the ideas presented in a paragraph are usually of unequal importance and require varying degrees of emphasis. 18. ...
All of the following are methods of placing extra stress on an idea *EXCEPT*
A. repeating it in a number of forms
B. placing it in the middle of the paragraph
C. placing it either at the beginning or at the end of the paragraph
D. underlining it

Questions 19-25.
DIRECTIONS: Questions 19 to 25 concern the subject of report writing and are based on the information and incidents described in the paragraph below. (In answering these questions, assume that the facts and incidents in the paragraph are true.)

On December 15, at 8 a.m., seven Laborers reported to Foreman Joseph Meehan in the Greenbranch Yard in Queens. Meehan instructed the men to load some 50-pound boxes of books on a truck for delivery to an agency building in Brooklyn. Meehan told the men that, because the boxes were rather heavy, two men should work together, helping each other lift and load each box. Since Michael Harper, one of the Laborers, was without a partner, Meehan helped him with the boxes for a while. When Meehan was called to the telephone in a nearby building, however, Harper decided to lift a box himself. He appeared able to lift the box, but, as he got the box halfway up, he cried out that he had a sharp pain in his back. Another Laborer, Jorge Ortiz, who was passing by, ran over to help Harper put the box down. Harper suddenly dropped the box, which fell on Ortiz' right foot. By this time Meehan had come out of the building. He immediately helped get the box off Ortiz' foot and had both men lie down. Meehan covered the men with blankets and called an ambulance, which arrived a half hour later. At the hospital, the doctor said that the X-ray results showed that Ortiz' right foot was broken in three places.

19. *What* would be the *BEST* term to use in a report describing the injury of Jorge Ortiz? 19. ...
A. Strain B. Fracture C. Hernia D. Hemorrhage

20. *Which* of the following would be the *MOST* accurate summary for the Foreman to put in his report of the incident? 20. ...
A. Ortiz attempted to help Harper carry a box which was too heavy for one person, but Harper dropped it before Ortiz got there.
B. Ortiz tried to help Harper carry a box but Harper got a pain in his back and accidentally dropped the box on Ortiz' foot.

C. Harper refused to follow Meehan's orders and lifted a box too heavy for him; he deliberately dropped it when Ortiz tried to help him carry it.
D. Harper lifted a box and felt a pain in his back; Ortiz tried to help Harper put the box down but Harper accidentally dropped it on Ortiz' foot.

21. One of the Laborers at the scene of the accident was asked his version of the incident. *Which* information obtained from this witness would be *LEAST* important for including in the accident report? 21. ...
A. His opinion as to the cause of the accident
B. How much of the accident he saw
C. His personal opinion of the victims
D. His name and address

22. *What* should be the *MAIN* objective of writing a report about the incident described in the above paragraph? To 22. ...
A. describe the important elements in the accident situation
B. recommend that such Laborers as Ortiz be advised not to interfere in another's work unless given specific instructions
C. analyze the problems occurring when there are not enough workers to perform a certain task
D. illustrate the hazards involved in performing routine everyday tasks

23. *Which* of the following is information *missing* from the passage above but which *should be included* in a report of the incident? The 23. ...
A. name of the Laborer's immediate supervisor
B. contents of the boxes
C. time at which the accident occurred
D. object or action that caused the injury to Ortiz' foot

24. According to the description of the incident, the accident occurred *because* 24. ...
A. Ortiz attempted to help Harper who resisted his help
B. Harper failed to follow instructions given him by Meehan
C. Meehan was not supervising his men as closely as he should have
D. Harper was not strong enough to carry the box once he lifted it

25. *Which* of the following is *MOST* important for a foreman to *avoid* when writing up an official accident report? 25. ...
A. Using technical language to describe equipment involved in the accident
B. Putting in details which might later be judged unnecessary
C. Giving an opinion as to conditions that contributed to the accident
D. Recommending discipline for employees who, in his opinion, caused the accident

---

TEST 2

1. Lieutenant X is preparing a report to submit to his commanding officer in order to get approval of a plan of operation he has developed. 1. ...
The report starts off with the statement of the problem and continues with the details of the problem. It contains factual information gathered with the help of field and operational personnel. It contains a final conclusion and recommendation for action. The recommendation is supplemented by comments from other precinct staff members on how the recommendations will affect their areas of responsibility. The report also includes directives and general orders ready for the commanding officer's signature. In addition, it has two statements of objections presented by two precinct staff members.
Which one of the following, if any, is *either* an item that Lieutenant X *SHOULD HAVE INCLUDED* in his report and which is not mentioned above, *or* is an item which Lieutenant X *IMPROPERLY DID INCLUDE* in his report?
   A. Considerations of alternative courses of action and their consequences should have been covered in the report.
   B. The additions containing documented objections to the recommended course of action should not have been included as part of the report.
   C. A statement on the qualifications of Lieutenant X, which would support his expertness in the field under consideration, should have been included in the report.
   D. The directives and general orders should not have been prepared and included in the report until the commanding officer had approved the recommendations.
   E. None of the above, since Lieutenant X's report was both proper and complete.
2. During a visit to a section, the district supervisor criticizes the method being used by the assistant foreman to prepare a certain report and orders him to modify the method. This change ordered by the district supervisor is in direct conflict with the specific orders of the foreman. In this situation, it would be *BEST* for the assistant foreman to 2. ...
   A. change the method and tell the foreman about the change at the first opportunity
   B. change the method and rely on the district supervisor to notify the foreman
   C. report the matter to the foreman and delay the preparation of the report
   D. ask the district supervisor to discuss the matter with the foreman but use the old method for the time being
3. A department officer should realize that the *most usual* reason for writing a report is to 3. ...
   A. give orders and follow up their execution
   B. establish a permanent record
   C. raise questions
   D. supply information
4. A very important report which is being prepared by a department officer will soon be due on the desk of the district 4. ...

supervisor. No typing help is available at this time for the officer.
For the officer to write out this report in longhand in such a situation would be
- A. *bad;* such a report would not make the impression a typed report would.
- B. *good;* it is important to get the report in on time
- C. *bad;* the district supervisor should not be required to read longhand reports
- D. *good;* it would call attention to the difficult conditions under which this section must work

5. In a well-written report, the length of each paragraph in the report should be 5. ...
   - A. varied according to the content
   - B. not over 300 words
   - C. pretty nearly the same
   - D. gradually longer as the report is developed and written
6. A clerk in the headquarters office complains to you about the way in which you are filling out a certain report. It would be *BEST* for you to 6. ...
   - A. tell the clerk that you are following official procedures in filling out the report
   - B. ask to be referred to the clerk's superior
   - C. ask the clerk exactly what is wrong with the way in which you are filling out the report
   - D. tell the clerk that you are following the directions of the district supervisor
7. The use of an outline to help in writing a report is 7. ...
   - A. *desirable* in order to insure good organization and coverage
   - B. *necessary* so it can be used as an introduction to the report itself
   - C. *undesirable* since it acts as a straight jacket and may result in an unbalanced report
   - D. *desirable* if you know your immediate supervisor reads reports with extreme care and attention
8. It is advisable that a department officer do his paper work and report writing as soon as he has completed an inspection *MAINLY* because 8. ...
   - A. there are usually deadlines to be met
   - B. it insures a steady work-flow
   - C. he may not have time for this later
   - D. the facts are then freshest in his mind
9. Before you turn in a report you have written of an investigation that you have made, you discover some additional information you didn't know about before. Whether or not you re-write your report to include this additional information should depend *MAINLY* on the 9. ...
   - A. amount of time remaining before the report is due
   - B. established policy of the department covering the subject matter of the report
   - C. bearing this information will have on the conclusions of the report
   - D. number of people who will eventually review the report

10. When a supervisory officer submits a periodic report to the district supervisor, he should realize that the *CHIEF* importance of such a report is that it 10. ...
   A. is the principal method of checking on the efficiency of the supervisor and his subordinates
   B. is something to which frequent reference will be made
   C. eliminates the need for any personal follow-up or inspection by higher echelons
   D. permits the district supervisor to exercise his functions of direction, supervision, and control better

11. Conclusions and recommendations are usually better placed at the *end* rather than at the *beginning* of a report because 11. ...
   A. the person preparing the report may decide to change some of the conclusions and recommendations before he reaches the end of the report
   B. they are the most important part of the report
   C. they can be judged better by the person to whom the report is sent after he reads the facts and investigations which come earlier in the report
   D. they can be referred to quickly when needed without reading the rest of the report

12. The use of the same method of record-keeping and reporting by *all* agency sections is 12. ...
   A. *desirable, MAINLY* because it saves time in section operations
   B. *undesirable, MAINLY* because it kills the initiative of the individual section foreman
   C. *desirable, MAINLY* because it will be easier for the administrator to evaluate and compare section operations
   D. *undesirable, MAINLY* because operations vary from section to section and uniform record-keeping and reporting is not appropriate

13. The *GREATEST* benefit the section officer will have from keeping complete and accurate records and reports of section operations is that 13. ...
   A. he will find it easier to run his section efficiently
   B. he will need less equipment
   B. he will need less manpower
   D. the section will run smoothly when he is out

14. You have prepared a report to your superior and are ready to send it forward. But on re-reading it, you think some parts are not clearly expressed and your superior may have difficulty getting your point. 14. ...
   Of the following, it would be *BEST* for you to
   A. give the report to one of your men to read, and if he has no trouble understanding it send it through
   B. forward the report and call your superior the next day to ask whether it was all right
   C. forward the report as is; higher echelons should be able to understand any report prepared by a section officer
   D. do the report over, re-writing the sections you are in doubt about

15. The *BEST* of the following statements concerning reports is that 15. ...
    A. a carelessly written report may give the reader an impression of inaccuracy
    B. correct grammar and English are unimportant if the main facts are given
    C. every man should be required to submit a daily work report
    D. the longer and more wordy a report is, the better it will read
16. In writing a report, the question of whether or not to include certain material could be determined *BEST* by considering the 16. ...
    A. amount of space the material will occupy in the report
    B. amount of time to be spent in gathering the material
    C. date of the material
    D. value of the material to the superior who will read the report
17. Suppose you are submitting a fairly long report to your superior. The *one* of the following sections that should come *FIRST* in this report is a 17. ...
    A. description of how you gathered material
    B. discussion of possible objections to your recommendations
    C. plan of how your recommendations can be put into practice
    D. statement of the problem dealt with

Questions 18-20.

DIRECTIONS: A foreman is asked to write a report on the incident described in the following passage. Answer Questions 18 through 20 based on the following information.

On March 10, Henry Moore, a laborer, was in the process of transferring some equipment from the machine shop to the third floor. He was using a dolly to perform this task and, as he was wheeling the material through the machine shop, laborer Bob Greene called to him. As Henry turned to respond to Bob, he jammed the dolly into Larry Mantell's leg, knocking Larry down in the process and causing the heavy drill that Larry was holding to fall on Larry's foot. Larry started rubbing his foot and then, infuriated, jumped up and punched Henry in the jaw. The force of the blow drove Henry's head back against the wall. Henry did not fight back; he appeared to be dazed. An ambulance was called to take Henry to the hospital, and the ambulance attendant told the foreman that it appeared likely that Henry had suffered a concussion. Larry's injuries consisted of some bruises, but he refused medical attention.

18. An *adequate* report of the above incident should give as minimum information the names of the persons involved, the names of the witnesses, the date and the time that each event took place, *and* the 18. ...
    A. names of the ambulance attendants
    B. names of all the employees working in the machine shop
    C. location where the accident occurred
    D. nature of the previous safety training each employee had been given
19. The *only one* of the following which is *NOT* a fact is 19. ...
    A. Bob called to Henry B. Larry suffered a concussion
    C. Larry rubbed his foot
    D. the incident took place in the machine shop

20. *Which* of the following would be the *MOST* accurate summary of the incident for the foreman to put in his report of the accident? 20. ...
   A. Larry Mantell punched Henry Moore because a drill fell on his foot and he was angry. Then Henry fell and suffered a concussion.
   B. Henry Moore accidentally jammed a dolly into Larry Mantell's foot, knocking Larry down. Larry punched Henry, pushing him into the wall and causing him to bang his head against the wall.
   C. Bob Greene called Henry Moore. A dolly then jammed into Larry Mantell and knocked him down. Larry punched Henry who tripped and suffered some bruises. An ambulance was called.
   D. A drill fell on Larry Mantell's foot. Larry jumped up suddenly and punched Henry Moore and pushed him into the wall. Henry may have suffered a concussion as a result of falling.

Questions 21-25.

DIRECTIONS: Answer Questions 21 through 25 *only* on the basis of the information provided in the following passage.

A written report is a communication of information from one person to another. It is an account of some matter especially investigated, however routine that matter may be. The ultimate basis of any good written report is facts, which become known through observation and verification. Good written reports may seem to be no more than general ideas and opinions. However, in such cases, the facts leading to these opinions were gathered, verified, and reported earlier, and the opinions are dependent upon these facts. Good style, proper form and emphasis cannot make a good written report out of unreliable information and bad judgment; but, on the other hand, solid investigation and brilliant thinking are not likely to become very useful until they are effectively communicated to others. If a person's work calls for written reports, then his work is often no better than his written reports.

21. Based on the information in the passage, it can be concluded that opinions expressed in a report should be 21. ...
   A. based on facts which are gathered and reported
   B. emphasized repeatedly when they result from a special investigation
   C. kept to a minimum
   D. separated from the body of the report

22. In the above passage, the *one* of the following which is mentioned as a way of establishing facts is 22. ...
   A. authority B. communication
   C. reporting D. verification

23. According to the passage, the characteristic shared by *all* written reports is that they are 23. ...
   A. accounts of routine matters
   B. transmissions of information
   C. reliable and logical D. written in proper form

24. *Which* of the following conclusions can *logically* be drawn from the information given in the passage? 24. ...
   A. Brilliant thinking can make up for unreliable information in a report.

B. One method of judging an individual's work is the quality of the written reports he is required to submit.
C. Proper form and emphasis can make a good report out of unreliable information.
D. Good written reports that seem to be no more than general ideas should be rewritten.

25. *Which* of the following suggested ittles would be *MOST* appropriate for this passage? 25. ...
A. Gathering and Organizing Facts
B. Techniques of Observation
C. Nature and Purpose of Reports
D. Reports and Opinions: Differences and Similarities

TEST 3

Questions 1-5.
DIRECTIONS: The following is an accident report similar to those used in departments for reporting accidents. Answer Questions 1 to 5 using *only* the information given in this report.

ACCIDENT REPORT

FROM *John Doe* DATE OF REPORT *June 23*
TITLE *Sanitation Man*
DATE OF ACCIDENT *June 22* TIME *3* ~~AM~~ PM
PLACE *1489 Third Avenue* CITY *Metropolitan*

VEHICLE NO. 1 (City Vehicle)
OPERATOR *John Doe Sanitation Man* Title
VEHICLE CODE NO. *14-238*
LICENSE NO. *0123456*

VEHICLE NO. 2
OPERATOR *Richard Roe*
ADDRESS *498 High Street*
OWNER *Henry Roe*
ADDRESS *786 E 83 St*
LIC. NUMBER *5N1492*

DESCRIPTION OF ACCIDENT *Light green Chevrolet sedan while trying to pass drove into rear side of Sanitation truck which had stopped to collect garbage. No one was injured but there was property damage.*
NATURE OF DAMAGE TO PRIVATE VEHICLE *Right front fender crushed, bumper bent.*
DAMAGE TO CITY VEHICLE *Front of left rear fender pushed in. Paint scraped.*
NAME OF WITNESS *Frank Brown* ADDRESS *48 Kingsway*
John Doe BADGE NO. *428*
Signature of person making this report

1. Of the following, the *one* which has been omitted from this accident report is the 1. ...
A. location of the accident
B. drivers of the vehicles involved
C. traffic situation at the time of the accident
D. owners of the vehicles involved

2. The address of the driver of Vehicle No. 1 is not required because he 2. ...
A. is employed by the department
B. is not the owner of the vehicle
C. reported the accident D. was injured in the accident

3. The report indicates that the driver of Vehicle No. 2 was *probably* 3. ...
   A. passing on the wrong side of the truck
   B. not wearing his glasses
   C. not injured in the accident D. driving while intoxicated
4. The number of people *specifically* referred to in this report is 4. ...
   A. 3 B. 4 C. 5 D. 6
5. The license number of Vehicle No. 1 is 5. ...
   A. 428 B. 5N1492 C. 14-238 D. 0123456
6. In a report of unlawful entry into department premises, it is *LEAST* important to include the 6. ...
   A. estimated value of the property missing
   B. general description of the premises
   C. means used to get into the premises
   D. time and date of entry
7. In a report of an accident, it is *LEAST* important to include the 7. ...
   A. name of the insurance company of the person injured in the accident
   B. probable cause of the accident
   C. time and place of the accident
   D. names and addresses of all witnesses of the accident
8. Of the following, the *one* which is *NOT* required in the preparation of a weekly functional expense report is the 8. ...
   A. hourly distribution of the time by proper heading in accordance with the actual work performed
   B. signatures of officers not involved in the preparation of the report
   C. time records of the men who appear on the payroll of the respective locations
   D. time records of men working in other districts assigned to this location

KEYS (CORRECT ANSWERS)

TEST 1		TEST 2		TEST 3
1. B	11. B	1. A	11. C	1. C
2. C	12. B	2. A	12. C	2. A
3. A	13. A	3. D	13. A	3. C
4. B	14. A	4. B	14. D	4. B
5. B	15. C	5. A	15. A	5. D
6. D	16. D	6. C	16. D	6. B
7. C	17. A	7. A	17. D	7. A
8. D	18. B	8. D	18. C	8. B
9. A	19. B	9. C	19. B	
10. C	20. D	10. D	20. B	
	21. C		21. A	
	22. A		22. D	
	23. C		23. B	
	24. B		24. B	
	25. D		25. C	

PREPARING WRITTEN MATERIAL

PARAGRAPH REARRANGEMENT

COMMENTARY

The sentences which follow are in scrambled order. You are to rearrange them in proper order and indicate the letter choice containing the correct answer at the space at the right.

Each group of sentences in this section is actually a paragraph presented in scrambled order. Each sentence in the group has a place in that paragraph; no sentence is to be left out. You are to read each group of sentences and decide upon the best order in which to put the sentences so as to form as well-organized paragraph.

The questions in this section measure the ability to solve a problem when all the facts relevant to its solution are not given.

More specifically, certain positions of responsibility and authority require the employee to discover connections between events sometimes, apparently, unrelated. In order to do this, the employee will find it necessary to correctly infer that unspecified events have probably occurred or are likely to occur. This ability becomes especially important when action must be taken on incomplete information.

Accordingly, these questions require competitors to choose among several suggested alternatives, each of which presents a different sequential arrangement of the events. Competitors must choose the MOST logical of the suggested sequences.

In order to do so, they may be required to draw on general knowledge to infer missing concepts or events that are essential to sequencing the given events. Competitors should be careful to infer only what is essential to the sequence. The plausibility of the wrong alternatives will always require the inclusion of unlikely events or of additional chains of events which are NOT essential to sequencing the given events.

It's very important to remember that you are looking for the best of the four possible choices, and that the best choice of all may not even be one of the answers you're given to choose from.

There is no one right way to these problems. Many people have found it helpful to first write out the order of the sentences, as they would have arranged them, on their scrap paper before looking at the possible answers. If their optimum answer is there, this can save them some time. If it isn't, this method can still give insight into solving the problem. Others find it most helpful to just go through each of the possible choices, contrasting each as they go along. You should use whatever method feels comfortable, and works, for you.

While most of these types of questions are not that difficult, we've added a higher percentage of the difficult type, just to give you more practice. Usually there are only one or two questions on this section that contain such subtle distinctions that you're unable to answer confidently, and you then may find yourself stuck deciding between two possible choices, neither of which you're sure about.

EXAMINATION SECTION

DIRECTIONS: Each question consists of several sentences which can be arranged in a logical sequence. For each question, select the choice which places the numbered sentences in the MOST logical sequence. *PRINT THE LETTER OF THE CORRECT ANSWER IN THE SPACE AT THE RIGHT.*

1. I. A body was found in the woods. 1.___
II. A man proclaimed innocence.
III. The owner of a gun was located.
IV. A gun was traced.
V. The owner of a gun was questioned.

The CORRECT answer is:
A. IV, III, V, II, I
B. II, I, IV, III, V
C. I, IV, III, V, II
D. I, III, V, II, IV
E. I, II, IV, III, V

2. I. A man was in a hunting accident. 2.___
II. A man fell down a flight of steps.
III. A man lost his vision in one eye.
IV. A man broke his leg.
V. A man had to walk with a cane.

The CORRECT answer is:
A. II, IV, V, I, III
B. IV, V, I, III, II
C. III, I, IV, V, II
D. I, III, V, II, IV
E. I, III, II, IV, V

3. I. A man is offered a new job. 3.___
II. A woman is offered a new job.
III. A man works as a waiter.
IV. A woman works as a waitress.
V. A woman gives notice.

The CORRECT answer is:
A. IV, II, V, III, I
B. IV, II, V, I, III
C. II, IV, V, III, I
D. III, I, IV, II, V
E. IV, III, II, V, I

4. I. A train left the station late. 4.___
II. A man was late for work.
III. A man lost his job.
IV. Many people complained because the train was late.
V. There was a traffic jam.

The CORRECT answer is:
A. V, II, I, IV, III
B. V, I, IV, II, III
C. V, I, II, IV, III
D. I, V, IV, II, III
E. II, I, IV, V, III

5. I. The burden of proof as to each issue is determined before trial and remains upon the same party throughout the trial. 5.___
II. The jury is at liberty to believe one witness' testimony as against a number of contradictory witnesses.
III. In a civil case, the party bearing the burden of proof is required to prove his contention by a fair preponderance of the evidence.
IV. However, it must be noted that a fair preponderance of evidence does not necessarily mean a greater number of witnesses.
V. The burden of proof is the burden which rests upon one of the parties to an action to persuade the trier of the facts, generally the jury, that a proposition he asserts is true.
VI. If the evidence is equally balanced, or if it leaves the jury in such doubt as to be unable to decide the controversy either way, judgment must be given against the party upon whom the burden of proof rests.

The CORRECT answer is:
A. III, II, V, IV, I, VI
B. I, II, VI, V, III, IV
C. III, IV, V, I, II, VI
D. V, I, III, VI, IV, II
E. I, V, III, VI, IV, II

6. I. If a parent is without assets and is unemployed, he cannot be convicted of the crime of non-support of a child. 6.___
II. The term *sufficient ability* has been held to mean sufficient financial ability.
III. It does not matter if his unemployment is by choice or unavoidable circumstances.
IV. If he fails to take any steps at all, he may be liable to prosecution for endangering the welfare of a child.
V. Under the penal law, a parent is responsible for the support of his minor child only if the parent is *of sufficient ability*.
VI. An indigent parent may meet his obligation by borrowing money or by seeking aid under the provisions of the Social Welfare Law.

The CORRECT answer is:
A. VI, I, V, III, II, IV
B. I, III, V, II, IV, VI
C. V, II, I, III, VI, IV
D. I, VI, IV, V, II, III
E. II, V, I, III, VI, IV

7. I. Consider, for example, the case of a rabble rouser who urges a group of twenty people to go out and break the windows of a nearby factory. 7.___
II. Therefore, the law fills the indicated gap with the crime of *inciting to riot*.
III. A person is considered guilty of inciting to riot when he urges ten or more persons to engage in tumultuous and violent conduct of a kind likely to create public alarm.

IV. However, if he has not obtained the cooperation of at least four people, he cannot be charged with unlawful assembly.
V. The charge of inciting to riot was added to the law to cover types of conduct which cannot be classified as either the crime of *riot* or the crime of *unlawful assembly*.
VI. If he acquires the acquiescence of at least four of them, he is guilty of unlawful assembly even if the project does not materialize.

The CORRECT answer is:
A. III, V, I, VI, IV, II
B. V, I, IV, VI, II, III
C. III, IV, I, V, II, VI
D. V, I, IV, VI, III, II
E. V, III, I, VI, IV, II

8. I. If, however, the rebuttal evidence presents an issue of credibility, it is for the jury to determine whether the presumption has, in fact, been destroyed. 8.___
II. Once sufficient evidence to the contrary is introduced, the presumption disappears from the trial.
III. The effect of a presumption is to place the burden upon the adversary to come forward with evidence to rebut the presumption.
IV. When a presumption is overcome and ceases to exist in the case, the fact or facts which gave rise to the presumption still remain.
V. Whether a presumption has been overcome is ordinarily a question for the court.
VI. Such information may furnish a basis for a logical inference.

The CORRECT answer is:
A. IV, VI, II, V, I, III
B. III, II, V, I, IV, VI
C. V, III, VI, IV, II, I
D. V, IV, I, II, VI, III
E. II, III, V, I, IV, VI

9. I. An executive may answer a letter by writing his reply on the face of the letter itself instead of having a return letter typed. 9.___
II. This procedure is efficient because it saves the executive's time, the typist's time, and saves office file space.
III. Copying machines are used in small offices as well as large offices to save time and money in making brief replies to business letters.
IV. A copy is made on a copying machine to go into the company files, while the original is mailed back to the sender.

The CORRECT answer is:
A. I, II, IV, III
B. I, IV, II, III
C. III, I, IV, II
D. III, IV, II, I

10. I. Most organizations favor one of the types but always include the others to a lesser degree. 10.___
II. However, we can detect a definite trend toward greater use of symbolic control.
III. We suggest that our local police agencies are today primarily utilizing material control.
IV. Control can be classified into three types: physical, material, and symbolic.

The CORRECT answer is:
A. IV, II, III, I
B. II, I, IV, III
C. III, IV, II, I
D. IV, I, III, II

11. I. Project residents had first claim to this use, followed by surrounding neighborhood children. 11.___
II. By contrast, recreation space within the project's interior was found to be used more often by both groups.
III. Studies of the use of project grounds in many cities showed grounds left open for public use were neglected and unused, both by residents and by members of the surrounding community.
IV. Project residents had clearly laid claim to the play spaces, setting up and enforcing unwritten rules for use.
V. Each group, by experience, found their activities easily disrupted by other groups, and their claim to the use of space for recreation difficult to enforce.

The CORRECT answer is:
A. IV, V, I, II, III
B. V, II, IV, III, I
C. I, IV, III, II, V
D. III, V, II, IV, I

12. I. They do not consider the problems correctable within the existing subsidy formula and social policy of accepting all eligible applicants regardless of social behavior and lifestyle. 12.___
II. A recent survey, however, indicated that tenants believe these problems correctable by local housing authorities and management within the existing financial formula.
III. Many of the problems and complaints concerning public housing management and design have created resentment between the tenant and the landlord.
IV. This same survey indicated that administrators and managers do not agree with the tenants.

The CORRECT answer is:
A. II, I, III, IV
B. I, III, IV, II
C. III, II, IV, I
D. IV, II, I, III

13. I. In single-family residences, there is usually enough distance between tenants to prevent occupants from annoying one another. 13.___
II. For example, a certain small percentage of tenant families has one or more members addicted to alcohol.
III. While managers believe in the right of individuals to live as they choose, the manager becomes concerned when the pattern of living jeopardizes others' rights.
IV. Still others turn night into day, staging lusty entertainments which carry on into the hours when most tenants are trying to sleep.
V. In apartment buildings, however, tenants live so closely together that any misbehavior can result in unpleasant living conditions.
VI. Other families engage in violent argument.

The CORRECT answer is:
A. III, II, V, IV, VI, I B. I, V, II, VI, IV, III
C. II, V, IV, I, III, VI D. IV, II, V, VI, III, I

14. I. Congress made the commitment explicit in the Housing Act of 1949, establishing as a national goal the realization of *a decent home and suitable environment for every American family*. 14.___
II. The result has been that the goal of decent home and suitable environment is still as far distant as ever for the disadvantaged urban family.
III. In spite of this action by Congress, federal housing programs have continued to be fragmented and grossly underfunded.
IV. The passage of the National Housing Act signalled a new federal commitment to provide housing for the nation's citizens.

The CORRECT answer is:
A. I, IV, III, II B. IV, I, III, II
C. IV, I, II, III D. II, IV, I, III

15. I. The greater expense does not necessarily involve *exploitation*, but it is often perceived as exploitative and unfair by those who are aware of the price differences involved, but unaware of operating costs. 15.___
II. Ghetto residents believe they are *exploited* by local merchants, and evidence substantiates some of these beliefs.
III. However, stores in low-income areas were more likely to be small independents, which could not achieve the economies available to supermarket chains and were, therefore, more likely to charge higher prices, and the customers were more likely to buy smaller-sized packages which are more expensive per unit of measure.
IV. A study conducted in one city showed that distinctly higher prices were charged for goods sold in ghetto stores than in other areas.

The CORRECT answer is:

A. IV, II, I, III
B. IV, I, III, II
C. II, IV, III, I
D. II, III, IV, I

KEY (CORRECT ANSWERS)

1.	C	6.	C	11.	D
2.	E	7.	A	12.	C
3.	B	8.	B	13.	B
4.	D	9.	C	14.	B
5.	D	10.	D	15.	C

PREPARING WRITTEN MATERIAL

EXAMINATION SECTION

TEST 1

DIRECTIONS: Each question or incomplete statement is followed by several suggested answers or completions. Select the one that BEST answers the question or completes the statement. *PRINT THE LETTER OF THE CORRECT ANSWER IN THE SPACE AT THE RIGHT.*

1. The one of the following sentences which is LEAST acceptable from the viewpoint of correct usage is: 1.____
   A. The police thought the fugitive to be him.
   B. The criminals set a trap for whoever would fall into it.
   C. It is ten years ago since the fugitive fled from the city.
   D. The lecturer argued that criminals are usually cowards.
   E. The police removed four bucketfuls of earth from the scene of the crime.

2. The one of the following sentences which is LEAST acceptable from the viewpoint of correct usage is: 2.____
   A. The patrolman scrutinized the report with great care.
   B. Approaching the victim of the assault, two bruises were noticed by the patrolman.
   C. As soon as I had broken down the door, I stepped into the room.
   D. I observed the accused loitering near the building, which was closed at the time.
   E. The storekeeper complained that his neighbor was guilty of violating a local ordinance.

3. The one of the following sentences which is LEAST acceptable from the viewpoint of correct usage is: 3.____
   A. I realized immediately that he intended to assault the woman, so I disarmed him.
   B. It was apparent that Mr. Smith's explanation contained many inconsistencies.
   C. Despite the slippery condition of the street, he managed to stop the vehicle before injuring the child.
   D. Not a single one of them wish, despite the damage to property, to make a formal complaint.
   E. The body was found lying on the floor.

4. The one of the following sentences which contains NO error in usage is: 4.____
   A. After the robbers left, the proprietor stood tied in his chair for about two hours before help arrived.
   B. In the cellar I found the watchmans' hat and coat.
   C. The persons living in adjacent apartments stated that they had heard no unusual noises.
   D. Neither a knife or any firearms were found in the room.
   E. Walking down the street, the shouting of the crowd indicated that something was wrong.

5. The one of the following sentences which contains NO error in usage is: 5.___
   A. The policeman lay a firm hand on the suspect's shoulder.
   B. It is true that neither strength nor agility are the most important requirement for a good patrolman.
   C. Good citizens constantly strive to do more than merely comply the restraints imposed by society.
   D. No decision was made as to whom the prize should be awarded.
   E. Twenty years is considered a severe sentence for a felony.

6. Which of the following is NOT expressed in standard English usage? 6.___
   A. The victim reached a pay-phone booth and manages to call police headquarters.
   B. By the time the call was received, the assailant had left the scene.
   C. The victim has been a respected member of the community for the past eleven years.
   D. Although the lighting was bad and the shadows were deep, the storekeeper caught sight of the attacker.
   E. Additional street lights have since been installed, and the patrols have been strengthened.

7. Which of the following is NOT expressed in standard English usage? 7.___
   A. The judge upheld the attorney's right to question the witness about the missing glove.
   B. To be absolutely fair to all parties is the jury's chief responsibility.
   C. Having finished the report, a loud noise in the next room startled the sergeant.
   D. The witness obviously enjoyed having played a part in the proceedings.
   E. The sergeant planned to assign the case to whoever arrived first.

8. In which of the following is a word misused? 8.___
   A. As a matter of principle, the captain insisted that the suspect's partner be brought for questioning.
   B. The principle suspect had been detained at the station house for most of the day.
   C. The principal in the crime had no previous criminal record, but his closest associate had been convicted of felonies on two occasions.
   D. The interest payments had been made promptly, but the firm had been drawing upon the principal for these payments.
   E. The accused insisted that his high school principal would furnish him a character reference.

9. Which of the following statements is ambiguous? 9.___
   A. Mr. Sullivan explained why Mr. Johnson had been dismissed from his job.
   B. The storekeeper told the patrolman he had made a mistake.
   C. After waiting three hours, the patients in the doctor's office were sent home.
   D. The janitor's duties were to maintain the building in good shape and to answer tenants' complaints.
   E. The speed limit should, in my opinion, be raised to sixty miles an hour on that stretch of road.

10. In which of the following is the punctuation or capitalization faulty? 10.___
   A. The accident occurred at an intersection in the Kew Gardens section of Queens, near the bus stop.
   B. The sedan, not the convertible, was struck in the side.
   C. Before any of the patrolmen had left the police car received an important message from headquarters.
   D. The dog that had been stolen was returned to his master, John Dempsey, who lived in East Village.
   E. The letter had been sent to 12 Hillside Terrace, Rutland, Vermont 05701.

Questions 11-25.

DIRECTIONS: Questions 11 through 25 are to be answered in accordance with correct English usage; that is, standard English rather than nonstandard or substandard. Nonstandard and substandard English includes words or expressions usually classified as slang, dialect, illiterate, etc., which are not generally accepted as correct in current written communication. Standard English also requires clarity, proper punctuation and capitalization and appropriate use of words. Write the letter of the sentence NOT expressed in standard English usage in the space at the right.

11. A. There were three witnesses to the accident. 11.___
   B. At least three witnesses were found to testify for the plaintiff.
   C. Three of the witnesses who took the stand was uncertain about the defendant's competence to drive.
   D. Only three witnesses came forward to testify for the plaintiff.
   E. The three witnesses to the accident were pedestrians.

12. A. The driver had obviously drunk too many martinis before leaving for home. 12.___
   B. The boy who drowned had swum in these same waters many times before.
   C. The petty thief had stolen a bicycle from a private driveway before he was apprehended.

D. The detectives had brung in the heroin shipment they intercepted.
E. The passengers had never ridden in a converted bus before.

13. A. Between you and me, the new platoon plan sounds like a good idea. 13.___
B. Money from an aunt's estate was left to his wife and he.
C. He and I were assigned to the same patrol for the first time in two months.
D. Either you or he should check the front door of that store.
E. The captain himself was not sure of the witness's reliability.

14. A. The alarm had scarcely begun to ring when the explosion occurred. 14.___
B. Before the firemen arrived on the scene, the second story had been destroyed.
C. Because of the dense smoke and heat, the firemen could hardly approach the now-blazing structure.
D. According to the patrolman's report, there wasn't nobody in the store when the explosion occurred.
E. The sergeant's suggestion was not at all unsound, but no one agreed with him.

15. A. The driver and the passenger they were both found to be intoxicated. 15.___
B. The driver and the passenger talked slowly and not too clearly.
C. Neither the driver nor his passengers were able to give a coherent account of the accident.
D. In a corner of the room sat the passenger, quietly dozing.
E. The driver finally told a strange and unbelievable story, which the passenger contradicted.

16. A. Under the circumstances I decided not to continue my examination of the premises. 16.___
B. There are many difficulties now not comparable with those existing in 1960.
C. Friends of the accused were heard to announce that the witness had better been away on the day of the trial.
D. The two criminals escaped in the confusion that followed the explosion.
E. The aged man was struck by the considerateness of the patrolman's offer.

17. A. An assemblage of miscellaneous weapons lay on the table. 17.___
B. Ample opportunities were given to the defendant to obtain counsel.

C. The speaker often alluded to his past experience with youthful offenders in the armed forces.
D. The sudden appearance of the truck aroused my suspicions.
E. Her studying had a good affect on her grades in high school.

18. A. He sat down in the theater and began to watch the movie. 18.___
B. The girl had ridden horses since she was four years old.
C. Application was made on behalf of the prosecutor to cite the witness for contempt.
D. The bank robber, with his two accomplices, were caught in the act.
E. His story is simply not credible.

19. A. The angry boy said that he did not like those kind of friends. 19.___
B. The merchant's financial condition was so precarious that he felt he must avail himself of any offer of assistance.
C. He is apt to promise more than he can perform.
D. Looking at the messy kitchen, the housewife felt like crying.
E. A clerk was left in charge of the stolen property.

20. A. His wounds were aggravated by prolonged exposure to sub-freezing temperatures. 20.___
B. The prosecutor remarked that the witness was not averse to changing his story each time he was interviewed.
C. The crime pattern indicated that the burglars were adapt in the handling of explosives.
D. His rigid adherence to a fixed plan brought him into renewed conflict with his subordinates.
E. He had anticipated that the sentence would be delivered by noon.

21. A. The whole arraignment procedure is badly in need of revision. 21.___
B. After his glasses were broken in the fight, he would of gone to the optometrist if he could.
C. Neither Tom nor Jack brought his lunch to work.
D. He stood aside until the quarrel was over.
E. A statement in the psychiatrist's report disclosed that the probationer vowed to have his revenge.

22. A. His fiery and intemperate speech to the striking employees fatally affected any chance of a future reconciliation. 22.___
B. The wording of the statute has been variously construed.
C. The defendant's attorney, speaking in the courtroom, called the official a demagogue who contempuously disregarded the judge's orders.

D. The baseball game is likely to be the most exciting one this year.
E. The mother divided the cookies among her two children.

23. A. There was only a bed and a dresser in the dingy room. 23.___
B. John is one of the few students that have protested the new rule.
C. It cannot be argued that the child's testimony is negligible; it is, on the contrary, of the greatest importance.
D. The basic criterion for clearance was so general that officials resolved any doubts in favor of dismissal.
E. Having just returned from a long vacation, the officer found the city unbearably hot.

24. A. The librarian ought to give more help to small children. 24.___
B. The small boy was criticized by the teacher because he often wrote careless.
C. It was generally doubted whether the women would permit the use of her apartment for intelligence operations.
D. The probationer acts differently every time the officer visits him.
E. Each of the newly appointed officers has 12 years of service.

25. A. The North is the most industrialized region in the country. 25.___
B. L. Patrick Gray 3d, the bureau's acting director, stated that, while "rehabilitation is fine" for some convicted criminals, "it is a useless gesture for those who resist every such effort."
C. Careless driving, faulty mechanism, narrow or badly kept roads all play their part in causing accidents.
D. The childrens' books were left in the bus.
E. It was a matter of internal security; consequently, he felt no inclination to rescind his previous order.

KEY (CORRECT ANSWERS)

1. C	6. A	11. C	16. C	21. B
2. B	7. C	12. D	17. E	22. E
3. D	8. B	13. B	18. D	23. B
4. C	9. B	14. D	19. A	24. B
5. E	10. C	15. A	20. C	25. D

TEST 2

DIRECTIONS: Each question or incomplete statement is followed by several suggested answers or completions. Select the one that BEST answers the question or completes the statement. *PRINT THE LETTER OF THE CORRECT ANSWER IN THE SPACE AT THE RIGHT.*

Questions 1-6.

DIRECTIONS: Each of Questions 1 through 6 consists of a statement which contains a word (one of those underlined) that is either incorrectly used because it is not in keeping with the meaning the quotation is evidently intended to convey, or is misspelled. There is only one INCORRECT word in each quotation. Of the four underlined words, determine if the first one should be replaced by the word lettered A, the second replaced by the word lettered B, the third replaced by the word lettered C, or the fourth replaced by the word lettered D. *PRINT THE LETTER OF THE REPLACEMENT WORD YOU HAVE SELECTED IN THE SPACE AT THE RIGHT.*

1. Whether one depends on fluorescent or artificial light or both, adequate standards should be maintained by means of systematic tests. 1.___
   A. natural B. safeguards
   C. established D. routine

2. A policeman has to be prepared to assume his knowledge as a social scientist in the community. 2.___
   A. forced B. role
   C. philosopher D. street

3. It is practically impossible to indicate whether a sentence is too long simply by measuring its length. 3.___
   A. almost B. tell C. very D. guessing

4. Strong leaders are required to organize a community for delinquency prevention and for dissemination of organized crime and drug addiction. 4.___
   A. tactics B. important C. control D. meetings

5. The demonstrators who were taken to the Criminal Courts building in Manhattan (because it was large enough to accommodate them), contended that the arrests were unwarrented. 5.___
   A. demonstraters B. Manhatten
   C. accomodate D. unwarranted

6. They were guaranteed a calm atmosphere, free from harrassment, which would be conducive to quiet consideration of the indictments. 6.___
   A. guarenteed B. atmospher
   C. harassment D. inditements

Questions 7-11.

DIRECTIONS: Each of Questions 7 through 11 consists of a statement containing four words in capital letters. One of these words in capital letters is not in keeping with the meaning which the statement is evidently intended to carry. The four words in capital letters in each statement are reprinted after the statement. Print the capital letter preceding the one of the four words which does MOST to spoil the true meaning of the statement in the space at the right.

7. Retirement and pension systems are essential not only to provide employees with a means of support in the future, but also to prevent longevity and CHARITABLE considerations from UPSETTING the PROMOTIONAL opportunities for RETIRED members of the career service. 7.___
   A. charitable B. upsetting
   C. promotional D. retired

8. Within each major DIVISION in a properly set up public or private organization, provision is made so that each NECESSARY activity is CARED for and lines of authority and responsibility are clear-cut and INFINITE. 8.___
   A. division B. necessary C. cared D. infinite

9. In public service, the scale of salaries paid must be INCIDENTAL to the services rendered, with due CONSIDERATION for the attraction of the desired MANPOWER and for the maintenance of a standard of living COMMENSURATE with the work to be performed. 9.___
   A. incidental B. consideration
   C. manpower D. commensurate

10. An understanding of the AIMS of an organization by the staff will AID greatly in increasing the DEMAND of the correspondence work of the office, and will to a large extent DETERMINE the nature of the correspondence. 10.___
    A. aims B. aid C. demand D. determine

11. BECAUSE the Civil Service Commission strongly feels that the MERIT system is a key factor in the MAINTENANCE of democratic government, it has adopted as one of its major DEFENSES the progressive democratization of its own procedures in dealing with candidates for positions in the public service. 11.___
    A. Because B. merit
    C. maintenance D. defenses

Questions 12-14.

DIRECTIONS: Questions 12 through 14 consist of one sentence each. Each sentence contains an incorrectly used word. First, decide which is the incorrectly used word. Then, from among the options given, decide which word, when substituted for the incorrectly used word, makes the meaning of the sentence clear.

EXAMPLE:
The U.S. national income exhibits a pattern of long term deflection.
A. reflection
B. subjection
C. rejoicing
D. growth

The word *deflection* in the sentence does not convey the meaning the sentence evidently intended to convey. The word *growth* (Answer D), when substituted for the word *deflection*, makes the meaning of the sentence clear. Accordingly, the answer to the question is D.

12. The study commissioned by the joint committee fell compassionately short of the mark and would have to be redone. 12.___
A. successfully
B. insignificantly
C. experimentally
D. woefully

13. He will not idly exploit any violation of the provisions of the order. 13.___
A. tolerate B. refuse C. construe D. guard

14. The defendant refused to be virile and bitterly protested service. 14.___
A. irked B. feasible C. docile D. credible

Questions 15-25.

DIRECTIONS: Questions 15 through 25 consist of short paragraphs. Each paragraph contains one word which is INCORRECTLY used because it is NOT in keeping with the meaning of the paragraph. Find the word in each paragraph which is INCORRECTLY used and then select as the answer the suggested word which should be substituted for the incorrectly used word.

SAMPLE QUESTION:
In determining who is to do the work in your unit, you will have to decide just who does what from day to day. One of your lowest responsibilities is to assign work so that everybody gets a fair share and that everyone can do his part well.
A. new B. old C. important D. performance

EXPLANATION:
The word which is NOT in keeping with the meaning of the paragraph is *lowest*. This is the INCORRECTLY used word. The suggested word *important* would be in keeping with the meaning of the paragraph and should be substituted for *lowest*. Therefore, the CORRECT answer is choice C.

15. If really good practice in the elimination of preventable injuries is to be achieved and held in any establishment, top management must refuse full and definite responsibility and must apply a good share of its attention to the task. 15.___
A. accept B. avoidable C. duties D. problem

16. Recording the human face for identification is by no means the only service performed by the camera in the field of investigation. When the trial of any issue takes place, a word picture is sought to be distorted to the court of incidents, occurrences, or events which are in dispute. 16.___
A. appeals B. description
C. portrayed D. deranged

17. In the collection of physical evidence, it cannot be emphasized too strongly that a haphazard systematic search at the scene of the crime is vital. Nothing must be overlooked. Often the only leads in a case will come from the results of this search. 17.___
A. important B. investigation
C. proof D. thorough

18. If an investigator has reason to suspect that the witness is mentally stable, or a habitual drunkard, he should leave no stone unturned in his investigation to determine if the witness was under the influence of liquor or drugs, or was mentally unbalanced either at the time of the occurrence to which he testified or at the time of the trial. 18.___
A. accused B. clue C. deranged D. question

19. The use of records is a valuable step in crime investigation and is the main reason every department should maintain accurate reports. Crimes are not committed through the use of departmental records alone but from the use of all records, of almost every type, wherever they may be found and whenever they give any incidental information regarding the criminal. 19.___
A. accidental B. necessary
C. reported D. solved

20. In the years since passage of the Harrison Narcotic Act of 1914, making the possession of opium amphetamines illegal in most circumstances, drug use has become a subject of considerable scientific interest and investigation. There is at present a voluminous literature on drug use of various kinds. 20.____

A. ingestion
B. derivatives
C. addiction
D. opiates

21. Of course, the fact that criminal laws are extremely patterned in definition does not mean that the majority of persons who violate them are dealt with as criminals. Quite the contrary, for a great many forbidden acts are voluntarily engaged in within situations of privacy and go unobserved and unreported. 21.____

A. symbolic
B. casual
C. scientific
D. broad-gauged

22. The most punitive way to study punishment is to focus attention on the pattern of punitive action: to study how a penalty is applied, to study what is done to or taken from an offender. 22.____

A. characteristic
B. degrading
C. objective
D. distinguished

23. The most common forms of punishment in times past have been death, physical torture, mutilation, branding, public humiliation, fines, forfeits of property, banishment, transportation, and imprisonment. Although this list is by no means differentiated, practically every form of punishment has had several variations and applications. 23.____

A. specific
B. simple
C. exhaustive
D. characteristic

24. There is another important line of inference between ordinary and professional criminals, and that is the source from which they are recruited. The professional criminal seems to be drawn from legitimate employment and, in many instances, from parallel vocations or pursuits. 24.____

A. demarcation
B. justification
C. superiority
D. reference

25. He took the position that the success of the program was insidious on getting additional revenue. 25.____

A. reputed
B. contingent
C. failure
D. indeterminate

KEY (CORRECT ANSWERS)

1. A	6. C	11. D	16. A	21. D
2. B	7. D	12. D	17. D	22. C
3. B	8. D	13. A	18. C	23. C
4. C	9. A	14. C	19. D	24. A
5. D	10. C	15. B	20. B	25. B

TEST 3

DIRECTIONS: Each question or incomplete statement is followed by several suggested answers or completions. Select the one that BEST answers the question or completes the statement. *PRINT THE LETTER OF THE CORRECT ANSWER IN THE SPACE AT THE RIGHT.*

Questions 1-5.

DIRECTIONS: Question 1 through 5 are to be answered on the basis of the following:

You are a supervising officer in an investigative unit. Earlier in the day, you directed Detectives Tom Dixon and Sal Mayo to investigate a reported assault and robbery in a liquor store within your area of jurisdiction.

Detective Dixon has submitted to you a preliminary investigative report containing the following information:

- At 1630 hours on 2/20, arrived at Joe's Liquor Store at 350 SW Avenue with Detective Mayo to investigate A & R.
- At store interviewed Rob Ladd, store manager, who stated that he and Joe Brown (store owner) had been stuck up about ten minutes prior to our arrival.
- Ladd described the robbers as male whites in their late teens or early twenties. Further stated that one of the robbers displayed what appeared to be an automatic pistol as he entered the store, and said, *Give us the money or we'll kill you*. Ladd stated that Brown then reached under the counter where he kept a loaded .38 caliber pistol. Several shots followed, and Ladd threw himself to the floor.
- The robbers fled, and Ladd didn't know if any money had been taken.
- At this point, Ladd realized that Brown was unconscious on the floor and bleeding from a head wound.
- Ambulance called by Ladd, and Brown was removed by same to General Hospital.
- Personally interviewed John White, 382 Dartmouth Place, who stated he was inside store at the time of occurrence. White states that he hid behind a wine display upon hearing someone say, *Give us the money*. He then heard shots and saw two young men run from the store to a yellow car parked at the curb. White was unable to further describe auto. States the taller of the two men drove the car away while the other sat on passenger side in front.
- Recovered three spent .38 caliber bullets from premises and delivered them to Crime Lab.
- To General Hospital at 1800 hours but unable to interview Brown, who was under sedation and suffering from shock and a laceration of the head.
- Alarm #12487 transmitted for car and occupants.
- Case Active.

Based solely on the contents of the preliminary investigation submitted by Detective Dixon, select one sentence from the following groups of sentences which is MOST accurate and is grammatically correct.

1. A. Both robbers were armed. 1.___
   B. Each of the robbers were described as a male white.
   C. Neither robber was armed.
   D. Mr. Ladd stated that one of the robbers was armed.

2. A. Mr. Brown fired three shots from his revolver. 2.___
   B. Mr. Brown was shot in the head by one of the robbers.
   C. Mr. Brown suffered a gunshot wound of the head during the course of the robbery.
   D. Mr. Brown was taken to General Hospital by ambulance.

3. A. Shots were fired after one of the robbers said, *Give us the money or we'll kill you.* 3.___
   B. After one of the robbers demanded the money from Mr. Brown, he fired a shot.
   C. The preliminary investigation indicated that although Mr. Brown did not have a license for the gun, he was justified in using deadly physical force.
   D. Mr. Brown was interviewed at General Hospital.

4. A. Each of the witnesses were customers in the store at the time of occurrence. 4.___
   B. Neither of the witnesses interviewed was the owner of the liquor store.
   C. Neither of the witnesses interviewed were the owner of the store.
   D. Neither of the witnesses was employed by Mr. Brown.

5. A. Mr. Brown arrived at General Hospital at about 5:00 P.M. 5.___
   B. Neither of the robbers was injured during the robbery.
   C. The robbery occurred at 3:30 P.M. on February 10.
   D. One of the witnesses called the ambulance.

Questions 6-10.

DIRECTIONS: Each of Questions 6 through 10 consists of information given in outline form and four sentences labelled A, B, C, and D. For each question, choose the one sentence which CORRECTLY expresses the information given in outline form and which also displays PROPER English usage.

6. Client's Name - Joanna Jones 6.___
   Number of Children - 3
   Client's Income - None
   Client's Marital Status - Single
   A. Joanna Jones is an unmarried client with three children who have no income.
   B. Joanna Jones, who is single and has no income, a client she has three children.

C. Joanna Jones, whose three children are clients, is single and has no income.
D. Joanna Jones, who has three children, is an unmarried client with no income.

7. Client's Name - Bertha Smith 7.___
Number of Children - 2
Client's Rent - $105 per month
Number of Rooms - 4
A. Bertha Smith, a client, pays $105 per month for her four rooms with two children.
B. Client Bertha Smith has two children and pays $105 per month for four rooms.
C. Client Bertha Smith is paying $105 per month for two children with four rooms.
D. For four rooms and two children client Bertha Smith pays $105 per month.

8. Name of Employee - Cynthia Dawes 8.___
Number of Cases Assigned - 9
Date Cases were Assigned - 12/16
Number of Assigned Cases Completed - 8
A. On December 16, employee Cynthia Dawes was assigned nine cases; she has completed eight of these cases.
B. Cynthia Dawes, employee on December 16, assigned nine cases, completed eight.
C. Being employed on December 16, Cynthia Dawes completed eight of nine assigned cases.
D. Employee Cynthia Dawes, she was assigned nine cases and completed eight, on December 16.

9. Place of Audit - Broadway Center 9.___
Names of Auditors - Paul Cahn, Raymond Perez
Date of Audit - 11/20
Number of Cases Audited - 41
A. On November 20, at the Broadway Center 41 cases was audited by auditors Paul Cahn and Raymond Perez.
B. Auditors Raymond Perez and Paul Cahn has audited 41 cases at the Broadway Center on November 20.
C. At the Broadway Center, on November 20, auditors Paul Cahn and Raymond Perez audited 41 cases.
D. Auditors Paul Cahn and Raymond Perez at the Broadway Center, on November 20, is auditing 41 cases.

10. Name of Client - Barbra Levine 10.___
Client's Monthly Income - $210
Client's Monthly Expenses - $452
A. Barbra Levine is a client, her monthly income is $210 and her monthly expenses is $452.
B. Barbra Levine's monthly income is $210 and she is a client, with whose monthly expenses are $452.
C. Barbra Levine is a client whose monthly income is $210 and whose monthly expenses are $452.
D. Barbra Levine, a client, is with a monthly income which is $210 and monthly expenses which are $452.

Questions 11-13.

DIRECTIONS: Questions 11 through 13 involve several statements of fact presented in a very simple way. These statements of fact are followed by 4 choices which attempt to incorporate all of the facts into one logical sentence which is properly constructed and grammatically correct.

11. I. Mr. Brown was sweeping the sidewalk in front of his house. 11.___
II. He was sweeping it because it was dirty.
III. He swept the refuse into the street
IV. Police Officer Green gave him a ticket.

Which one of the following BEST presents the information given above?
A. Because his sidewalk was dirty, Mr. Brown received a ticket from Officer Green when he swept the refuse into the street.
B. Police Officer Green gave Mr. Brown a ticket because his sidewalk was dirty and he swept the refuse into the street.
C. Police Officer Green gave Mr. Brown a ticket for sweeping refuse into the street because his sidewalk was dirty.
D. Mr. Brown, who was sweeping refuse from his dirty sidewalk into the street, was given a ticket by Police Officer Green.

12. I. Sergeant Smith radioed for help. 12.___
II. The sergeant did so because the crowd was getting larger.
III. It was 10:00 A.M. when he made his call.
IV. Sergeant Smith was not in uniform at the time of occurrence.

Which one of the following BEST presents the information given above?
A. Sergeant Smith, although not on duty at the time, radioed for help at 10 o'clock because the crowd was getting uglier.
B. Although not in uniform, Sergeant Smith called for help at 10:00 A.M. because the crowd was getting uglier.
C. Sergeant Smith radioed for help at 10:00 A.M. because the crowd was getting larger.
D. Although he was not in uniform, Sergeant Smith radioed for help at 10:00 A.M. because the crowd was getting larger.

13. I. The payroll office is open on Fridays. 13.___
II. Paychecks are distributed from 9:00 A.M. to 12 Noon.
III. The office is open on Fridays because that's the only day the payroll staff is available.
IV. It is open for the specified hours in order to permit employees to cash checks at the bank during lunch hour.

The choice below which MOST clearly and accurately presents the above idea is:
A. Because the payroll office is open on Fridays from 9:00 A.M. to 12 Noon, employees can cash their checks when the payroll staff is available.
B. Because the payroll staff is only available on Fridays until noon, employees can cash their checks during their lunch hour.
C. Because the payroll staff is available only on Fridays, the office is open from 9:00 A.M. to 12 Noon to allow employees to cash their checks.
D. Because of payroll staff availability, the payroll office is open on Fridays. It is open from 9:00 A.M. to 12 Noon so that distributed paychecks can be cashed at the bank while employees are on their lunch hour.

Questions 14-16.

DIRECTIONS: In each of Questions 14 through 16, the four sentences are from a paragraph in a report. They are not in the right order. Which of the following arrangements is the BEST one?

14. I. An executive may answer a letter by writing his reply on the face of the letter itself instead of having a return letter typed. 14.___
II. This procedure is efficient because it saves the executive's time, the typist's time, and saves office file space.
III. Copying machines are used in small offices as well as large offices to save time and money in making brief replies to business letters.
IV. A copy is made on a copying machine to go into the company files, while the original is mailed back to the sender.

The CORRECT answer is:
A. I, II, IV, III
B. I, IV, II, III
C. III, I, IV, II
D. III, IV, II, I

15. I. Most organizations favor one of the types but always include the others to a lesser degree. 15.___
II. However, we can detect a definite trend toward greater use of symbolic control.
III. We suggest that our local police agencies are today primarily utilizing material control.
IV. Control can be classified into three types: physical, material, and symbolic.

The CORRECT answer is:
A. IV, II, III, I
B. II, I, IV, III
C. III, IV, II, I
D. IV, I, III, II

16. I. They can and do take advantage of ancient political and geographical boundaries, which often give them sanctuary from effective police activity. 16.___
II. This country is essentially a country of small police forces, each operating independently within the limits of its jurisdiction.
III. The boundaries that define and limit police operations do not hinder the movement of criminals, of course.
IV. The machinery of law enforcement in America is fragmented, complicated, and frequently overlapping.

The CORRECT answer is:
A. III, I, II, IV
B. II, IV, I, III
C. IV, II, III, I
D. IV, III, II, I

17. Examine the following sentence, and then choose from below the words which should be inserted in the blank spaces to produce the best sentence. 17.___
The unit has exceeded _____ goals and the employees are satisfied with _____ accomplishments.
A. their, it's
B. it's, it's
C. its, there
D. its, their

18. Examine the following sentence, and then choose from below the words which should be inserted in the blank spaces to produce the best sentence. 18.___
Research indicates that employees who _____ no opportunity for close social relationships often find their work unsatisfying, and this _____ of satisfaction often reflects itself in low production.
A. have, lack
B. have, excess
C. has, lack
D. has, excess

19. Words in a sentence must be arranged properly to make sure that the intended meaning of the sentence is clear. The sentence below that does NOT make sense because a clause has been separated from the word on which its meaning depends is: 19.___
A. To be a good writer, clarity is necessary.
B. To be a good writer, you must write clearly.
C. You must write clearly to be a good writer.
D. Clarity is necessary to good writing.

Questions 20-21.

DIRECTIONS: Each of Questions 20 and 21 consists of a statement which contains a word (one of those underlined) that is either incorrectly used because it is not in keeping with the meaning the quotation is evidently intended to convey, or is misspelled. There is only one INCORRECT word in each quotation. Of the four underlined words, determine if the first one should be replaced by the word lettered A, the second one replaced by the word lettered B, the third one replaced by the word lettered C, or the fourth one replaced by the word lettered D. *PRINT THE LETTER OF THE REPLACEMENT WORD YOU HAVE SELECTED IN THE SPACE AT THE RIGHT.*

20. The alleged killer was occasionally permitted to excercise in the corridor. 20.___
    A. alledged B. ocasionally
    C. permited D. exercise

21. Defense counsel stated, in affect, that their conduct was permissible under the First Amendment. 21.___
    A. council B. effect
    C. there D. permissable

Question 22.

DIRECTIONS: Question 22 consists of one sentence. This sentence contains an incorrectly used word. First, decide which is the incorrectly used word. Then, from among the options given, decide which word, when substituted for the incorrectly used word, makes the meaning of the sentence clear.

22. As today's violence has no single cause, so its causes have no single scheme. 22.___
    A. deference B. cure C. flaw D. relevance

23. In the sentence, *A man in a light-grey suit waited thirty-five minutes in the ante-room for the all-important document*, the word IMPROPERLY hyphenated is 23.___
    A. light-grey B. thirty-five
    C. ante-room D. all-important

24. In the sentence, *The candidate wants to file his application for preference before it is too late*, the word *before* is used as a(n) 24.___
    A. preposition B. subordinating conjunction
    C. pronoun D. adverb

25. In the sentence, *The perpetrators ran from the scene*, the word *from* is a 25.___
    A. preposition B. pronoun
    C. verb D. conjunction

KEY (CORRECT ANSWERS)

1. D
2. D
3. A
4. B
5. D

6. D
7. B
8. A
9. C
10. C

11. D
12. D
13. D
14. C
15. D

16. C
17. D
18. A
19. A
20. D

21. B
22. B
23. C
24. B
25. A

ANSWER SHEET

ST NO. __________ PART ______ TITLE OF POSITION ____________________
(AS GIVEN IN EXAMINATION ANNOUNCEMENT - INCLUDE OPTION, IF ANY)

ACE OF EXAMINATION ____________________ DATE __________
(CITY OR TOWN) (STATE)

RATING

USE THE SPECIAL PENCIL. MAKE GLOSSY BLACK MARKS.

Each item: A B C D E

1	26	51	76	101
2	27	52	77	102
3	28	53	78	103
4	29	54	79	104
5	30	55	80	105
6	31	56	81	106
7	32	57	82	107
8	33	58	83	108
9	34	59	84	109
10	35	60	85	110

Make only ONE mark for each answer. Additional and stray marks may be counted as mistakes. In making corrections, erase errors COMPLETELY.

11	36	61	86	111
12	37	62	87	112
13	38	63	88	113
14	39	64	89	114
15	40	65	90	115
16	41	66	91	116
17	42	67	92	117
18	43	68	93	118
19	44	69	94	119
20	45	70	95	120
21	46	71	96	121
22	47	72	97	122
23	48	73	98	123
24	49	74	99	124
25	50	75	100	125

ANSWER SHEET

TEST NO. ____________ PART ______ TITLE OF POSITION ______________________________
(AS GIVEN IN EXAMINATION ANNOUNCEMENT - INCLUDE OPTION, IF ANY)

PLACE OF EXAMINATION ______________________________ DATE ______________
(CITY OR TOWN) (STATE)

RATING

USE THE SPECIAL PENCIL. MAKE GLOSSY BLACK MARKS.

1 A B C D E	26 A B C D E	51 A B C D E	76 A B C D E	101 A B C D E
2 A B C D E	27 A B C D E	52 A B C D E	77 A B C D E	102 A B C D E
3 A B C D E	28 A B C D E	53 A B C D E	78 A B C D E	103 A B C D E
4 A B C D E	29 A B C D E	54 A B C D E	79 A B C D E	104 A B C D E
5 A B C D E	30 A B C D E	55 A B C D E	80 A B C D E	105 A B C D E
6 A B C D E	31 A B C D E	56 A B C D E	81 A B C D E	106 A B C D E
7 A B C D E	32 A B C D E	57 A B C D E	82 A B C D E	107 A B C D E
8 A B C D E	33 A B C D E	58 A B C D E	83 A B C D E	108 A B C D E
9 A B C D E	34 A B C D E	59 A B C D E	84 A B C D E	109 A B C D E
10 A B C D E	35 A B C D E	60 A B C D E	85 A B C D E	110 A B C D E

Make only ONE mark for each answer. Additional and stray marks may be counted as mistakes. In making corrections, erase errors COMPLETELY.

11 A B C D E	36 A B C D E	61 A B C D E	86 A B C D E	111 A B C D E
12 A B C D E	37 A B C D E	62 A B C D E	87 A B C D E	112 A B C D E
13 A B C D E	38 A B C D E	63 A B C D E	88 A B C D E	113 A B C D E
14 A B C D E	39 A B C D E	64 A B C D E	89 A B C D E	114 A B C D E
15 A B C D E	40 A B C D E	65 A B C D E	90 A B C D E	115 A B C D E
16 A B C D E	41 A B C D E	66 A B C D E	91 A B C D E	116 A B C D E
17 A B C D E	42 A B C D E	67 A B C D E	92 A B C D E	117 A B C D E
18 A B C D E	43 A B C D E	68 A B C D E	93 A B C D E	118 A B C D E
19 A B C D E	44 A B C D E	69 A B C D E	94 A B C D E	119 A B C D E
20 A B C D E	45 A B C D E	70 A B C D E	95 A B C D E	120 A B C D E
21 A B C D E	46 A B C D E	71 A B C D E	96 A B C D E	121 A B C D E
22 A B C D E	47 A B C D E	72 A B C D E	97 A B C D E	122 A B C D E
23 A B C D E	48 A B C D E	73 A B C D E	98 A B C D E	123 A B C D E
24 A B C D E	49 A B C D E	74 A B C D E	99 A B C D E	124 A B C D E
25 A B C D E	50 A B C D E	75 A B C D E	100 A B C D E	125 A B C D E